"*Baptists and the Communion of Saints* is a feast to relish. Not only does it offer substantive and convincing proposals for a properly Baptist approach to this issue, it is a sterling example of constructive theology."

—**Dan R. Stiver**, *Cook-Derrick Professor of Theology, Logsdon School of Theology, Hardin-Simmons University*

"An important and timely book on one of the most neglected articles of the Apostles' Creed, *Baptists and the Communion of Saints* explores what it means for believers to share together life in Christ in this world—and the next—along the boundaries of space and time that both separate and unite the church militant, triumphant, and vigilant."

—**Timothy George**, *Dean of Beeson Divinity School, Samford University and Chair, Doctrine and Christian Unity Commission, Baptist World Alliance*

Baptists and the Communion of Saints

A Theology of Covenanted Disciples

Paul S. Fiddes

Brian Haymes and Richard Kidd

BAYLOR UNIVERSITY PRESS

Scripture quotations, where not an author's own translation, are from the New Revised Standard Version Bible, copyright 1989, Division of Christian Education of the National Council of the Churches of Christ in the United States of America. Used by permission. All rights reserved.

Cover Design by Kara Davison, Faceout Studio
Cover image: The dome of Andrew Gerow Hodges Chapel, Beeson Divinity School, Samford University, Birmingham, Alabama. Artist Petru Botezatu. Photograph by Kevin Boyd, 2008.

Andrew Gerow Hodges Chapel at Beeson Divinity School was consecrated in 1995 and is spoken of as "A Sermon in Stone" for its witness to the Gospel message through sacred art and architecture. The chapel is named in honor of Andrew Gerow Hodges, close personal friend and advisor to the late Mr. Ralph Beeson. A variety of worship services takes place in Hodges Chapel throughout the year. Beeson is an evangelical, interdenominational theological school. The doors of Hodges Chapel are open to welcome all visitors.

Library of Congress Cataloging-in-Publication Data

Fiddes, Paul S.
  Baptists and the communion of saints : a theology of covenanted disciples / Paul S. Fiddes, Brian Haymes, and Richard Kidd.
  238 pages cm
  Includes bibliographical references and index.
  ISBN 978-1-4813-0089-6 (pbk. : alk. paper)
  1. Communion of saints. 2. Baptists—Doctrines. I. Title.
  BT972.F53 2014
  262'.73--dc23

                              2013045458

CONTENTS

INTRODUCTION

Paul S. Fiddes

The chapel of Beeson Divinity School in Birmingham, Alabama, has a quite extraordinary dome depicting the Communion of Saints.[1] (*It can be seen on the cover of this book.*) Ninety feet above the chapel floor, at the center of the dome, the glorified Jesus Christ is portrayed with arms outstretched to embrace the world, with the marks of suffering still on his hands. Behind him, right at the center, there are thousands of faces, a "great cloud of witnesses," representing *all* Christian disciples throughout the ages. They are, quite clearly, all "saints." In a circle around the edge of the dome are a number of named saints, sixteen witnesses to Christ drawn from the history of the church—who between them cross all the boundaries of the Christian churches, of ethnicity, and of gender—together with six named martyrs from the twentieth-century church. Among these, six Baptist "saints"—John Bunyan, John Leland, William Carey, Lottie Moon, Charles Spurgeon, and William Wallace—are depicted in company with such saints of the wider church as Perpetua and Felicitas, Augustine, Athanasius, Thomas Aquinas, Martin Luther, John Calvin, Toyohiko Kagawa, and Dietrich Bonhoeffer. It is, perhaps, not surprising that the Divinity School, while preparing men and women of all Christian denominations for the ministry, is attached to a Baptist university (Samford).

This book might be regarded as the verbal commentary on this visual image. It offers an approach, from a Baptist perspective, to the doctrine of the Communion of Saints. It takes a Baptist standpoint, but it is not only written for Baptists; I and my fellow authors hope that Christians of all denominations will find some illumination in it about Christian fellowship with "saints" (all disciples) and "the saints" (the named witnesses).

The visual image communicates effectively, of course, in its own right, but for those who would like it, this book teases out the theology that the image implies. Yet the reader should be aware that, although this book contains some serious theology, it is not just a book full of concepts. The book sets out to make practical suggestions about how the doctrine of the Communion of Saints might come alive in Baptist settings, and about how believing in it might make a difference to the way Baptists understand the church, prepare their worship, care for the dying and the bereaved, and celebrate baptism and the Lord's Supper. Furthermore, the theology that we present is interwoven with experience and story, quite extensively drawing on our own life narratives. To this extent the book offers the practice of "theology as biography."[2]

One of my fellow authors, Richard Kidd, has clearly gained much from his experience of spending time with Baptist churches in South America and South Africa, and he recounts the developing story of how various theologians and other thinkers have influenced his own thought. He also reflects theologically on a series of personal experiences that have stayed vividly in his memory; these open up questions for him about the often unnoticed connections between people, and about a continuing "connectedness" with those who have died. My other fellow author, Brian Haymes, reflects theologically on such experiences as his call to Christian ministry and his visits to the Carmel convent in Lisieux where St. Thérèse was a nun. His experience of pastoral ministry also provides him with a constant reference point; for instance, he recalls welcoming ecumenical visitors to the church where he was minister in the center of London, only to have them ask, "Where is Mary and where are the saints?" What appeared so significant to them as Christians was absent from this Baptist building for worship. That experience set him thinking, he says, about what Baptists might be missing and has prompted much of his theological exploration of our theme. Though we do not explicitly mention it, all three of us have also been profoundly shaped, in our doing of theology, by the experience of being principals (in American terms, presidents) of colleges preparing candidates for Baptist ministry, serving between us for over fifty years in these offices.

Unlike my two coauthors, I do not refer explicitly to my own life experiences in the two chapters for which I have been mainly responsible. I take the privilege now, therefore, to bear personal witness that I have been deeply influenced in the theology I present in my chapters in this book by experiences of meeting fellow Baptists throughout the world through travels with the Baptist World Alliance. As I have written elsewhere,

> I have stood with fellow Baptists at a service in Sam Sharpe Square in Montego Bay, Jamaica, a place named in memory of the Baptist deacon and slave who was executed for his protest against the British slave system. I have prayed with fellow Baptists by the side of the Han river in Seoul, Korea, and witnessed several thousand young people being baptized—not in a media spectacle, but each one greeted personally by his or her pastor. I have lectured with fellow Baptists in the University of Timisoara, Romania, near the square where more than fifty young people (Baptists among them) were killed in the revolution of 1989 as they demonstrated for freedom, shouting, "God exists." I have shared in a Sunday morning service in the black township of Tembisa near Johannesburg where the previous night Zulu Inkatha terrorists had massacred nearly a hundred people, and I experienced Zulu and Chosa Baptists worshipping together there in acceptance of each other. I have sat with Baptists in Cuba, listening to the way that they understand mission in their neighbourhood, led by a pastor who was serving as a Deputy in the government of Fidel Castro, and suffering rejection by fellow Christians because of this involvement in politics. I have received hospitality from Baptists in Myanmar, and admired the way that the many ethnic groups express their faith and their hopes for their common society, despite governmental oppression, through their different styles of song and dance.[3]

I have also stood with Baptists in Jordan, beside the Jordan River in the area where Jesus was baptized, when one hundred young people made open profession of being Arab Christians by being baptized in his footsteps. All these experiences, and more, have opened to me the vision of a church universal and confirmed my belief in the centrality of the doctrine of the Communion of Saints.

Indeed, the first time that I saw the dome of the chapel at Beeson, I was part of a delegation from the Baptist World Alliance engaging in a five-year-long theological conversation with representatives from the Roman Catholic Church, the report of which has now been published.[4] A significant part of our time together, which I believe influenced our theological dialogue on "The Word of God in the Life of the Church," was a visit that our hosts at Beeson wanted us to make to the Birmingham Civil Rights Institute—which presented many records of the struggle against racial discrimination in Birmingham—and to the African-American Sixteenth Street Baptist Church. In this church, on Sunday, September 15, 1963, in the midst of the civil rights movement, a bomb exploded that had been planted by white extremists, and four girls were killed. They are, without doubt, among the myriads of witnesses not greatly known except to their friends and families, just as Martin Luther King, who was active in the Birmingham demonstrations, is among the public, named witnesses of the Christian church. We conducted our conversations in that meeting aware of our ongoing communion with these particular saints, as well as with those portrayed on the dome over the space where we worshipped.

But is the "Communion of Saints" a Baptist theme at all? Can one really speak of a Baptist approach to it? This is the question raised in the very first chapter, and an answer begins there, which the rest of the book sets out to expand. Although there has been a lively online conversation recently about whether Baptists should create a "Calendar of Saints" and—if so—who should be on the list,[5] there does not seem to be another book entirely devoted to the issue of Baptists and the doctrine of the Communion of Saints. It will not, I think, spoil the adventure of reading the book if I reveal here that our Baptist approach will be based on the heritage of "covenant" in Baptist thinking.

Readers, indeed, will notice that there are three underlying theological impulses in this book. The first is to bring ideas of "communion" and "covenant" together—as the title indicates—to understand the "Communion of Saints" in terms of a "Covenant of Saints." We three authors collaborated (with others) in the writing of a book nearly thirty years ago entitled *Bound to Love: The Covenant Basis of Baptist Life and Mission*,[6] and we have been glad to see the way that talk of covenant has since been revived among Baptists. The present book might be regarded as a sequel to the first, after a greater experience of life and ministry.

The second impulse is an engagement with a theological and pastoral issue. Is it possible to practice a fellowship of prayer and mutual support with faithful disciples who have died, without losing a confidence in our direct fellowship with the triune God which needs no human mediators, or without falling into an unhealthy obsession with communication with the dead?

The third impulse is a constant wrestling with a theological conundrum. None of the authors takes a dualistic view of the human being: that is, none of us thinks that a soul detaches from the body at death and continues to exist in a disembodied form. Our hope lies not in such ideas of Greek philosophy, but in what the biblical image of the resurrection of the body in a future new creation points toward. But if this is our hope, in what sense can we speak of a "communion" of saints here and now? How can we today have a fellowship with those who have died if they are not souls continuing somewhere without bodies?

I will not spoil our readers' discoveries by telling them here our answer to these questions, but readers will not be surprised to find they are something to do with the covenant that God makes and sustains. As authors, we hope that exploring these theological and pastoral questions will be of relevance to many who are not Baptists but who may be interested to read what three Baptists have to say about these issues.

All this is to underline that this book is not an edited collection of separate essays on a theme, but a jointly written book that builds an argument from the first chapter to the last. The chapters are only identified by names because most of them contain autobiographical material that needs to be personally owned; we want readers to follow our developing experience as well as our arguments. We are mainly responsible for two chapters each, but in a sense all the chapters have been coauthored, and we hope to show this by putting all our names on the last chapter, where we ask, "What difference, then, does holding this doctrine make?"

It has taken us more than four years to write this book together. We have discussed several drafts of every chapter with each other in most-enjoyable meetings and over convivial meal tables, and revised them in the light of each other's comments. In the writing of the book, we have experienced just a fragment of the communion that we are promised in the Communion of Saints. While we have much of a common mind, we still each have different emphases, which the reader will, no doubt, notice. Yet in discussing our contributions, our minds have been changed by each other, and our hope is that our readers may be willing to have their minds changed as well.

I

WHY TALK ABOUT THE SAINTS?

Brian Haymes

A book on the Communion of Saints by Baptists may occasion
some surprise, not least among Baptists. The saints, as they have
come to be popularly conceived, do not figure much if at all in Baptist services of worship, prayers, architecture, or doctrinal reflections.
Unlike others, Baptists do not usually dedicate buildings to named
saints.[1] They celebrate local church anniversaries but not in the form
of patronal festivals. They usually keep no calendar of saints,[2] nor list of
martyrs. There are few statues in their places of worship, or paintings.
Rarely in their various collections of hymns do they take up the theme
of the Communion of Saints. There are no prayers to the saints in the
resource books compiled to help those leading prayer and worship, and
very few commemorating particular named saints. In sum, the saints,
including Mary, are noticeable by their visible absence. All of which
might suggest that the doctrine of the Communion of Saints and all
that it expresses is at least marginal to the life and faith of the Baptists.

Such a judgment might be fair but possibly superficial. For example, none of us really knows what goes on in the personal prayers and
devotions of individual Baptists, some of whom have been known to
use a rosary as an aid to prayer. Many a local pastor is aware of church
members whose relationship to those who have died remains strong
and features in their understanding of the Lord's Supper. Such theological responses may be imperfectly formed, but they are real enough in

personal spiritualities. And, of course, much depends on what is meant by the word "saints" and how such persons are to be identified.

One aspect of what we are exploring in this book concerns the situations that have arisen as the church has moved through its history, proclaiming the gospel of God but not without the kinds of theological challenges and changes in which Baptists, among others, have been caught up. We are all heirs to magnificent insights into the ways of God as well as those human limitations that attend all reflections on the divine. Baptists are children of the Reformation, which means they may see some things very clearly but other matters through blurred lenses. Could it be again the case that we who are Baptists are right in what we affirm but not so correct in what we choose to deny or ignore? Might the doctrine and the attendant practices relating to the Communion of Saints be a case in point?

Saints in the New Testament

The New Testament uses the word "saint" in an open and direct way. It is Paul's chosen word for the church members he addresses in his letters (Rom 1:7; 1 Cor 1:2; Phil 1:2). The saints ("holy ones," *hagioi*) are those baptized into Christ, born of the Spirit, sharing the new creation of which the risen Christ is in all senses the head. Their calling had ethical implications, and there is evidence in the text to show how carefully such matters were taken. However, the early Christians were saints not because of their moral achievements, or even martyrdom, but because they were "in Christ." They waited the coming day of resurrection in hopeful confidence. Even in such a disarranged church as in Corinth, the apostle called church members "saints." What is particularly striking is the corporate nature of this being in Christ, in affirmation of which Paul uses the metaphor of the one body. Against an individualistic, atomistic approach, which is often taken to these matters in not a little contemporary popular theology, the New Testament has a strong corporate emphasis. The saints, those living and dead, are one in Christ, sharing the life of God's new creation. Of the sixty-four times the word "saint" appears in the New Testament, it is always in the plural. Through Christ and in Christ, the saints share the life of God in Trinity. They live in the covenant of saving grace, the work of God, awaiting the end of all things.

In the Letter to the Hebrews, the writer explores the meaning of faith by recalling those who, from creation, exhibited faithfulness to God and God's purposes, in their living, even if their moral qualities admittedly were not always godly. These remarkable women and men are commended for their active faithful trust in God. The writer pictures them as a great cloud of witnesses (Heb 12:1), which could mean that they serve as examples of faithfulness and its price and so have become a kind of biblical roll of honor. Or might it be that the writer pictures them as those living in God who now look upon us, we whose time for discipleship and witness has come? These surround the living as a continuing presence, inseparably related in Christ. Separated from us the living, says the writer, they cannot be made perfect (Heb 11:40).

But two factors immediately required further thought in the New Testament era. First was the fact that some saints were dying before the expected end. What was their destiny? Paul's pastoral response was to argue that those who had "fallen asleep" were asleep in Christ, still waiting with the living for Christ's coming reign, at which point all, both the living and the dead, in Christ would be changed (1 Cor 15:51-57). "Being in Christ," who was the first to be raised from the dead, described the state of Christians both "asleep" and still living. In that sense, all were held together in Christ, in the covenant of communion that death could not destroy. It is as if the New Testament recognizes a boundary in death but that the boundary is not absolutely separating, because of the resurrection of the crucified Jesus. In the book of Revelation, the imagery is developed so that we are given pictures of the saints at worship and prayer. Sleep is not an encompassing enough metaphor, for here the saints are active, sharing the purposes of God in prayer and celebrating their joy in praise (Rev 7:9-17; 21:3-4).

The other factor for the early church to reckon with was martyrdom. We are not long into reading the story as Luke tells it when we encounter the first martyr death. Stephen is killed as he bears witness, reflecting in his dying the way of Christ (Acts 7:54–8:3). It becomes clear that to be baptized into Christ is to be a member of a martyr church. Indeed, it was not long before some Christians spoke of two baptisms: the first of water, the second of blood.[3] Thus, the New Testament affirms saints both visible and invisible, but all are saints because of their being in Christ by the gracious work of God. It is important to note that the object of Stephen's petition is the glorified Jesus, the one whom the martyrs worship. Stephen's martyr death is set forth not as an act of witness that has seriously and unfortunately gone wrong, but as the paradigm of Christian life and witness, following Christ of the cross. Following Jesus is very different from following a philosophical lead, such as that supplied by Socrates. Christians are called to follow a person whose authority is constituted by the resurrection. It means that sharing the body of Christ involves more than obeying a formal ethic. It is participation in the body of the living Christ. In this sense the New Testament assumes that the virtues for martyrdom are no different from those of faithful Christian living. Martyrdom is not the calling of the select few but an aspect of the commitment of the whole church, the martyr church.

Early Baptists understood saints in this manner, as a title for all members of the witnessing church. They used the word "saint" in their confessions but, in good Reformation discipline, always with reference to the living church members, following the pattern of the New Testament epistles, using the term to refer to church members, all those called to the new humanity in and through Christ. The (Particular Baptist) London Confession of 1644, citing in the margin many of the texts we have referred to above along with others, asserts in paragraph 33:

> That Christ hath here on earth a spirituall Kingdome, which is the Church, which he has purchased and redeemed to himselfe, as a peculiar inheritance: which Church, as it is visible to us, is a company of visible Saints, called and separated from the world, by the word and Spirit of God, to the visible profession of the faith of the Gospel, being baptized into that faith, and joined to the Lord, and each other, by mutuall agreement, in the practical injoyment of the Ordinances, commanded by Christ their head and King.[4]

The saints in this communion blest are the living members of the church. The Second (Particular Baptist) London Confession of 1677, in chapter 27 entitled "On the Communion of Saints," likewise keeps the emphasis on the visible church that includes the whole household of God, all those who in every place call upon the name of the Lord Jesus.[5] The later sections in the confession, on life after death and the last judgment, again only use the word "saint" with reference to living members of the church on earth. The (General Baptist) *Orthodox Creed* of 1679 similarly has an article entitled "Of Communion of Saints," which refers to "one mystical body of Christ" made up of all baptized Christians, in which there should be "fellowship and communion in each other's sufferings or afflictions" and where members "partake of each other's gifts."[6] This clearly has living saints in mind, going on to urge giving to the poor among them.

But it was understood, both in the New Testament and among early Baptists, that those who had died in Christ had not left the fellowship of the church. Being baptized into Christ, they shared his resurrection life and his eschatological future. The distinction is not between the dead and the living, for all the saints are alive in Christ. The church is this Communion of Saints, on earth and in heaven, united in Christ, participating in the life of God by the Spirit. Because of our understanding of baptism, Baptists might well be placed to recover the significance of this dynamic relationship, which is the Communion of Saints, being that whole community of those graced by the Spirit of God who participate in the holiness of God.

Thus, the church on earth is one with those who now are a great cloud of living witnesses (Heb 12:1). To recall some other New Testament affirmations, the boundary between heaven and earth is blurred in the expanded fellowship of the saints, as the martyred servants of God cry out, "How long?" (Rev 6:9-11). These saints are not inactive, for their prayers rise up to God (Rev 8:3-5), and as together they sing a new song (Rev 14:1-5), their prayers are caught up into the eternal intercession of our one High Priest. So there emerges a picture of a continuous congregation, one holy communion in prayer and praise. By grace, all are raised into Christ's eschatological future. And those who have died are not the saints at inactive rest but rather those who offer praise to God and presumably continue to share God's longing for the complete coming of the kingdom on earth, the new creation. This Communion of Saints then is a reality in which the church on earth participates by prayers, in the Eucharist, in faithful service, waiting for the fulfillment of all things in Christ. We shall return to this theme later, after following the historical development of the doctrine a little further.

The Cult of the Saints

The rise of the more Catholic understanding of the saints, often called the cult of the saints, is well documented.[7] It almost certainly had its initial impetus in increased martyrdoms and the memory of the martyrs of the early centuries. Early expressions of the cult included the recording of the stories and the gathering of relics. Early Christianity was a countercultural force at odds with prevailing religious and political assumptions. Since the context was that of the Roman Empire, with its own tests of loyalty to Caesar and the gods, any other form of religious loyalty had dangerous political implications. Christians became objects of discontent from both the official powers and the populace who might blame them for various disasters. Some early Christians attempted defenses of fellow disciples by arguing that their behavior was no threat to the common good and did not make them bad citizens. The Apologies of Justin Martyr are an illustration of this reporting and argument.[8]

Another form of literary record developed in the second century as the stories of the martyrs and their deaths were recorded. The telling of these stories by one local church community was a means of keeping the memory of their witness alive for other communities of the faith. Examples of these texts would include the *Martyrdom of Polycarp*, written to help those under instruction grow into full discipleship, and the moving record of the martyrdoms of the women Perpetua and Felicitas.[9] These full texts described the suffering, the passion, of the martyrs. Martyrdom was a public spectacle and in that sense political. In the arena a struggle of intense cosmic proportions was being fought out between the "powers" in their death throes and Christ in his body. So Origen could encourage those who have been brought to the place of testing:

> A great multitude is assembled to watch you when you combat and are called to martyrdom. It is as if we said that thousands upon thousands gather to watch a contest in which the contestants of outstanding reputation are engaged. When you will be engaged in the conflict you can say with Paul: *We are made a spectacle to the whole world and to angels and to men.* The whole world, therefore, all the angels on the right and on the left, all men, both those on the side of God and the others—all will hear us fighting the fight for Christianity.[10]

In this context, martyrdom was thought of as a gift and calling. To seek it was morally wrong. The "suicide martyr" has no place in Christian thinking. Given the prospect of glory, the temptation was strong to do the right thing for the wrong reason.[11] But the church is called to bear the cross of Christ and inevitably becomes a martyr church. Martyrs do not die for *reasons*, as if their death had some explanation other than Christ. They die in and for and with Christ. The martyrs are remembered by the church as followers of Jesus. Their being remembered is a guard against any self-deception by contemporary and future Christians as to the meaning of discipleship. The calling of Christ is to walk the path of the cross. Thus, it has been argued that the developing disciplines, in the early church, of prayer, Scripture readings, alms giving, acts of penitence, and attendance at the Eucharist were ways by which Christians grew in strength and were prepared for the possibility that they would be called to make the act of final witness. Not all were faithful unto death. Such was the case of Quintus the Phrygian who saw the beasts, was afraid, and recanted, offering incense and taking the oath at the entreaty of the Roman Proconsul.[12] More than personal shame would result from the disciples who withdrew and recanted in the public arena. To be ashamed of Christ was no light matter (Mark 8:38).

Martyrdom was therefore a feature of the church of the early centuries, certainly in the pre-Constantinian period. Recognition of genuine martyrs and saints was largely a local matter, as some lives were received as being especially significant in their witness to Christ, there being no central authority of the church. From early days, however, the memory of the saints and martyrs was a feature of church life. Shrines were developed at the place of martyrdom, which became places of pilgrimage, and relics were collected, an illustration of which is given recalling the martyrdom of Polycarp:

> So [following his death and burning] we afterwards took up his bones, more valuable than precious stones and finer than gold, and laid them where it was fitting. There the Lord will permit us, as shall be possible to us, to assemble ourselves together in joy and gladness, and to celebrate the birthday of his martyrdom, alike in memory of them that have fought before and for the training and preparation of them that are to fight hereafter.[13]

Thus, some saints were remembered on the day of their death or martyrdom or birth, days of commemoration. Eucharist would be celebrated, expressing the understanding that in the saints there was a drawing near of God as their lives and martyrdom had a special power of disclosure. The celebration of the Eucharist also underlined the connection between the martyr's life and death and the cross of Christ, which led in turn to the thought that the saints, living in Christ, would intercede for the living and the dead.

After Constantine's decision to embrace rather than persecute the church, there was a decline in the numbers of martyrs. However, during the middle ages, the cult of the saints developed. The veneration of relics increasingly became an important feature of common religious life, one consequence of which was economic. A trade in relics resulted, allied with monetary gains relating to places of pilgrimage. Issues of authorization and formal canonization became more urgent. Much popular expression of faith focused on the shrines of the local saints, who often had a nationalistic or group identity. The cult of the saints became a major feature of Christian devotion in days when the use of Latin, with a priest operating behind a rood screen, only made general participation in worship more demanding and exclusive.

The processes of canonization themselves were an expression of the power of religious authorities. The lists of those canonized in the Western churches were dominated by popes, bishops and other priests, kings, princes, and benefactors. There were very few women, and married women with children hardly appear at all.[14] The gracious work of God seemed to be very socially and economically focused. It is possible that the whole idea of the intercession of the saints came to reflect the hierarchical form of society. In such days it was necessary to have a friend in court if the ear of the king or prince were to be caught. Might the saints be understood as those who especially had the ear of God? If that was the understanding, here was a situation ripe for theological development.

Early Baptists and the Saints

With the Reformation came a reappraisal of the saints and the cult that had developed. One important difference with regard to the early days of the Christian era was that now Christians were persecuting

Christians. Arguments about the true church, its governance, and its membership meant that whoever had the power to do so brought death with them—the destroying of heretics or the affirmation of martyrs according to the prevailing theological point of view. Christians were both the prosecutors and the persecuted. Catholics killed Protestants, Protestants killed Catholics, and both, when in political power, killed Dissenters such as Anabaptists. The power of the state allied to religious convictions is always a serious, potentially fearsome matter.

Insofar as Baptists were caught up into the Reformation movement, as we have already noticed, the basic affirmations of the saints as church members in Christ became dominant. No other mediators were necessary in the light of Christ. Devotion to the saints ran the risk of idolatry: worshipping and praying to the creature rather than the Creator. It ran the danger of compromising the unique and necessary work of Christ. The assertion of the Bible's authority, in contrast to the claims of the tradition of the church's teaching that had developed, meant that the being and role of the saints was reexamined. So there came the biblical perspective that we have already indicated is the understanding of early Baptists. Did anything important get lost in these arguments?

To return to the biblical perspective for a moment, using "saint" as a designation of members of the early church expressed their being in continuity with Israel. The saints were only special in the sense that they were called of God in covenant love. They were not otherwise a special group of people. God had called a people to be God's own, blessing them in order that they should be a blessing. Here in the divine call to be a holy nation, a priestly kingdom, was the identity of Israel and the church (Exod 19:6; 1 Pet 2:9; Rev 5:10). Such people, ordinary as they were in many respects, were called to share something of God's "otherness." Their vocation was a work of divine grace, but it carried serious moral implications. So the designation "saint" in the New Testament carries these earlier overtones of calling by the faithful covenant-making God, and such calling came to mean Christlikeness, the virtues of faithfulness, hope, and love as embodied in Jesus the Lord. This called and gathered nature of Israel and the church, grounded in the purposes of the covenant-making God for all creation is an important feature of the doctrine of the Communion of Saints.

Historically, the phrase "Communion of Saints" is a late entrant into the Apostles' Creed. It does not appear at all in the Nicene-Constantinopolitan Creed. Nor is it a scriptural phrase, although as is the case with other doctrinal terms the building blocks are clear enough in the Bible as we have indicated already. The Apostles' Creed locates the Communion of Saints in this section: "I believe in the Holy Spirit, the holy catholic church, the communion of saints, the forgiveness of sins, the resurrection of the body, and the life everlasting." Communion, *koinonia*, has frequent usage with a rich range of meanings in Scripture and tradition. It means sharing, mutual interests, generosity, participation in goods, sufferings, and grace. It means fellowship with Christ in the Spirit, sharing the blessings of Christ's death and resurrection as part of his body. It entails living in the mission of God with others in mutual care expressed not the least in hospitality and eucharistic living. Such is the nature of the church, sharing by gracious calling the life of God in Trinity (2 Cor 13:13). It is by this calling and participation in the life of the triune God that the church is the holy people of God whose members are called saints. The church is holy because it is the body of Christ, because its members, living or dead, are inseparable from Christ. And they belong together, regardless of race, gender, tribe, or time, because they are called of God.

The phrase Communion of Saints, *sanctorum communio*, admits of two different translations and meanings. If sanctorum is taken to be neuter plural, then the phrase might well be taken to mean participating in holy things, the life and worship of the Church, and most notably the Eucharist. If, however, it is taken as masculine plural, then it will refer to the martyrs and saints, alive and dead, who together with Christ are his body. It is unnecessary to choose between these two readings; indeed, it might be unwise to do so. Paul certainly seems to see an important connection between the two possible interpretations when he argues, "The cup of blessing that we bless, is it not a sharing in the blood of Christ? The bread that we break, is it not a sharing in the body of Christ? Because there is one bread, we who are many are one body. For we all partake of the one bread" (1 Cor 10:16-17). Thus, the historical Jesus, the prophet from Nazareth in Galilee, and the Christ of God—present as promised among his people in the Eucharist—are identified. The saints share this one communion blessed.

In the light of this biblical understanding of the church as a "holy" community, we turn to the issues this teaching poses for Baptists. Baptists, along with others in the sixteenth and seventeenth centuries following the Reformation, stressed that becoming a Christian and a church member was both a work of God's grace and the free decision of the individual believer. Having faithful Christian parents did not of itself make you a disciple of Jesus. That was a personal matter, involving hearing a call to discipleship, trusting the promises of God, and responding in faith to God's initiative. The call of God was gracious, without threat or coercion. No one, least of all God in Christ, was to put pressure on another to walk the way of Jesus (John 6:66-67). This emphasis on liberty of conscience in matters of religion was an essential feature of Baptist life and faith from the very first. Famously, it was Thomas Helwys, the leader of the first Baptist church in England in 1612, who made a direct plea to the ruling monarch for liberty of conscience when it came to the relationship between God and any human being.[15] This growing emphasis on the individual, which began to flourish in the Reformation in the questioning of authority, was to come to fuller bloom in the Enlightenment stress on the autonomy of each person in matters of morals, politics, and faith. It might be argued that this emphasis on the individual, where it is coupled with a loss of historical sense and identity, has gone too far as an understanding of what it is to be a human being. It is an overemphasis that Baptists have been tempted to make, which in its own turn has led to the weakening of a sense of community, the corporate sense of Christian identity, and the significance of being the church.

The implication of responding to the gracious call of God in Christ, signified in baptism, therefore was a crucial issue for Baptists. It related to the question of where the true church was to be found and who were its members. Infant baptism gave credence to a church whose membership was national, with respect to the faith of the monarch or prince, and hereditary, with regard to family allegiance. Children were baptized into the faith of the parents and the nation. But this was the inherited faith of the parents or prince, and—whereas it might seem that bringing the child for baptism was an important act of loyalty and trust in the gracious God—it overlooked that essential personal response necessary for baptism, discipleship, and church membership. The church is a fellowship of Christian believers, disciples who have—of their own will and choice, enabled by grace—chosen to respond to God's call. This is the believers-church tradition to which Baptists belong. The London Confession of 1644 offered the following definition of the Christian church: namely, "a company of visible Saints, called and separated from the world, by the word and spirit of God, to the visible profession of the faith of the Gospel, being baptized into that faith, and joined to the Lord, and each other, by mutuall agreement, in the practical injoyment of the Ordinances, commanded by Christ their head and King."[16]

Baptism and a New Humanity of Saints

We have already noted that Baptists referred to church members baptized into Christ as "saints." They were the holy ones because they shared the life of the holy God through Christ in the power of the Spirit. Being baptized was more than a personal act of witness to individual faith. It was more than an act of obedience by one who sought to follow Jesus. There were ontological and corporate implications at stake.

The Christ into whose name we are baptized is the one who announced the presence of the kingdom of God. In his life and work, he revealed the challenge of the rule of God to all that might resist that divine purpose. So works of healing and exorcism were a significant part of Jesus' message. So also were his actions in including those who were otherwise excluded and marginalized: women, foreigners, enemies, children, and sinners. Being a disciple meant, at the very least, being drawn into the way of this kingdom. Those who followed might well be described as "blessed" (Matt 5:1-12), but the way was far from comfortable. For Jesus, the consequence of his convictional way of life was the cross. Under political pressure that was in those days inevitably allied with religious dogma, he was crucified and buried. It is no surprise that following Christ led to being a martyr church. However, the Christ whom the church proclaims is the Risen One, raised by the power of God, "declared to be Son of God with power according to the spirit of holiness by resurrection from the dead, Jesus Christ our Lord" (Rom 1:4). Here is God's work of salvation in Jesus, a work encompassing the forgiveness of sins, the restoration of relationships, the healing of wounds by suffering love, and the announcement of the undoing of death. The church proclaims Christ crucified and risen, the triumph of God, the new creation in which death no longer has dominion. In the Bible story, the only God we know is one who has a fundamental relationship with creation, and the only humanity we know is one inseparably related to God, needing a salvation it cannot of itself supply. The story the Bible tells records fractures and threats to this relationship, of ways in which it is seriously distorted, of how it is recalled in prophetic challenge and imagery to the covenant way, and of how it is restored in Jesus. The image of God in humanity is badly scarred but never totally obliterated in the scriptural perspectives. So, there is something both old and new in the resurrection of Jesus from the dead. It is old in that it is, from the beginning, the work of God. It is new in that for God and ourselves something new comes to be in the life, death, and resurrection of Jesus the Christ.

Paul speaks of this as "new creation" (2 Cor 5:17). Too easily have Baptists interpreted such a text within a very narrow individual focus. We enthusiastically sing, "I am a new creation," and properly rejoice in what Jesus has done for us. But the new creation in Christ is corporate. It is a new world, one both present and in the making. It is one where death is no more, nor crying, for former things have passed away (Rev 21:1). In Jesus Christ, creation is being restored, the promise of a new heaven and a new earth being fulfilled. It is shared by the one new humanity in Christ. The church is called to live this way, resisting old distinctions of religion, economics, and gender (Gal 3:28) and living without the dividing walls of hostility (Eph 2:14-22). Christ brings reconciliation and peace, the restoration of relationships. When we are baptized into Christ, therefore, it is into this new humanity. There is an essential corporateness, for the church is called to live this new humanity. For all its diversity, it is the one body of Christ. No part can claim independence from the others, and Christ alone is head (1 Cor 12:12-27).

Therefore, in spite of its essential individuality of response, baptism has this corporate dimension. Those in Christ are united in him. Thus the church is composed of those who live the life in Christ now on earth, serving the cause of God's kingdom by living in it, and those who have died but still live in Christ, awaiting the promised end. Christians, those alive and those dead-as-alive are one in the risen Christ. There are saints on earth and saints "in heaven." They are together in God. Together they are the church, the Communion of Saints.

Thus this doctrine of the church enlarges our common under-standing of being the church that is tempted not to go far beyond the experience of the local gathering of Christians. An insistence on the so-called autonomy of the local congregation has always had this Achilles heel.[17] The local congregation gathered in Christ is the church but is not all there is to being the church. For that, the whole com-pany of God's people, alive and dead, are necessary, and we cannot be the church in its fullness without one another. To ignore or forget the saints is to diminish our calling in Christ. It is to live as an impover-ished church. In and through Christ we are one new people of God, the living and the dead.

Together, those in Christ constitute a royal priesthood. Baptists have consistently asserted the priesthood of all believers. Often this has been understood in ways dominated by pervasive individualism and anticlericalism, claiming for example that since "my relationship to God" is personal, then "I need no other intermediary." If we go directly to the Father through the Son in the power of the Spirit, then we can pray on our own. Without wishing to deny that affirmation, a further dimension of meaning of priesthood is suggested in the doctrine of the Communion of Saints. Jesus Christ is the one who is our Great High Priest, and he intercedes for us. Insofar as we are one in him—saints alive on earth and those departed in Christ—might we not think of ourselves as the one priesthood of all believers in and under Christ our head? An essential aspect of this priesthood is to offer prayers for the world, focused in the divine prayer for the coming of the kingdom, the doing of God's will on earth. Christ prays for us. The Spirit takes up our earthly inarticulate groans, and so they become prayer to the Father, even as "the Spirit intercedes for the saints according to the will of God" (Rom 8:27). In Revelation, the martyrs' prayer is the great cry "How long?"—expressing their desire to see the vindication and fulfillment of all things in and through Christ (Rev 6:10). We might then think of the saints, on earth and in heaven, constituting one priesthood in Christ, praising God and praying for all those for whom God continues to long in saving love. Might not the saints in glory still have their contribution to make in the ongoing work of Christ until all things are delivered to the Father (1 Cor 15:24)?

If these things are so, then until that final time the work of prayer will have significance for the world that it scarcely recognizes, as the church shares in the life of God, longing in love for the praise and glory of God in all things restored in Christ. So we might think of the saints praying for us out of their love and desire for God's kingdom revealed in Christ. They pray, not because we ask for their help, but unbidden in the bonds of love as those who share the life of God in Trinity. And in this living community, sharing the life of God, might we not remember them in prayers of gratitude and concern, even as the bonds of love are not broken by death, and we are united in Christ?[18] The imagery Paul offered out of his pastoral concern for the dead in Christ was the metaphor of sleep (1 Cor 15:6). However, the picture of passive waiting, unconsciously aware of the ongoing struggles of the coming kingdom, hardly does justice to the imagery of those sharing by grace the active life of God. The possibility arises that our prayers, inseparably linked with those of the saints, might do more than our individualistic models could ever consider. It might well be that the world is sustained by the prayers of the saints in the intercessions of Christ and the Spirit, expressing the gracious love and patient care of God.

Saints and "The Saints"

All of this suggests a broader understanding of church than is usual in Baptist circles. The church includes the living and the dead-as-alive in Christ. We belong in a community of saints, the holy ones who share by grace the covenant love and life of God. In Christ we are inseparably related to Mary, Peter, John, Stephen, Justin, Perpetua, Francis, Clare, Benedict, Thomas Becket, Dietrich Bonhoeffer, Martin Luther King, Dorothy Day, Oscar Romero, Mother Teresa, and countless others. All these and more are, with us, the living church. That they are so very different from us and from one another is significant. We learn that there are many ways of following Christ and being what in our day we are called to be. The fact that all of them are sinners, some spectacularly so, reminds us that we are forgiven, all of us heirs of grace. They witness to the meaning of enduring faithful discipleship to which we are called. They show us in different ways what following Jesus looks like. They are witnesses to what God can do in and with the church. The covenant we share is undeserved by us all. It is a gift from the gracious God. The memory of the saints therefore is an important matter for us. They remind us of our identity in Christ and ways by which we might live as faithful disciples of Jesus. The saints are part of our story, which, we believe, is the story of God in the world. We shall not understand our identity and calling without them.

It is popular to dismiss the call to be saints as unrealistic if not actually undesirable. The saints are holy, and that term deserves serious reflection. "Holiness" is misunderstood if it focuses exclusively on moral qualities. This is a common mistake with regard to the saints, whose endurance and moral qualities are often outstanding, even unnerving. The martyrs can disturb us by their dedication and readiness to sacrifice and suffer. But holiness in the biblical context refers not in the first instance to moral perfection but to the mystery of God. God is holy, the source of holiness. Holiness describes the ways of God, so impacting our understanding of justice and righteousness. God's holiness implies truth, faithfulness, love, and glory, the weighty radiance of God's presence in the world. Such holiness and glory of God is never directly perceived by humankind, but we are given glimpses in the lives of the faithful servants of God, the saints. Human beings can reflect the divine glory, even as they participate in the life and ways of God. God's glory may also be glimpsed in history, in events affirming the gifts of liberation and peace, affirming God's presence among us.

Particularly and uniquely, this is the case in Jesus Christ, possessed of glory as of the Father's only Son, full of grace and truth (John 1:14). Holiness is therefore a matter of belonging to God, the Holy One, participating in God's will and ways and so reflecting God's glory. As Elizabeth Johnson puts it, "In the abstract, the notion of divine holiness stands for infinite otherness and separation—the Godness of God; but in the concrete, glory as well as other metaphors function as a hermeneutic of holiness that affirms the elusive Holy One is powerfully near in and through the wondrous processes of nature, the history of struggle for freedom and life, and communities where justice and peace prevail."[19] We might be specific and add, in the lives of the saints, those whose lives are a divine disclosure. Such people are saintly because of their relationship with God, revealed in the specific context of their discipleship. The covenant call of the Holy God, to be holy because God is holy, is the ground of their consecration, their reflecting of the glory of God. Such holiness is part of the divine search for humankind. It is relational. In Jesus, it obviously is not hierarchical, as later canonization implied. This covenant community, the church, is the Communion of Saints, participating in the holy life of God and reflecting that holiness in faithful living. It is a work of grace.

With early Baptists we will want to affirm that this holiness, this power of disclosure of the Holy One, is the vocation of all those called into the covenant community. All members are saints. But at the same time, in some lives there appears to be a particular disclosure that calls for attention, such that we are inclined to stretch grammar and call them "*the* saints." There is one holy community, but within this we can recognize "saints *and* the saints," however blurred the difference might be between them. We find spiritual gain in commemorating particular saints and even creating a calendar of them, though in different communities some lives will stand out in a way that is appropriate for that group of people, and no calendar can be the "standard" one for the whole church. It is in accord with our theological discussion so far to stress that the particular power of disclosure in certain lives is not due to any personal merit of the disciples concerned, and is not even *due* to any heroic character or groundbreaking actions that they performed, though this may often be *true* of them. The grace of God within them has been the same as in all saints, but we may say that the particular circumstances of their life of discipleship have given special opportunity for the holiness and glory of God that is in all disciples' lives, to become visible in a way that rouses our attention, startles us, and calls for imitation.[20] There will always be an ambiguity and overlap between "saints" and "the saints," and we should use the term in a way that makes room for this continual uncertainty of identification. But some disciples are still recognizable as "the saints," due to the initiative of God and the sheer contingencies and accidents of history.

There are twentieth century examples who will be commonly recognized like this. Dietrich Bonhoeffer, Oscar Romero, Dorothy Day, Thomas Merton, and Mother Teresa of Calcutta are all recognized by common acclamation as those who memorably disclose something of the challenge and grace of God in human life. They express the alternative values of the kingdom of God, which involves living a different way. They are all sinners, some persistently so, never quite overcoming the demons that tormented them. Criticisms can be brought against all of them on social and political grounds. But they express the calling of "the chosen race, the royal priesthood, a holy nation, God's own people" (1 Pet 2:9). To remember them and others is to be inspired by the Spirit. To think that we are part of this company by grace is humbling and exalting at the same time.

All this helps us understand the apostolic call to imitation. Paul praises the Thessalonians by providing an example for other Christians as they imitate the Lord, his servant Paul, and Paul's companions (1 Thess 1:6-8). In the case of the Corinthians, however, it is more a case of Paul arguing that such imitation will be a source of unity relating to his calling and God-given authority (1 Cor 4:16). This apostolic admonition is part of the story of an early Christian community trying to find its way in the life of Christ. The crucial matter for Paul is that the community members should imitate Christ in their relationships and trust. In the Letter to the Ephesians 5:1-2, the urge is to be imitators of God. Recalling the lives of God's "holy ones" therefore is a creative feature of discipleship, the journey to which we are committed in the company of Christ. It is not a matter of copying in exactitude the deeds the saints have performed, so much as being led into new insights for our pilgrimage by their example. The saints are our, sometimes subversive, companions in the fellowship of the church. So "the communion of saints becomes the cloud of witnesses, surrounding those who cry for justice with encouragement and blessing, lending the support to their own interest for personal and social transformation."[21]

Commemorating the Saints among Baptists

So how might all this begin to show itself in Baptist churches? It would be a very strange and impoverished Baptist congregation that did not have its stories of saints. God has always given people who have helped the rest of us in our pilgrimage because of their insights, quality of life, and the wisdom that comes from openness to the Spirit. Stories are told of individuals and events that have given to the local congregation the character it has. The tradition of church anniversary might well be a time for such memories to be recalled and assessed. As an alternative to the common practice of bringing in a notable preacher, the local congregation might take the anniversary as an opportunity to recall its saints and their influence. This need not be a backward-looking stance so much as a recalling of how God has used such disciples in the past and how God's call and covenant might be celebrated now. Some research into the congregation's history might bring to light important events, attitudes, and individuals now forgotten. The church in its worship may well benefit from paying attention to a catholic calendar of saints, a practice which might well shed light on present issues of witness, loyalty, and faithfulness, by recalling—for example—Thomas Helwys (religious liberty), William Carey (the call to mission), and William Knibb (the struggle against slavery and racism). Keeping All Saints Day in public worship would be an enrichment of any congregation.

How might this be done? Here are some illustrations of how local congregations and wider groups of Baptist Christians have enlarged their understanding of the faith and of their call to be the church. The first is the Church of the Lamb of God, in San Salvador, El Salvador, visited by two of the authors of this volume in the 1990s. In this Baptist church, the memory of the civil war was still keen among the members, and, for the majority, the scars had not completely healed. Members of the church had been among those who had been imprisoned and tortured and were among the "disappeared." This small congregation, numbering less than thirty children and adults, placed photographs of the "disappeared" on the communion table. This meant that when the Lord's Supper was shared—the congregation standing in a circle spreading out from the sides of the table—the church alive and dead was being remembered in the love and life of Christ. Other congregations in Central and South America that had known the taking of members in this way would at Communion have their names called, at which the congregation responded with the affirmation "Presente!"

Another example comes from the occasion of the celebration of the first seventy-five years of life of the American Baptist Convention. Its worship session included the following litany, written by the Baptist historian William Brackney:

Leader: Let us recall the works of God in the American Baptist family—75 years as pilgrims in grace in Long Beach, Fargo, Philadelphia,

Matadi, Bangalore, and Shanghai . . . praying, planning, struggling, working together.

Response: We remember the faithful paths of our mothers and fathers, sisters and brothers, the people of God, pilgrims in grace . . .

Leader: Through multiple wars, economic crises, times of apathy and upheaval, we have ministered to each other by sharing common resources and gifts as pilgrims in grace . . . In a broken world we have sought to unite yellow, red, black, and white in justice and reconciliation, in peace and security, in strength and dignity . . .

Response: We sense God's Spirit among us, pilgrims in grace.

Leader: As did our forebears, Helen Montgomery, Henry Morehouse, Luther Wesley Smith, Martin Luther King, Jr., and Isabel Crawford, we continue to be faithful to our mission, to act boldly and prophetically, to dare to be pilgrims in grace.

Response: Let us, O God become anew the people of God, pilgrims in grace. Continue to call thy people, O God, to a recommitment to our historic principles of soul liberty and new life in Christ. Continue to lead us, thy pilgrims in grace, less we miss your Kingdom's goal. In the name of Jesus Christ, the author and finisher of our faith. Amen.[22]

A similar example was the commemoration of representative figures from four centuries of Baptist history, at a worship service organized by the Baptist World Alliance in 2009 celebrating the formation in 1609 of the first Baptist church in Amsterdam.[23] After some forty well-known names from all continents of the world were remembered, the litany also made mention of those many saints without name whose contributions to the living tradition of Baptist faith and practice are indispensable, including "members of our churches and congregations who live out the story in hope and in fear, in safety and in danger."[24]

It is not unknown for congregations in North America to make a special celebration of All Saints Day. For example, in one congregation, in the weeks before November 1, a "book of life" is made available at a prominent place, and members are invited to write into it the names of people, church members, and others in history who have impressed them and in their stories help the present members on their journey. Over the weeks this can amount to several hundred names, recalling earlier church members and the greater history of the Christian church. All these names are then printed in the worship bulletin of the worship service. Each name is celebrated by a small candle in the place of worship. The names of church members who have died in the last year are read out as the community comes to Communion. It is the testimony of the congregation that having come to honor the saints of God, they have left with the experience of being part of a great story of God's people who have honored them.

Similarly, at a recent retreat I conducted with a company of Baptists from various congregations, the invitation was given to list around the worship room the names of those in history who continued to inspire and teach us. The historical and theological range of those so commemorated gave its own sense of the great company to which we belong. Participants spoke of the sense of being one with these followers in Christ. It enriched the sense of worship with angels and archangels and all the company of heaven.

A final example comes from the Canonmills Baptist Church in Edinburgh, Scotland. At Christmas, when memories of not a few families will be stirred, recalling those members who used to be present but have died in the last year, the church takes an opportunity—provided by a large Christmas tree set in the one of the squares near the city center—to sponsor lights to shine in their named memory. Hence the "presence" of these saints is recognized at the festival of the Incarnation. They are remembered as part of the body that still seeks the peace of the city.

It may also be the case that in some congregations the Communion of Saints finds regular focus in the intercessory prayers of the church. For example, on June 20, 1923, at Ramsden Road Baptist Church in Balham, England, Robert Veysey de Carle Thompson—a student of Regent's Park College—was ordained. He was to serve with the Baptist Missionary Society. The order of service includes the Communion service with an order of prayers listed: a prayer of confession, a prayer for the Holy Spirit, a prayer of thanksgiving, and then, following participation in the bread and wine, a "Prayer for the Communion of Saints."[25] We do not know, of course, the content of these prayers, so the Communion of Saints may well refer to general intercessions, since such prayers do not appear elsewhere in the service order. But coming at the conclusion of Communion, it is more likely that the church recalled the saints and gave thanks for them and a continuing participation of them, along with the congregation, in the life of Christ. The hymn that followed includes these lines: "Yet she on earth hath union / with God the Three in One, / and mystic sweet communion / with those whose rest is won."[26]

In these and other ways, some congregations have affirmed the doctrine of the Communion of Saints and by so doing have deepened their understanding of being the church of Christ. Doubtless, there are other stories to be told. Some of them are personal, with rich surprises for those concerned, and I wish to tell one here in conclusion. In 1901 a service of thanksgiving was held at the West Street Baptist Church in Rochdale, England, in celebration of the lives of the Reverend and Mrs. T. W. Piggott and their twelve-year-old son Wellesley. On July 9, 1900, these three with others had suffered martyrdom for Christ. They were in China with the Baptist Missionary Society, serving in the Shou-Yang Mission. During the Boxer Uprising, ten other members of the mission suffered a similar fate that day, including one other child. It is recorded that as they made the two-day journey to the place of execution in open carts, Mr. Piggott, whose hands were manacled, nonetheless preached earnestly to the crowds whenever the cart stopped by the way. He preached to the last.[27] One of the Piggott's company, Wang-Tan-Jen, because of his known zeal for Christ, was specifically ordered to defile the cross on which he stood if he wished to save his life. He refused and was killed immediately.

At the service of remembrance and thanksgiving in Rochdale in 1901, the preacher flashed out the question, "Who will take their place?" A seventeen-year-old man stood up—a clerk in the accounts department of a local mill, baptized the previous November—and declared he would go. His name was Henry Raymond Williamson. He went eventually to prepare for ministry at the Bristol Baptist College, where he showed a particular aptitude for language study, and in 1908 applied to the Baptist Missionary Society. He was accepted for service in China, as was another member of the West Street Baptist Church, Miss Emily Stevens, who was engaged to be married to Williamson.

Their service given in China lasted until 1938, during which time Williamson became a well-respected scholar-Christian.[28] He returned to England and gave further service as a member of the Headquarters

Staff of the Baptist Missionary Society, and in 1951 he was President of the Baptist Union. Upon his return to England, he became a member of the Cheam Road Baptist Church in Sutton, Surrey. I myself was a much younger member of that church, and I was also to go the Bristol Baptist College with the encouragement of H. R. Williamson. Each vacation we would meet to talk about the past term and the calling to ministry. At my service of ordination to Christian ministry in July 1965, the ordination prayer was led by Dr. H. R. Williamson. Thus one young man and the church of which he was a member, in a comfortable part of England, were in contact and fellowship with those who had literally given their all for Christ. In a direct line of vocation by the covenant-making God, we were part of the martyr church. Such a memory remains deeply moving and inspiring. Memory is a powerful and creative form of solidarity. To forget the saints is to be impoverished indeed.

MEMORY AND COMMUNION

Richard Kidd

Reflecting on Memories

This chapter—which takes up the theme of memory, introduced so powerfully in Brian Haymes' account of his own ordination to ministry—is an experiment in critical reflection on experience. I need to make this clear from the beginning, as it has a number of implications for both the form and the content of all that follows. Each unit of exploration I offer sets out from the description of a particular memory, usually my own, either called to mind in the immediacy of writing, or lifted from fragments of journals written over a period of years. I have no intention of claiming for these memories an intellectual weight in excess of their just deserts; they are in the end no more than *my* memories, with all the incompleteness and fragility that memories always have—one of the themes that will receive more detailed attention within the body of this chapter. The only real measure of such proposals as I offer, then, lies in the reader's assessment of the quality of my critical reflection, and with it the value of the connections that are made with other material gleaned from a wider corpus of Christian reflection on experience.

My particular memories have been chosen on the basis of little more than a "gut feeling" that they are in some way significant for my own spiritual journeying—often they seem almost to choose themselves. Immediately, of course, use of the word "feeling" has its

limitations. It is a concept that is open to such a wide variety of interpretations, and there is a danger that the very use of this term will lead
some readers to undervalue the place these memories hold in my life.
These are, however, significant feelings that have already stood some
preliminary tests of critical analysis, and survived; they do not deserve
to be dismissed as "mere" feelings, even if my faith-life does not stand
or fall by them. In fact, few of the ideas explored here are actually core
to the faith I live by—nor, indeed, the faith I hope to die by. It is not
that they tackle issues that are unimportant for faith—the memories
I recall and my reflections on them are genuinely significant for the
faith I live by, and have clear implications for my understanding of
God—but they remain ideas that are still very much "up for grabs,"
and I quite expect them to undergo further evolution as a result of my
own continuing reflection. Already, however, my experience is that the
twin concepts of "remembering" and "memory" have been circulating
somewhere just below the surface of my consciousness for most of my
Christian pilgrimage, and their importance has been fed from a wide
range of sources, within and beyond the Christian community.

It is not insignificant, for example, that I am strongly drawn to
the core motifs in Marcel Proust's classic, *A la recherche du temps perdu*
(*In Search of Lost Time*);[1] I am deeply drawn to the idea of repeatedly
revisiting particular intimations that surface from the past, better to
understand my present experience. From early in *Du côté de chez Swann*
(1913), the first of the six volumes, in a flowing stream of prose, Proust
explores in minute detail seminal moments from early childhood,
which remain for a lifetime as powerful to shape and transform the
present. Best known is his memory of a "madeleine," a small sponge
cake with a distinctive shell-like shape:

> And suddenly the memory appeared. That taste was the taste of the little
> piece of madeleine which on Sunday mornings at Combray (because that day
> I did not go out before it was time for Mass), when I went to say good morn-
> ing to her in her bedroom, my Aunt Léonie would give me after dipping it in
> her infusion of tea or lime-blossom.[2]

A simple incident of memory becomes in Proust's novel the focus for
extensive reflections on the place and energy of memories in later life.
I know this experience too—not perhaps focused around an encounter

with a "madeleine," but I have no shortage of other madeleine moments amongst my own recollections.

I am also drawn to the poems of Craig Raine, who shows a similar commitment to the continual revisiting of personal histories. "The Onion, Memory," a poem that provided the title for one of Raine's early published collections, includes the following lines:

> It is the onion, memory,
> that makes me cry.[3]

This is a hugely powerful metaphor that functions in a variety of intriguing ways: not least, it invites us to explore the layering of memory in all its complexity, and it emphasizes the potency of memory to shape our present moment, sometimes reducing us to tears.

My gut feeling, then, is that the experience of memory is fundamental to my experience of faith, and that it is deeply interconnected with an elusive intuition that somehow my own faith-life is intimately interconnected with the lives and memories of others, widely scattered across time and place. It is this intuition I explore in this chapter as a contribution to the overall theme of the Communion of Saints.

"Living" Memory and Hope

All great spiritual movements live "from" and "in" the memory of their founders and founding events. Israel remembers Moses and the crossing of a particular sea, as the event recorded in Exodus 14:21-31 is recalled throughout Israel's history as a peculiarly formative moment. Christians remember Jesus and a specific death outside the walls of Jerusalem, and it has often been noted that each of the three Synoptic Gospels uses around half of its respective texts to explore the final stages and death of its leading character. Indeed, Christians highlight both "memory" and "remembering" in their most distinctive community ritual, the Lord's Supper (or Communion meal), calling each other to "remembrance." As is well known, in 1 Corinthians 11:24 and elsewhere, the Greek word is anamnesis, much more than a casual recalling, but an invitation to feel for and to know the resurrection presence and the life-giving energy of the one who is remembered.

There have been many attempts to capture in paraphrase the fuller meaning of the crucial Corinthian text, "Do this in remembrance of

me." I have often experimented with different paraphrases of this seminal instruction. As far as I can recall, the trigger came in an early collection of prayers by the United Reformed Church author Alan Gaunt,
best known for his work as hymn writer, where I found the words, "Do
this to make my presence known." Other variations of my own have
included "Do this and live the memory of me" and "Do this and let
my memory come alive amongst you." But every experiment of this
kind introduces distractions as well as elucidations, and ultimately has
its own limitations. The crucial point is that memory—far from being
a merely mechanical device to replay newsreel from the distant past,
somewhat akin to a high-quality digital recording—has the potential to
occasion something enormously dynamic and vital, in which all kinds
of "coming alive" begin to happen.

Memory, however, does not just stand alone in our quest for meaning. It is hard to imagine "living well" in the present moment without
the twin foundational supports of "memory" and "hope" orienting us
to the past and the future, respectively. Jürgen Moltmann made the
point very strongly in his groundbreaking *Theology of Hope*,[4] and this
motif has remained crucial for his theological development ever since.

In early life, memory is still embryonic and slender, while hope is
open ended and soon becomes expansive. As life unfolds, the balance
shifts, often almost unnoticed, and in later years memory can become
increasingly wide ranging and deep; conversely, hope can become more
narrowly and sharply focused. In the case of a long life, memory as
"active recall" typically begins to fail, although, long after stories can
be articulated, formative people and events from the distant past can
remain hugely significant. In the normal flow of life, however, where
one or the other, memory or hope, is threatened or radically truncated,
perhaps by disease or by forced confinement, "living well" seriously
suffers.

Traces of Those Long Gone

It has been my own experience, corroborated in the testimony of
many others, that when in later life we begin to revisit the "well of
memory," seeking to understand more fully the people we have now
become, attention naturally focuses on those formative years through
childhood into early adolescence. This has, of course, been the staple

of psychology ever since it first began to take shape as a distinctive science in the early twentieth century. Sigmund Freud famously proposed models mapping the ways in which human development is formatively shaped by relationships with the father and the mother: with the mother drawing on the language of the ancient Greek mythology of Oedipus, and with the father drawing on the dramatic Hebrew and other mythologies of patricide.[5] Few today take Freud at face value; a hermeneutic of suspicion has rightly pointed up the biased perspective generated by his own distorting male experience, as also the imbalanced sample of clients, largely comprising vulnerable women already manifesting symptoms of ill mental health. However, the core motif, the potent influence of childhood experience, is beyond question. Building on and radically critiquing Freud, Melanie Klein, for example, focused more explicitly on the experience of male and female children, rather than adult females, and Kleinian analysis continues to provide another mapping of the correlation between early experience and later life.[6] Today it is commonplace in a wide range of therapies to encourage the exploration of early memories, in the expectation that their discovery will contribute to a process of growing wholeness and health. Indeed, the significance of memory is now understood not only in relation to particular formative events, but in the whole process of human development.

I am especially struck by the measure to which people, most of whom for much of our lives have remained largely forgotten, are actually still very much "alive" and, in some sense, "at work" within us. It is as though the impact of their past encounter, however brief, has left some kind of trace, has become incarnated in us, as it were, so that secretly they continue to live within us and through us. It is noticeable, however, that in beginning to try and express this, I have found it necessary to push at the limits of language, to begin to tell a story rather than provide an explanation, even drawing on a complex metaphor like incarnation to suggest a creative way of exploring my theme.

I, like others, have no difficulty at all in remembering particular mentors and teachers, now long gone, who still profoundly shape the person I am today, so that the very way I see the world continues to be informed by their ways of seeing—so much so, that it is as if they are still actively present with us. Mrs. Whitaker, for example, still enables my spirit to thrill in the presence of early twentieth-century visual art. Mr. Parker still enables me to problem solve in an incisive and systematic way, even though today's problems are poles apart from the disciplines of mathematical physics through which he so deeply influenced the shape of my teenage mind. And the cloud of witnesses is legion: all those peculiar relationships with parents and significant others who, for better or worse, laid the trails that now enable and disable my ability to reach the full potential of human maturity. We might reasonably say that this is the very fabric of our development as humans. This is why it is not necessary in each new generation to "reinvent the wheel" over which our forebears have already sweated and devoted their energy. We can take up the baton, continue the race where they have left it, their ideas and aspirations continuing, for good or ill, to shape our own futures. The philosopher Karl Popper draws attention to the way that human knowledge is, for instance, systematically laid down in a collective memory, much of it stored in libraries and archives.[7]

In the history of Christian theology, this mode of connecting with the past has typically been identified with the concept of tradition—which is why Baptists, along with many other Protestants, have struggled to incorporate this insight into their broader mindset. Such a clear choice has been made in favor of Scripture over tradition, so that the baby has been thrown out with the baptismal water, and we have lost hold of the ability to articulate something that, in reality, is no less dear to us than it is to others. When we trawl the collective memory of our own Baptist spiritual parents, be it Thomas Helwys, John Smyth, Charles Haddon Spurgeon, John Clifford, or whoever is the flavor of the era, we are no less allowing the stories of the saints to shape us than others in less Bible-centered traditions.

One particular personal memory comes to mind as I work at this chapter. In 1994, shock waves ran through our college community with news of the sudden and tragic death of one of our recently ordained ministerial students, Tim Clay. He died in a climbing accident. Tim and I had become special friends; he and I ran our first half marathon together, and we sailed together on significant trips off the south coast of England down to the Channel Islands and the Brittany Coast. Tim had already shown remarkable pastoral skills in his work at the local children's hospice, and so much about him challenged my own spiritual and pastoral aspirations. He had an infectious smile, often accompanied by a phrase that still readily comes to mind: "I'd go for it!" he would say. He would and he did!

For days after the news of his death, my head was spinning with memories, agitated and disturbed by the struggle to begin to make sense of this loss. I still remember a train journey returning to Manchester from a meeting in Edinburgh when I began to pen the following words. I am not sure how best they should be described, a kind of "prose poem" perhaps; I find the process of formulating patterns of words like this to be a very significant way of sharpening my understanding of my own experience and what it is I want to say about it. This particular prose poem is recorded here because it begins to chart the kind of ideas that are fundamental to this chapter. This is what I wrote that day in November 1994:

> Ever your own person
>> it was from strength
>> you opened yourself to a suffering world.
> We saw it when,
>> opening your mind to mindless pain,
>> you turned around
>>> not just in mind
>>> but in living, which turned around
>>>> the lives of others too.
> Often I saw you alone:
>> in a crowd,
>> or in the silence of a race,
>> or once, at the bow
>>> in a threatening sea,
>> smiling inwardly at I knew not what,
>>> listening, watching . . .
> "I'd go for it!" you said,
>> and I found courage to sail through dangerous waters.
> "I'd go for it!" you said,
>> and gently pointed up my failure to hold fast
>>> the radical believing
>>> which once I'd pointed up for you.

And now there is so much I want to ask you:
>so much I could learn
>but this time you have withdrawn beyond the crowd,
>>beyond the bow.

But still I feel you give me courage;
>still you speak as long as memory lives,
>and I listen, attentive to your words.
My prayer . . .
>that I may find grace to become
>one small embodiment
>>of your resurrection to eternal life.

It is that phrase in the last lines, "one small embodiment of your resurrection to eternal life," that has become increasingly significant for
me. This was the first time I had managed to formulate such a thought,
but, as the following sections reveal, it is a thought that has come to
take a very important place in my continuing reflection.

The Emergence of "Becoming"

I also remember, as a young theologian, first beginning to discover patterns of philosophy and theology, largely gathered around the word
"process," which gave voice to my growing intuition that memory does
in fact occupy a very significant role in forming and enabling our present reality. Like the birth of psychology, much of the seminal work
also took shape in the final decades of the nineteenth century and the
early decades of the twentieth century, a period in which major shifts
took place in human self-understanding, especially within European
cultures. After centuries of the preeminent emphasis on "being," with
its "great chain"[8] and its static anchorage in the "eternal now," out of
that ferment of fresh thinking we broadly call the Enlightenment came
a new emphasis on "becoming," and "process" in reality. Many famous
names are implicated in the story: Hegel, Darwin, Marx, and Freud
amongst them. From the perspective of a theologian, the works of
Henri Bergson and Teilhard de Chardin come especially to mind. Bergson, in his groundbreaking *Creative Evolution* (first published 1907),[9]
began to provide philosophical models broad enough to contain the
new paradigms following Darwin. Teilhard de Chardin, wearing the

double robes of paleontologist and Jesuit priest, began to combine a Bergsonian model with new ways of imaging Christ as the "Omega Point" toward which the creative process had long been moving—most famously in his *The Phenomenon of Man* (first published 1959).[10]

All this and more came as a breath of fresh air to someone like myself who was desperate to discover fresh metaphors that would help my spiritual imagination deal with ideas of the "heavenly" without introducing insuperable complications, dualistic separations, and inconceivable otherness. More recently I have drawn inspiration from a movement in the visual arts, the futurists, dating from much the same period.[11] From the second decade of the twentieth century—also inspired by Bergson, amongst others—vorticists like Giacomo Balla Carlo Carrà, and Kasimir Melevich, not content with the "static" limitations of classic iconography, began to experiment with images that would catch more powerfully the unfolding patterns of movement generated by the revolutionary technologies of their day: moving bicycles, trains, and the people who populate them. "Becoming" was increasingly taking its place as integral within the nature of being.

The new thinking spanned a very wide spectrum of intellectual disciplines indeed. Another manifestation of these ideas in the early decades of the twentieth century appeared in Einstein's twin theories of relativity, special and general,[12] paving the way for an emerging "quantum" view of the world: a view within which time is no longer simply reducible to an infinite sequence of timeless instants. Rather, time is always and only known as a quantum of finite duration, a "moment of becoming," a *movement* in which something actually happens, A becomes B. In the language of a mathematics originating with Werner Heisenberg, when dealing with measurement of energy and time on a quantum scale, neither the energy nor the time can ever be zero.[13] The practical outcome is that the precise instant is something forever inaccessible to the human observer; the *extended moment*, even if infinitesimal in duration, is all we can ever discover. This becomes especially significant at the quantum scale, where any activity by the observing subject inevitably disturbs the observed object in the very act of observation.

Based on this, amongst Einstein's many amazing contributions to our ability to conceptualize the universe we inhabit was his deconstruction of the idea of simultaneity, the notion that we could ever all agree what the present moment actually looks like. Without simultaneity, the possibility of a coherent concept of an "eternal now" soon begins to melt. Einstein showed that whether A and B are simultaneous events, or whether A is momentarily before B or B is momentarily before A, is a matter of relative judgment, depending on the "rest frame" of the observer. The best we ever can do is to explore the inner dynamics of the extended span of a moment. This is practically and conceptually immensely challenging and deeply elusive, but it provides a fundamental focus for fascination in human life.

Our best possible endeavor as humans is thus to explore the dynamics of the "moment of becoming"—which is precisely what the early "process" physicist-philosopher-theologian Alfred North Whitehead pioneered with such extraordinary brilliance. Few today would want to stake their entire worldview on the models that Whitehead proposed. Many fields of human self-understanding, including process philosophy and process theology themselves, have moved on substantially since his day, but we would be foolish indeed not to revisit and feed on some of his richest insights.

The Making of the Present

I am especially drawn to Whitehead's and later process theologians' analysis of the way that each present moment of becoming is constituted, made what it is, by a vast network of connections linking back to a wealth of prior events. If we stay initially with Whitehead's original proposals, set out at length in *Process and Reality* (1929),[14] past events become, as it were, incarnate in each new moment of possibility. It is as if there were an immense cone—full of past times and places, reminiscent of Einstein's space-time cones of the knowable past and future (*figure 1*)—that focuses in on the present as we come to know it.

In Einstein's diagram that I have reproduced on the next page, the volumes within the space-time cones represent all the possible moments of space-time past and future with which a present observer has potential for contact—the transport of information limited, as it is, by the speed of light. On this model, therefore, it is possible to imagine other events "outside" the cones that are feeding into and out of the present moment; but, though such events are conceivable, they

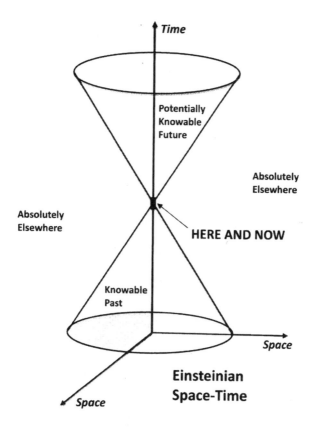

Figure 1

are "absolutely elsewhere," and can never become the content of our human observation.

A Whiteheadian equivalent of this diagram recognizes that there is a vast array of events "back there" in sundry times and places from which it is possible to map trails of influence finally connecting into the present moment; correspondingly, there is a vast array of possible futures to which this moment might contribute an as yet unformed influence. There are, however, as in Einstein's model, pasts that have no connection to our present, and futures that cannot possibly be ours (events outside the cones, in his mapping; see *figure 2*).

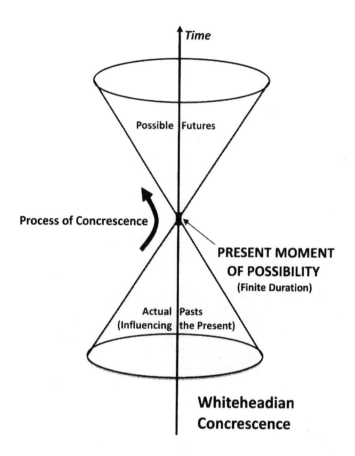

Time

Possible |Futures

Process of Concrescence

PRESENT MOMENT
OF POSSIBILITY
(Finite Duration)

Actual |Pasts
(Influencing |the Present)

Whiteheadian
Concrescence

Figure 2

My interest in this chapter concerns the way that events in the past shape the events of my own experience in the present moment, this moment of "becoming." Whitehead's language for describing the way in which the past makes actual its influence on the present is "concrescence."[15] So, illustrating this in narrative form, it is possible to describe the way the encounters with particular people in my past become objectified in my present experience. If, for example, I tell part of my own story, it will include traumatic moments, like the one when at the age of six I was unjustly reprimanded and humiliated for the first time in front of a class of peers—and the connecting links are still very much alive, still having power to shape my present moments.

I could also include events at which I myself was not even present: the exposure to chemical gas of my grandfather in the trenches of the First World War, which also lives in my present through the stories I heard at my grandmother's knee. I could include events utterly remote from my own time and place, which have woven their way into the fabric of my life, like the martyrdom of Polycarp in the late first century of the Christian era. A chain of connections runs from their first recording nearly two millennia ago, through to the day I first read about this death in Stevenson's *New Eusebius* as a ministerial student, so that now, from time to time, it resonates in my own mind, usually uninvited, when I am tempted to lose grip on my own testimony to the love of Christ. "For eighty and six years have I been his servant, and he has done me no wrong, and how can I blaspheme my King who saved me?"[16] says Polycarp, when threatened by death; and suddenly, who I am and what I can become is in measure reconstituted by Polycarp's presence. I must certainly include the death of Jesus of Nazareth at the hands of Roman soldiers "under Pontius Pilate," utterly immersed as the account is in complex and passionate patterns of interpretation and reinterpretation. This death has become thoroughly incarnate in my own life, on a scale quite unlike any other prior moment in human history of which I am aware.

In summary, then, my "becoming" in each present moment, in some still hard-to-define sense, incarnates and perpetuates the vitality of my friend Tim, my harsh and unjust schoolteacher, my maternal grandfather, the elder Polycarp, and this extraordinary man, Jesus of Nazareth. Their anamnesis is really significant in who I am becoming. In different ways, appropriate to each, I have become, as it were, a minor participant in their "resurrection to eternal life." And what is true of these five is also true of a host of others; I am joined in a living way into the stories of a vast multitude of God's creatures, and amongst them all, crucially, I can testify to a central truth of my life: that Christ lives resurrected in me.

However, the limitation, especially using the original Whiteheadian model, is that objectification of former lives is just that, and leads to a concept of "objective immortality," which looks unlikely to embrace

the kind of vitality, the subjective immortality, to which I am in measure struggling to give expression in a full understanding of the Communion of Saints. People live on, objectified in the memory of others,
but what can we also say about their living on as personal subjects in
their own right, with all the potential development of their personality
that may have an effect on us now?[17] Memory as objectification is providing a useful model for describing part of the way past events shape
my present experience, but it falls short in describing the entirety of
the experiences on which I have been seeking to reflect. Certainly it
seems to offer no space for an active, subjective influence of others,
now dead, on my life in the present moment. This is a serious limitation, and I shall return to it a little later in the chapter.

Humanity as Corporate

All of this might seem to have strayed rather a long way from the physics of Einstein and the philosophy of Whitehead—but perhaps not. I
do not want to suggest that they have "explained away" what is happening in this irreducible mystery that is our human becoming. What
I do want to say is that they have provided me with fresh models and
metaphors that help me to talk about the experience of this mystery
with at least some measure of coherence and consistency. Whitehead
has opened up a line of thinking that provides very helpful ways of conceiving crucial elements of the processes by which we relate to people
who are lodged in our memories, and the fact that this does not serve
to elucidate other issues relating to the continuing influence of those
now dead should not detract from the value of these particular insights.

The model, as explored so far, does yield other dimensions of
significance for our exploration into the Communion of Saints, not
least if we shift the emphasis to the plurality implied in the concept
of communion. The Whiteheadian model already affirms a profoundly
interconnected understanding of human identity. It affirms corporate
identity as being of central importance for human self-understanding.
This, of course, comes as nothing new to the Hebrew and Christian
religious traditions, but it is fair to say that, for much of its two millennia, too much Western Christian theologizing has been massively
overlaid with the Hellenistic patterns of thought that have channeled
us into an all-pervasive individualism.

It is, in fact, only relatively recently that Christian scholars have begun to reappropriate a much more thoroughgoing notion of corporate identity that flourished so well through most of our Hebrew scriptures. For centuries, Western Christians have been taught to read Hebrew and Greek scripture through Platonic and Neoplatonic lenses. This was so much so that we had forgotten how to read the great names of the Pentateuch as tribal communities and not just as individual pilgrims: Abraham and Isaac and Jacob. We have forgotten to read the Letters of Paul the apostle as from the pen of one deeply immersed in Hebrew culture, hearing his wrestling with the relationship between "flesh" and "spirit," two whole states of human life, as an invitation to a crude dualism of soul and body,[18] setting the clock of wisdom back more than two thousand years. This is not, however, a matter of straight alternatives: either an individual or a social view of human being. Individuals are rightly important in a Christian understanding of persons; it is the "-ism" in individualism that does the harm, when individuals are considered as islands, as if the origin and formation of a person were independent of belonging in community.

These rediscoveries of a profound truth about human identity as essentially communal, however, have not been gained without cost. On my own journey, I first learned to think beyond the model of an isolated individual from the stories of two deeply pained communities. I learned them first from the mid-twentieth-century theologians of Latin America, who saw through the myth of individualism and its crushing effects on the poor of their lands, and who began to affirm "being in community" with new energy and commitment. Starting from the simple biblical premise that when one part of the body suffers, all suffer, they began to cut through the hypocrisy of church and state, which were both making rationalizations of a necessary division between rich and poor. They began to mobilize newly "conscientized" communities, initiating processes of social transformation that would be significant for not only themselves but the wider world too.[19] Much of this came to me first through the writings of Gustavo Gutiérrez,[20] and later through José Comblin.[21] This was consolidated by hands-on experience during a brief but personally formative visit to El Salvador, where I met Christians, Baptists and Catholics together, living in impressively sacrificial ways that translated the theory into visible practice.

Similar insights have also emerged in recent years as indigenous African theologies have had increasing impact in the northern hemisphere. Many of us began to learn and experience what is termed in several African languages *ubuntu*, an ancient model of corporate identity deeply rooted in pre-Christian African cultures. Ubuntu is a very rich concept, not easily translated into contemporary English. Found widely in African cultures in a variety of guises, this Zulu/Xhosa word expresses a deep conviction that humans cannot and do not exist in isolation one from another. "My" humanity and the humanity of the whole community are profoundly interconnected. Ubuntu makes it clear that my humanity is not a project I can tackle alone, for "my" humanity and yours are interlinked. It is ubuntu that undergirds the experience that strikes many Europeans so forcibly in the form of extremely generous hospitality to the stranger, but it goes much deeper than that. It is ubuntu that determines levels of sharing and communal support structures that are now quite unknown in most Western communities.

I also learned these and related insights from the rapidly emerging women theologians of the same era, who began to point out a dimension of male inadequacy in the dearly held doctrines of individualism. Why, they asked, are men so typically concerned with their own sinfulness, their own salvation, their own eternal destiny, as if any of these make sense without the salvation of us all?[22] Their writings impacted me deeply, and I have gladly watched the gradually widening influence of their deeply Christian insights. The invitation, then, from Latin America, from Africa, and from many of our most gifted women theologians is to begin to take a new pleasure in our corporate identity as human beings, to discover a real contentment in the loss of self as individual and the finding of self in the community of God.

No Easy Solution

It might feel that this last exploration was something of a diversion, so now we must begin to pull the strands of this chapter together. What does it look like to take "memory" seriously in the exploration of human identity? The first answer is that it does not look like an easy solution. The models of memory I am exploring do not offer quick answers or provide "explanations" for the mystery of human personality or our hopes for personal identity beyond these mortal lives.

Indeed, in some ways these models and metaphors make it even harder to give an account of the mystery we call human life. But the lack of ease alone should not deter us.

There is a complex philosophical issue that needs exploration around the question about objective and subjective immortality. In terms of the Communion of Saints and a theology of memory, the question is whether the influence of past saints on our lives today is simply a matter of us responding to the residue of their lives objectively, but statically, implanted in the networks that frame our current experience. Or does it make sense in any way to think about a continuing incarnation of their active subjectivity, such that past saints somehow actively prompt the now of my own story? Is there a living dimension to the continuing presence of the saints, living that is in the sense of their continuing intentional activity? This is indeed a complex question, and I think it unlikely that it will be resolved in a way that will command universal acceptance. These issues as they relate to process models of God have been carefully mapped in the writings of Marjorie Suchocki,[23] and have been further refined in the written responses of David Griffin,[24] and my own coauthor Paul Fiddes.[25] All three are seeking ways that a process model might be developed and refined so as to accommodate a more active sense of lasting human survival evident in the shaping of later human experience, and ultimately, of course, in the memory and experience of God.

Suchocki states the problem very clearly and makes proposals for modifications to the process models as we know them through the writings of Whitehead and later by Charles Hartshorne.[26] She revisits the process of "concrescence," seeking to discover, in each brief event that comprises the totality of life in the world, a lasting residue of aliveness that remains to be caught up again in the future in active ways. Her own proposal struggles to describe coherently how it might be that this myriad of moments, strung together as it were to describe a life, might hold that continuity and connectedness in the longer term, which might be called "life" in the memory of God. Griffin explores a model with resonances to a more traditional idea of a soul that survives death. Fiddes suggests that a coherent model, one which is sufficient to deal with the totality of human experience, demands we also see it in concert with an understanding of resurrection, a creative act of God when "God recreates persons on the basis of God's living their lives vicariously for them, now raising them to participate fully in the dance of God's triune relations."[27]

My coauthor will explore the idea of resurrection further in chapter 4, but for the purposes of this chapter I much prefer to leave the account I am attempting as simply providing insights within the more limited scope of a discussion about memory, ours and God's. I do want to affirm here, however, that the idea points me to the place where I think the most helpful insights accessible to us are likely to be located, that is, by thinking more fully about what it means for our lives to be lived within the life of God. I want to suggest a connection here with another modeling of life in God: that which underpins the writings of Thomas Merton, and works with a distinction between a "true" and a "false" self.[28] It is no surprise to me that we might need the help of a mystical writer like Merton at this point, because it seems to me we are reaching the boundaries of philosophy's intrinsic ability to provide a single coherent model of a reality that I believe to be shot through with unsubstitutable mystery. Thinking back to the section on cosmological physics, I am struck by a growing, relatively recent, consensus that begins to cast doubt on the theoretical possibility of a single unified theory of everything, the great scientific dream very much alive from the days of Einstein through to the late twentieth century. Increasingly, the message from the exponents of string theory and M-theory seems to be that the project could well be flawed. Stephen Hawking in his most recent popularization, *The Grand Design*,[29] clearly suggests that the best humans might ever be able to achieve is a collection of models, each fitted to the description of clusters of experimental data, but intrinsically incapable of interconnections in the way that would reduce these models to a single, all-embracing whole. My own sense is that something similar is at work in the modeling of the kinds of human experiential data that become the content of theological reflection. Many theological models might well yield significant insight into part of the human experience; it might even be that in time these models can be reduced in number to a minimal few that together touch most of what we want to report—but never, perhaps, to a single unity.

Another way to put it is that I am not expecting a theory of memory, human or divine, to provide a single coherent model for understanding the mystery of the Communion of Saints. Two key aspects of any discussion about memory come immediately to mind as warning that we should be cautious not to overestimate our powers of explanation. The first is that we humans have a remarkable ability to deceive ourselves when it comes to matters of identity and self-awareness. This is part of the package we call corporate sin. We are all too familiar with the power associated with the control of history—a major theme in Orwell's *1984* scenario—and where there is power there is usually the abuse of power. I remember the impact on me of reading Edouard Hoornaert's *The Memory of the Christian People*, which came out of the Latin American liberation movement mentioned above;[30] it was the first time I was exposed to a radical retelling of the early history of the Christian movement, rehabilitating many of the players, like the Montanists of second-century Asia Minor, that I had previously been taught to dismiss with the label "heretic." My experience is that, quite commonly, further exploration of movements traditionally rejected as dangerous to orthodoxy yields rich and valuable insights that were written out of the history because of their threat to the hierarchy. Staying with the illustration of Montanism, I have now been encouraged to recognize in it a creative grassroots movement in early Christianity, with significant insights into the ministries of women, and the theology of the Holy Spirit.

If I am to engage creatively with my own memory, I will need all the skills of critical scrutiny I can lay my hands on. I like the phrase "a hermeneutic of suspicion," well known from the work of Paul Ricoeur. The exploration of memory should not be undertaken lightly, nor, ideally, alone. Spiritual companions and communities of faith are not just luxuries, but par for the course. I can, for example, use my personal memories of the abusive behavior of others to license my own lack of discipline and self-control; understanding influences can become an excuse rather than a prompt for transformation.

A second caution concerns the way that memories steadily transmute with retelling and the passage of time. This is, of course, the basis of one very significant dynamic of healing, and has great anthropological importance. As Miroslav Volf explores so creatively,[31] the healing of memories is a complex cluster of processes, one dimension of which is a kind of anesthesia, left to us as a gift out of the evolutionary process.

We all know the cathartic value of repeatedly retelling the story of a recent accident, and the comfort that comes as the shock gradually becomes integrated with the larger narrative of our lives. But the shifting sand of memory can also become the basis for self-deception. Each time we recall an event of our past life, the new event, the "recollection," is itself a new event, and the remembering of the new event irretrievably alters the earlier remembering. Around the fortieth anniversary of the first landing of a human on the moon, one astronaut was reported to say that when he had told the story more than a thousand times, it became ever harder to know the difference between truth and falsehood about details. In some instances, it is even hard to know whether there was an original event at all. As we "remember" and there is a fresh coming together of traces from the past with additional information and knowledge from the present, there can be a radical change in how we relate to the past, for good or ill.

Blending these reflections with my exploration of process ideas, at least inasmuch as this had taken shape in my own mind by the mid-1990s, I remember writing this short piece, seated on a thrifty tussock overlooking the Sound of Iona, on a beautiful summer afternoon in August 1996:

It is no small thing for us
> to remember;
not merely
> the regret of
> > promise broken,
> > opportunity missed,
the pain of
> grief revisited—
> real though these are.

Much more,
> each time a memory is re-collected
> > it is changed,
> > > forever, and in measure lost;
> > fused with fresh connections,
> > > new interpretations,

which, when re-stored,

fade into that

eternal blur

which will become our final now.

And God is the chief exemplification!

Reading these words more than a decade later still resonates much with my spirit, but I would no longer want to retain the penultimate lines. "Eternal blur" and "final *now*" no longer tell the truth as I see it, not least because of much more sustained reflection on the final line about God and "chief exemplification"—Alfred North Whitehead again![32] This is the big line, with radical implications for how we understand the place of "becoming" in the being of God. This is the line that demands we see becoming, not as an afterthought or an add-on to the deepest nature of reality; rather, it is integral to the nature of everything, God included.

Community in God

"And *God* is the chief exemplification." This is truly the trump card. In other words, everything I have so far explored about the way that past events become lastingly incarnate in my own *human* being is also true of God, the *divine* being. Nothing is lost; everything is caught up into the memory of God. If we take this route, then one clear implication is that there is genuine kinship between God's remembering and my remembering; in other words, reflection on the dynamics of my own memory process will not be entirely deceptive in the way I think about God's memory too. This is another point at which I find the connection to Merton and writings of other more mystical authors helpful again.[33] If Merton is right, and when I discover my true self what I am actually uncovering is God active in me—or to put it the other way round my only true life is my life "in God"—then I begin to trace a model in which my subjectivity is something that only makes sense in the here and now in immediate connection with the activity of God. I in Christ and Christ in me—this is my hope. This is being alive. If this works as a model of being alive today, is there not huge potential to carry this model over into the continuing life of God where those "true selves," alive in God, continue to be at one with me in a dynamic "living" way, in community with me, whose true self is also alive even now in the same Christ? I am most alive, after all, when I am not self-centered at all, but when God is alive in me and I am centered in God.

Now caution intervenes again. Suddenly I am nervous that I might be overstretching a human limitation in my capacity to model a mystery. I am reading these powerful images—"true self," "in Christ"—as metaphors and not as explanations of the sort that every kind of reductionism loves to favor. A deep conviction of mine is that persons are not accessible to reduction, to resolution free of intrinsic mystery.

In my continuing quest for models that rise to the challenge of issues raised in this chapter, I am also greatly attracted to the language that becomes increasingly the coinage of Baptist and other theologians around the world—that is, to language about *participation* in the life, the Trinitarian life, of God. At first sight, it might have seemed that this model of incarnate remembrance is still too mechanical, too impersonal, not lively enough. But if, indeed, we are dealing with embodiment into the life of God, the possibility for genuine vitality is again open ended.[34] Not only am I helped to understand more fully what it might mean to be interconnected with the lives of a vast community of God's creatures, past and present, but I also have the makings of a model for giving such account as I am able of my hope for the future.

If all this is credible as critical reflection on experience, it demands a radical reenvisioning of human and Christian identity, especially amongst Protestant dissenting communities like the Baptists, who have all too easily been overwhelmed by the tide of individualism and put too much of their energy into the basket of individual survival. Our hope must be to discover a fresh understanding of what it means to celebrate ubuntu, our lives completely and utterly bound up and integrated with the lives of the whole human community—not seeing this negatively as if others were a millstone around the neck of our own salvation, but positively recognizing all that is on offer in this particular kind of loss of self and gain of the whole. Only then we can see lasting living participation in the memory of God, as the highest possible affirmation of life and hope. On this model, the memory of God becomes more than an occasion for the pleasure of God, as also an occasion of deep pleasure for us who live "in Christ" in communion with God and all God's people.

Let us thank God, then, for the emphases that have graced our particular Baptist history: an emphasis on continually listening to Scripture, and an emphasis on radical openness to the rule of Christ. In these must rest our hope of continuing reformation and, amidst it all, a very different perception of what it means to belong in a vast Communion of Saints, spanning the immensity of time and place.

3

HOPE, STRANGENESS, AND
INTERCONNECTIONS

Richard Kidd

"So will I ever see him and be with him again?" This is the agoniz-
ing question many a widow would articulate to her pastoral visitor—
if only, that is, she could be confident that her question would elicit
genuine and serious consideration. It is one of those cases where too
much "Yes" or too much "No" proves equally superficial, pastorally
and humanly inadequate. "Yes *and* No," however, can sound so easily
like evading the question. And yet, "Yes" and "No" are both necessary
to be true to the human, biblical, and theological complexity of this
question.

On the one hand, Jesus did not encourage his hearers to run away
with the idea that a future beyond the grave is simply "more of the same,"
even if written in a larger font. The peculiarly private bonds explored
in a lifetime of married love will not be carried over, or certainly not
in exact continuation, he says to the Pharisees (Mark 12:18-27)—so,
there is no point in pushing seeming contradictions for those who are,
sometimes of necessity, married several times. There is no point in trying to force categories forged out of the stuff of daily experience, in
order to transfer their descriptive capacities directly into the language
of heaven. Never, indeed, is it more important than on issues like these
to remind ourselves that we are dicing with metaphors; sometimes the
metaphors will simply break down, and sometimes all six faces of the
dice will be needed to gain even limited purchase on the reality we
aspire to describe.

So "No," I do not think I will "see" my dad again—I mean *in the exact way* that I remember him in my early childhood, when he passed to me his carpenter skills at the bench in our workshop, or as I remember him taking my hand and speaking a blessing over me in the minutes immediately prior to his death at the ripe old age of ninety-two. My experience is, however, that he still comes to me in my mind's eye—or, perhaps, as artist Bridget Riley so cannily calls it, my eye's mind.[1] He arrives at unexpected moments, both waking and sleeping, usually to bless me, recognizable by his characteristic smile, and this is a sufficiently significant component of my life experience that I am forced to wrestle with its potential theological significance. I am not at all willing to read these as ghostly appearances, but that does not mean they are not, in some important sense, real. They are "real" dreams, both daydreams and night dreams, and they are hugely significant for my personal well-being. They fit well with the models of objectified memory I explored in the previous chapter, but I find still myself compelled to ask if there is more to "being with him" than skeptically, in modern reductionist mode, I might rush to believe. If being with him has some real measure of meaning for me in the "now" of my present life, then why can this not also be so beyond my own death when, as it were, he and I will share in something of the same "beyondness"? So "Yes," there is something in my own experience, as well as in the received wisdom of the Christian tradition, that forces me to say more than a simple "No."

But not every metaphor will work for us on such delicate ground. To pick up an appropriate measure of the "Yes" and the "No," we will need to find, for example, ways to articulate more emphasis on a corporate than on an individual dimension of human being. We will also need to find a way, as I explore it in this chapter, to begin our thinking with something that happens "in God" rather than something that happens "on earth," whether it be this one or some "new earth."

A Corporate Future?

So, how much mileage is there in the theme of a future corporate identity? I am not at this stage ruling out the importance of individuality, but we do need to test out what happens when we push at the boundaries. For a start, it is not difficult to demonstrate that the overall theme of interconnectedness has gained hugely in vitality in recent time. Cosmologists now stretch our minds with the idea that certain subatomic particles are twinned across the entire universe, their quantum states synchronized like dancers in a vast cosmic ballet. Whether the specific term "Gaia" is invoked or not,[2] serious science as well as serious religion has become immensely interested in exploring those senses within which the whole order of the universe might betray a level of interconnection, as yet little explored or understood. We hear it in the oftentimes overburdened terminology of ecology, and its narrative descriptions of the whole, that attempt to draw on a wide range of metaphors gleaned from the parts. So, for example, the planet might be said to "react" to the pressure of specific environmental changes, the implication being that there is something more organic, almost something conscious, than "mere" reactivity in a mechanical system. Already, narratives have taken shape suggesting that planet earth as a whole has strategies for survival reaching way beyond what we might have guessed from knowledge of the parts. Ecological *niches* do not disappear lightly without complex "attempts" by the whole to secure their survival; there is, as it were, a pressure for the preservation, maybe even the increase, of diversity. I have to remind myself, however, whether as ecoscientist or as theologian, that this is all metaphorical talk, although no less important for that. It is just too easy to slide from the metaphorical into the literal, almost accidentally buying into the discredited notion that the literal is somehow a superior carrier of truth.

I have long been impressed with the thought that, in the development of human understanding, the consequences of increasing complexity are not always logically predictable simply based on information available from the prior conditions. A specific childhood memory comes immediately to mind. In the very first weeks of secondary-school science, I learned that when iron filings and sulfur are combined by heat to form a ferrous compound, there appear some quite unpredictable characteristics in the more complex material that is formed: how, for example, visually it relates to the yellow and gray of its component parts, and whether it will or will not have the magnetic properties of its ferrous constituent. In reality, it is neither gray nor yellow, but an odd color very much its own, and it is not magnetic at all!

Even at first hearing this, as a schoolboy, this struck me as highly significant—that the rigors of a deterministic universe are not as simple as the reductionist culture of the 1960s was trying to tell me—and I tucked the memory away, little knowing how strongly it would resurface in future years. But return it did when, as a young theologian, I began to read Teilhard de Chardin's inspiring narrative of the cosmic evolutionary process.[3] Teilhard de Chardin identified moments in the increasing complexity of the universe when, as he saw it, the intrinsically unpredictable emerges—effectively releasing into the universe a new and previously unknown dimension of reality. These, for example, he located in the transition from inorganic to organic systems, in the transition from purely reactive systems to those that seemingly manifest an element of choice, and in the transition to the human in which a new narrative of spiritual identity becomes meaningful.[4] The narrative continues, then, through Christ to an "Omega Point," one in which an utterly unpredictable possibility for the human emerges, seen uniquely in the Christ, and signaling a potential for us all, the possibility of a genuine new humanity.

Now, as they say in the great sagas, this was all a very long time ago, and the development of diverse sciences has given us humans a hugely more substantial grasp of the mechanisms of such a process than anything accessible to Teilhard de Chardin in the early years of the twentieth century. In the meantime, however, similar ideas were further developed by Paul Tillich in the third volume of his *Systematic Theology*, where he mapped a possible orderly model for understanding an emerging sequence of dimensions of existence in the universe—from the inorganic, through the organic and the psychological, eventually to the spiritual.[5] Tillich aptly chooses the metaphor "dimension," rather than "stratum" or "layer," to avoid some of the inevitable misunderstanding that might accompany these inevitably hierarchical words. One thing that interests me is the measure to which our apparent wisdom in all these matters is ever and only *ex eventu*, after the event, and today I am not at all sure that it is wise to assume that the intrinsically unpredictable, something perhaps even beyond what we now know as the spiritual, is closed with respect to future happenings—and a higher "dimension" of human interconnectedness might just be one such theme.

Every now and again, even in the twenty-first century, we can get a taste of human corporate interconnectivity, which takes us by surprise. Could it be, for example, that the World Wide Web is pushing at the boundaries of a new human possibility? Certainly it is already offering us a plethora of metaphors with which to explore new ways of thinking. Much as the flutter of a butterfly's wings is said to create sufficient local atmospheric disturbance to effect a shift in global weather systems, so it seems that the "flutter" of a seemingly trivial individual human action can generate enormous transformations in global patterns of human behavior—and this effect goes far beyond simply influencing public opinion. The World Wide Web increasingly provides metaphors that suggest enormous possibilities for transformational change. The touch, accidental or deliberate, on a keyboard in a remote corner of the world can now destabilize global money markets and make an impact on the life or death of already starving children on the other side of the globe.

The potential for a higher, or perhaps deeper, level of human interconnectivity reaches much further, however, than anything that can be described as the mechanism of the Internet. And it is not at all surprising that it has been novelists and poets who frequently seem to feel their way toward these unknown futures more effectively than those limited to the partial strategies of scientists who are still overlocked into a positivistic paradigm. As H. G. Wells demonstrated very clearly, science fiction can sometimes run way ahead of science fact.[6]

All I want to say at this point is that there is nothing fundamentally incredible, even in the modern era, in speaking about another kind of human potential, a corporate human identity before which even the African experience of ubuntu pales into insignificance,[7] the kind of thing Christians have been exploring from the start with a concept like being "in Christ," interconnected in a real *koinonia*, something so much more than any individual's making.[8] Baptists should feel good about this, because part of the genius of our own movement has always been our delight in the local experience of *koinonia* in the communities we call congregations, people gathered by the spirit of God who find that they can see emerging, out of their togetherness and interconnectedness, something quite unpredictable, a mind that is more than the sum of their own individual contributions, something we dare to call "the mind of Christ." This quest to find "the mind of Christ" has been at the heart of our church meetings and meetings of churches in associations and assemblies.

Reference is frequently made to the use of this phrase in Philippians 2:5. Sadly, however, over the centuries its meaning has too often been reduced to something little more than membership in a club, in the sense of a fellowship of the already like minded. Baptist tradition at its best has claimed something much more surprising, a mind that emerges amongst those who might otherwise never have anything in common, something that emerges simply because all are *in Christ*. So, a legitimate, perhaps compulsory, Baptist ambition today might be to push this to the furthest limit, "losing" ourselves in Christ and finding another kind of mind, as yet only tasted in part. "For to me, living is Christ," says Paul (Phil 2:20). "Christ in you, the hope of glory" (Col 1:27).

I have often found myself needing to use a term like "strangeness" to describe those moments of interconnection in life that, whether they are susceptible to logical explanation or not, nonetheless register themselves powerfully in our lives, our memories, and our futures. One of those moments of strangeness that sharply focused my own attention occurred on retreat at the Jesuit house at St. Beuno's in North Wales. It was 2006, and for a whole decade I had frequently found myself using my visit in 1996 to the rose garden at the University of Central America in San Salvador as a focus for inspiration and further reflection. The garden was planted in memory of the six priests and their two housekeepers brutally murdered in 1989 by the military in the middle of the civil war. In the nearby museum is a photograph of one of the priests, Father Ignaçio Ellacuría, then rector of the seminary, face down on the ground outside his residence at the university. It was taken on the morning after the killings, and it is not difficult to identify the bullet holes in the back of his head where the shells passed through his skull into the ground on which he had been laid. A deep impression from Ellacuría's life and death stayed with me long after my visit. We had, in some ways, a great deal in common—and yet there is so much that leaves us poles apart. I too have been the equivalent of a rector in a seminary; I am now around the age that he was at the time of his death. But the differences are enormous. He lived the good news of Christ in such a way that it became strategically advantageous for the military to "take him out"—and many times I have found myself reflecting how little I have done that might even mildly rouse the forces of wickedness to such anger in the presence of the gospel. For many years I kept a small photograph of him pinned to the corner of my computer, as a kind of prompt to remind me how dangerous the good news of Jesus Christ can be for those who really find the courage to live it.

It was only on the last day of my guided retreat at St. Beuno's—at the end of a very significant silent experience lasting more than a week, a week in which I had passed in and out of the St. Beuno's chapel many dozens of times—that I chanced to glance at a small black and white picture that hangs by the sacristy. It contains tiny images of all the martyrs of the University of Central America, and in the center at the top is an identical copy of my own small picture of Ignaçio Ellacuría. That night it stopped me in its tracks. It was not that anything defying logic or due scientific process had occurred; it was simply a moment of strangeness when something lodged itself in my consciousness with unusual force. Next day, after explaining to my prayer guide that as a Baptist I had no framework for thinking about these things, I asked her whether it would make any sense to say that, in some "strange" way, that evening Ellacuría's life and mine might have touched, and what she would say about it. She simply said, "Today there is extra rejoicing in heaven!"—which I took to mean that Ellacuría himself was, in some sense, taking delight in my awakening awareness of the Communion of Saints.

Could it be that these strange human moments—the moments our metaphors struggle to express, when it feels proper to say things like "I believe that my dad (or Ignaçio Ellacuría) is praying with me"—do indeed make sense in the larger scheme of things? Could it be that to deny this is to betray an offer to embrace the unthinkable that God in Christ is always willing us to enjoy?

God in Us?

Another example of life's "strangeness" comes to mind. I can no longer be at all sure about its epistemological status; I feel that just what happened and how it should be interpreted must remain very much in the air. It was during my days as an undergraduate in King's College,

Cambridge, so that makes it 1971, more than forty years ago. I was still very young as a Christian believer, and hugely gullible for emotional exploitation. I had come into contact with a then highly innovative charismatic prayer group, just beginning to meet in Cambridge—recently inspired through contact with the work of David Watson in York. Heady days indeed! All of this left me with a disturbed and disturbing sense of longing to experience the immediacy of the Holy Spirit in more visible ways, as others around me at that time seemed to be discovering. On this particular day, I was the person appointed to read the Gospel at Evensong in King's College Chapel, famous the world over for its Christmas Eve carol service. Although I had read a lesson in King's Chapel quite often, it never ceased to be an inspiring and challenging thing to do. When I looked up the lectionary gospel for the day, particularly given my preoccupation with my own intensified search for the gifts of God, I was notably excited to find that I would be reading the dramatic words from Matthew 18:19—"if two of you agree on earth about anything you ask, it will be done for you "—so I was already alert to a heightened sense of drama.

There I was, then, suitably robed in gown and surplice, perhaps thirty seconds before leaving my seat in the choir to read at the lectern, when a stranger sitting next to me, without any words or other acknowledgment passing between us, handed me a scrappy torn-off sheet of paper on which he had just penned some words. This is what he had written:

> God in us
>
> trust
>
> trust
>
> else
>
> we're
>
> less
>
> than
>
> dust

I felt a kind of shock wave run through me, sensing that something quite extraordinary was happening, though quite what I really had no idea. I read the lesson with unusual conviction, returned to my seat still a little shaken, and tried to concentrate on the remains of the liturgy. When the service was over, I waited until almost everyone else had left the chapel, and then turned to the man, who showed no sign of rushing to leave, inquiring who he was and how I should understand the significance of the paper he had shown me. In one sense the story he told is quite simple and unremarkable, just one more thread in the everyday passage of time and of things, but in another sense I am not so sure.

He was, he said, a poet from the United States, visiting Cambridge for just one day, and, overwhelmed by the beauty of King's Chapel and the music of King's choir, he had penned these few words—immediately wanting to show them to someone. On that occasion, the someone turned out to be me. By this stage, as we sat in the quietness of the emptying chapel, he could see how shaken I actually was, but he never allowed me sufficient space to intimate that he might in any way have been functioning for me like a messenger from God—though I have always suspected he felt at least a hint of that in himself too. I invited him back to my rooms overlooking the River Cam and the famous bridge over the river in the grounds of the college for coffee and conversation. What American tourist could refuse an offer like that? We chatted for a while, although, for some reason I now cannot fathom, I ended up with no record of who he was or how I might be in touch with him into the future—and soon he went on his way. I have never seen him again, but the words he showed me on that flimsy scrap of paper have remained scorched on my mind as if it were yesterday—and perhaps, all these years later, I am still continuing to understand, little by little, more of what they could possibly be about.

The whole event felt strange—even as it was happening. Inevitably it all became interwoven with my personal search for some kind of charismatic renewal. As an event, I have certainly never forgotten it. Forty years later it comes back to mind with force as I reflect on the themes of this chapter. It recalls one of those moments of strangeness when something of the interconnectedness of our human narratives briefly becomes apparent. Furthermore, both in content and form, the whole event potentially hinges around a concept of "God in us"—and by implication therefore, symmetrically, "ourselves in God."

I remember my early years as a believer as ones in which "strange happenings" seemed to pass my way with much more frequency than, with hindsight, I recall for most of the intervening years. It is only in quite recent times, seemingly without invitation, that the frequency of my need to call on the language of "strangeness" has slowly risen on the scale again. Or is it just the perspective through which I choose to read events? Like the event in King's Chapel, none of them is strange in the sense that it is low on susceptibility to description and rational explanation; but all of them are strange "to me," because that is how they struck me, and because they do seem to make an impact on my own life and the lives of others in ways that matter more than run-of-the-mill matters, ways that have sometimes had lasting implications. One further illustration will suffice in making my point. This time it was late one evening on Stockport Station—very much deserted, and quite a hostile environment for the lone traveller. The only other person in sight was a young woman, and I recall thinking to myself that I ought to keep my distance, since a tall, bearded stranger might easily present as intimidating at that time of night.

But as I bought my ticket at the machine, I realized that she had taken the initiative to move much nearer, and was standing immediately at my side. As I turned to look, she said something like, "I have a terrible headache; it has been an awful day at the hospital." My first inclination was to look over my shoulder to check out the person she was speaking to—but soon I was left in no doubt that she was talking to me, and that she was making a lightly veiled plea for help. In retrospect, I can see that I had been right about her more than normal vulnerability; my guess is that she had a modest level of learning disability—which is something I have thought about and worked with from time to time over the years. It turned out we that were heading the same way, and I think it would be fair to say that in a strange kind of way I became her "guardian angel" for a while, until finally we said goodnight, me remaining on the train, as she got off and headed home. It could happen to anyone, any evening, yes; but it actually happened to me, that particular day, and it had a quality of strangeness, which makes me think about it again, all this time later, as I reflect about God at work "in me," "in us."

On reflection, the common factor between those early "charismatic" years and more recent times might be something about my own disposition to spiritual awareness. The presenting context more recently is my exploration of contemplative modes of spirituality, the kind I have learned to associate with Thomas Merton, Henri Nouwen, and others whose ways of thinking I now explore quite regularly on retreat in a place like St. Beuno's.[9] Increasingly I have come to think that the heightening that seems commonplace in the testimony of those caught into movements of charismatic renewal and the testimony of those who explore silent and contemplative forms are very much two sides of a single coin. Most obviously, you might say that when overwhelmed by the presence of God there are really only two possibilities and neither of them is conventionally verbal: either you pray in tongues, or you fall into silence.

I am writing about these things here because they seem to intimate a potential interconnectedness between human lives beyond the normality of day-to-day experience, and I cannot help but wonder if they are tiny foretastes of a human possibility still only minimally realized at this moment in human history. Perhaps they are the stuff of a more fully realized humanity, the kind that might also be known by those who are fully and finally "in God," beyond death. They occur from time to time, it seems, in every human culture and, I am guessing, to far more individuals than dare to bear public witness to them in the contemporary Western world. They were, of course, bread and butter in ancient Hebrew communities, who could speak more freely about them in narrative forms, without the fear of the rejection that we often face in our compulsively reductionist world. They are found at many of the great turning points in human history—when Abraham welcomed three strange guests at a table in the wilderness (Gen 18:1-10), when Moses became strangely aware of a burning bush that would not be consumed (Exod 3:1-12), when a woman in Jericho named Rahab aided two Israelite spies in the time of Joshua (Josh 2:1-21), and when the first Christian disciples became inexplicably aware that Jesus, even after his death, was still strangely active amongst them, even more so, perhaps, than in the days of their shared pilgrimage through the villages and countryside of Judaea.[10]

All these experiences, of course, resonate peculiarly well with the content of the "poem" presented to me that evening in Cambridge and with the phrase "God in us"—without which, the visitor was right, there would not be a lot to write home about but dust. I continue to explore new ways to feel for what this might mean—"God in us"—and what I think of as an equivalent phrase, "Christ in us." "Christ in me" seems to be quite a good description of this opening up of a westerner's normally inhibited experience. Thomas Merton was in no doubt that it is "Christ in me," "Christ in us," that is the key to almost everything of significance in spiritual experience.[11] It is experiences with an edge of strangeness that make the ancient stories of the Eastern church's "saints" seem so alien in the modern West, and yet at the same time make them so attractive to many contemporary readers.

I find myself both drawn to and hesitant about the idea of Christ being, in some very deep sense, "in me." Positively, it offers a meaningful, really quite thrilling framework for understanding the energetic, almost resurrectional explosion to which human beings testify at times of peculiar spiritual significance. Negatively, however, I hesitate: first, at the measure to which it might seem to override my personal freedom, and also to the apparent exclusivism of its overly closed Christian explanation of things. Perhaps another of my own "prose poems," written at a time when I was especially wrestling to understand the possible significance of experiences of this kind, offers a way through and beyond this discomfort. I titled it "God in Us," and it reads like this:

Christ,
God giving Godself in the world.
God giving Godself
in bud and leaf-burst
in all people and everywhere.
God giving Godself in me.
God giving Godself
in Confucius,
in the Buddha, in Mohammed
and for me, I do confess,
quite amazingly in Jesus.

I am choosing in this prose poem a very particular way of understanding the concept of Christ—or better perhaps "Christness"—through the dynamic concept of "God giving Godself." I am also recognizing that such giving can take a multitude of forms and expressions. I have long been attracted to the idea that there has to be more to Christness than Jesus,[12] although a Christian can never think of Christness *without* Jesus. As a Christian believer, I cannot separate "Christness" from the historic Jesus of Nazareth, but I want to say that others who do not count themselves as Christians find at least something of what I know through my encounter with the person of Jesus, while I want to confess his importance for me as clearly and coherently as I can. Intellectually this belongs with my conviction that "Christness," "God giving Godself," is a reality in all human beings everywhere, a precondition of our very humanity. This is a widely explored theological strategy and originally came most strongly to my own attention through the work of the Roman Catholic theologian Karl Rahner, with his idea of the "pre-concept" or "pre-apprehension" as a gift of God.[13] However, his language of the "anonymous Christian"[14] seems to me to be an imposition of the Christian label on those who do not own it for themselves, and I would rather speak of an "anonymous Christ."

So could these "strange happenings" be described as the "Christ in me," as it were, somehow effecting a connection between me and the same "Christ in others," providing a point of meeting in the one Christ? If I take, for example, my experience with the girl on the station, could it be that she, in her frail and somewhat broken state, was that evening especially open for the "Christ in her" to surface with unusually heightened clarity, my own attention alerted by her particular movements and words? I have long thought that many of the people I have known with significant learning disabilities have also demonstrated greater potential to manifest such openness, a quality that more able folk like myself too often close down in ourselves using our excessive hubris, self-confidence, and self-assurance. I am wondering if, on that evening, my own more than usual openness to Christ meant that the "Christ in me" could, as it were, effect a deep-level connection with the "Christ in her," such that a "strange happening," a moment of profound interconnection, was free to take place.

However, describing my experience in this way, if taken too literally, could easily undermine the subtlety of what I am trying to convey, turning our genuinely "strange" meeting into a merely mechanical process. What I am trying to articulate is deeply informed by my understanding of the mystery of God, and a sense that it is proper to speak of our meeting as some kind of movement in God, a meeting "in Christ."

The surprising thing, perhaps, is that we are not aware of such move-ments more normally as a part of human life—if indeed this is consti-tutive of our very being, as Karl Rahner and others have suggested. Thomas Merton would probably have said that our lack of awareness is a direct consequence of the priority we give to a "false self," a super-ficial human construction that obscures a deeper reality, the "true self," the self that becomes possible on account of its grounding in God.[15]

I merely offer these narratives in an attempt to illuminate some of the stranger things that happen to us. They certainly help me to make sense of a number of things I am struggling to understand. Thinking back to my encounter at King's in 1971, given that poets are, by trade, unusually dedicated exponents of openness, it is not at all surprising that it should be a poet who was intuitively open to this strange con-necting of persons.

This approach to what I am calling "strangeness" is very much con-nected with a theological conundrum that I first encountered years ago while exploring the theology of Paul Tillich. Tillich, like many others, became convinced early in his own theological pilgrimage that all theo-logical language is "symbolic"—that was his word, though today others might say "metaphorical" and mean much the same. My guess is that he would have been comfortable applying this term to my own exposi-tion of what it means to be "in Christ." Tillich never found, however, his own use of the term "symbolic" entirely convincing, and continued to explore whether in fact there might be at least one nonsymbolic (or nonmetaphorical) statement lurking somewhere in the background—a statement that would enable, as he said, the whole theological edifice to have at least one leg to stand on. In the first volume of his *System-atic Theology*, he toyed with "the statement that God is being-itself is a non-symbolic statement,"[16] as the possible leg, the one nonsymbolic statement. But its claim on him could not be sustained, and my under-standing is that he ended his life returning to the conviction that no such statement can be found.

I too share something of Tillich's unease; I too would like to find a leg on which the whole theological edifice can make its perch. I won-der if Tillich's error was that he repeatedly looked for a conceptual statement to break through what he experienced as an *impasse*. Surely that was always doomed to fail, because every conceptualization is bound to be susceptible to precisely the same symbolic analysis. Shifting the metaphor from legs to boots, Tillich was very much trying to lift himself up with his own bootstraps. Rather than a nonsymbolic or nonmetaphorical "leg," a more credible direction was that taken by Karl Rahner and others who worked from his transcendental Thomist perspective, when they wrote in terms of the "preconceptual," an a priori horizon that effectively bridges the epistemological gap between human experience and divine mystery.[17] The fact that this knowledge is preconceptual should not bring into question its reality or its crucial importance; it merely relocates its epistemological standing. The preconceptual givenness, the horizon, is very closely related to what I am calling "Christness," "God giving Godself" to us. It is "Christ in me"—the immediate, nonconceptual encounter, the most real encounter I can ever have—that is the ultimate hope of salvation, my own and others. "Christ in me" really is the key—to life, to faith, to salvation, and to future hope.

Ourselves in God?

Earlier I suggested a possible symmetry between the language of "God in us" and "ourselves in God." This invites further exploration. One of the most familiar ways that Christians define their relationship with God is to speak of themselves as being "in Christ." This is a rich metaphor. To be *en christo* is, amongst other things, a way of saying that we participate in all the existential benefits that are ours because of all that Christ is and all that Christ has done, and so because God is as God is. We are beneficiaries of all God's gracious gifts; among these are unconditional acceptance and thus freedom to act in the world, even when this freedom expresses itself in ways that are at odds with what God would prefer to choose for us. "In Christ" my prayers, if they are authentic, are best described as Christ praying in me, effective because it is Christ who holds my prayers for me and with me "in God." The Apostle Paul speaks of something like this, using the language of "Spirit" in Romans 8:26-27. This is why it makes sense to Christians when they pray to God, through Jesus Christ. It seems reasonable to me, then, that the prayers of all the saints, both living and departed, should operate in this way. So when I sense that there are those who continue to pray with me in God, be it Mary of Nazareth, Ignaçio

Ellacuría, my parents, or whomever, it is always and everywhere also God praying in them, in God. Christ praying through them, in Christ. It is a work of God as Spirit.

Our puzzling and tantalizing foretastes of this way of being "in Christ" suggest to me that the polarized distinction of individual and corporate identity might reasonably be thought to collapse when the fullness of "God in us" and "ourselves in God" is finally achieved. I cannot do more than dice with the metaphors; I wager on the mysterious, perhaps mystical, experience in the midst of life that my true self, acting most freely, is in reality God acting in me, and so by implication connecting me into the greater wholeness of an extended human community. This gives me confidence that to be entirely "oned" with others and with God need not negate the reality of my personal identity, my ability to become and to be myself.

One more memory has returned to mind; on the night of my own first coming to adult Christian faith, more than forty years ago, I was presented with a book in which my faith midwife had written a few words from the opening of the Second Letter of Peter. I have treasured it, both the book and quotation, and repeatedly it invites me back for further reflection. The core phrase is the writer's injunction that we should become "participants in the divine nature" (2 Pet 1:4). This is a phrase that has received sparse attention amongst Protestants generally and Baptists in particular, but has always been important in the Orthodox communions of the Eastern church. The Orthodox have never shied away from the idea of *theosis*, the conviction that we are caught into a process of divinization at the heart of God's work of salvation. In the twentieth century, more attention was given to the writings of the Eastern fathers, and a fresh encounter with what John Hick described as the Irenaean, as distinct from the Augustinian, traditions awakened new interest in the West of these Eastern ways of thinking.[18]

As I read the opening of 2 Peter today, it draws me back to the centrality of God, and specifically our life "in God." As we read in Paul's address to the Areopagus, "For 'In him we live and move and have our being' as even some of your own poets have said" (Acts 17:28). Once again it seems that it is poets who have been ahead of the game. The image of being a "participant in the divine nature" reminds me that at the core of all our human becoming is God; we are what we are, human, only because of the life of God in us. It also keeps me focused on God's ultimate goal for us all, to be liberated into the joy of God's own life.

An Even Greater Hope?

How, then, are these insights related to other great themes in the Christian tradition concerning our future hope, and in particular to the important motifs of "resurrection of the body" and "new creation"? The focus for my discussion in this chapter has been ways in which we might think coherently about our own experience of praying, and how this relates to the praying of those who have died before us, with whom, I have sought to argue, we share an elusive but deep communion in prayer, in Christ.

There are, however, these other great themes of hope on which I have hardly touched, and the next chapter will explore these more fully: it will suggest possible ways of connecting our sense of praying in communion with those recently departed, with an even larger perspective on God's still incomplete work of renewing the entirety of creation. The conviction I have been seeking to express here is simply this: that the saints are in some real sense praying with me even now, their prayers rising as, in the words of the seer of Patmos, a fragrant incense (Rev 8:3-4)—even if together we still await a general resurrection. My own convictions concerning the Communion of Saints are predominantly projections born of a confidence that grows out of my present experience. Having known this God in Christ, and tasted "in-Christness," we can trust that this is how it truly is, in God.

Is it possible for a Baptist to translate all this into a coherent and functional spirituality, a discipline of prayer that does at least some justice to experience, Scripture, and tradition? I have been experimenting for some time with a simple pattern of prayers, something like the patterns in the rosary. Within a cycle of repetitions, I have been looking for brief forms of words that express sufficiently of the deep content of my faith to function much as the "Jesus Prayer" functions for others in their respective traditions.

After reflection, I have arrived at two brief forms of prayers that seem to capture much that is true to my experience. The first is deliberately a variant on the Jesus Prayer, but picking up the crucial note about God in us. It reads:

> Jesus Christ, God in us, have mercy.

The second is a response to the famous prayer calling on Mary, as *Theotokos* or "God-bearer." The phrase I am keen not to lose in this prayer is the one that continually brings me back to a reminder of my own mortality, "the hour of my death," but it also seeks to name the relationship of my own prayers to the prayers of those who have gone before me. It reads:

> All you, gathered into God, pray with me now and in the hour of my death.

These, then, I offer as prayers to express a trust in the Communion of Saints, made strong in the spirit of future hope.

4

Praying with Mary and All the Saints

Paul S. Fiddes

If we are Catholics, Orthodox, or Anglicans, we will be reminded at the Eucharist that we do not pray alone. The words of the liturgy tell us that we celebrate the death and resurrection of the Lord in the company of "Mary and all the saints," and our prayers of thanksgiving and intercession are mingled with theirs. In one form of the eucharistic prayer in the Catholic Mass, the priest recalls Mary, the apostles, and all the saints and then prays, "May we praise you in union with them, and give you glory."[1] Similarly, in Anglican *Common Worship*, the celebrant prays "that we, in company with [naming a particular saint, often Mary] and all the Saints may praise and glory you for ever."[2] In the Orthodox Divine Liturgy of St. John Chrysostom, the priest prays that God will "make firm our steps through the prayers and intercessions of the glorious Mother of God and Ever-Virgin Mary, and of all your Saints."[3] Perhaps unsurprisingly, nothing similar can be found in the patterns for the Lord's Supper suggested in the recent volume *Gathering for Worship* published for the Baptist Union of Great Britain. The earlier Baptist *Orders and Prayers for Church Worship* (first published in 1960) does contain the prayer "And we praise thee for all thy servants departed this life in faith and fear," asking God that "we may . . . with them be made partakers of thy heavenly kingdom,"[4] but all mention of *sharing* our prayers with them is avoided.

Does this omission at the Lord's table matter? Does it matter that we avoid mentioning that we are praying with Mary and all the saints?

I suggest that it does, and explaining why will—I hope—give me an opportunity to pick up some threads from the preceding three chapters, as will reflecting on the prayer offered at the end of the last chapter, "All you, gathered into God, pray with me now and in the hour of my death." But, of course, the point at which we begin our discussion should not be with our own praying at all, but with the praying of Christ.

Sharing in the Intercession of Christ

In Hebrews 7:25–8:1, we are presented with the picture of Christ "sitting at the right hand of God" and praying, as the Great High Priest, to God the Father in the heavenly sanctuary:

> He holds his priesthood permanently, because he continues for ever. Consequently he is able for all time to save those who approach God through him, since he always lives to make intercession for them (7.25) . . . the main point in what we are saying is this: we have such a high priest who is seated at the right hand of the Majesty in the heavens (8.1).

This statement by an unknown author is strikingly similar to an expression used by the Apostle Paul, that Christ "who is at the right hand of God . . . intercedes for us" (Rom 8:34), suggesting that the heavenly intercession of Christ is a widespread tradition in the earliest church. Though it failed to get into the creeds, it is frequently mentioned by the church fathers. Later, it played a strong part in the theology of the Reformers, who appealed to it for support of such doctrines as that Christ carried his humanity into heaven, and that Christ—rather than the churchly priest—presents his own sacrifice to the Father as victim and priest.[5] However, the picture of Christ interceding with God the Father on our behalf does raise some uncomfortable ideas. It seems to imply that the Father is reluctant to forgive us, and needs the effective pleading of his own Son to move his heart, while much other biblical witness speaks of the compassionate God, always willing to forgive.[6] The returning son in Jesus' parable needs no spokesman on his behalf with the father, who runs to meet him and embraces him.

There seems then, in Hebrews 7:25, just the touch of having a powerful "advocate at court" to present our case,[7] and this can be (and has been) extended into the advocacy of Mary and the saints. Once God the Father is seen to be a distant and stern authority, calling for a more "human" intermediary in Christ, it is easy to extend the picture into an exalted Christ calling, in turn, for even more human intermediaries like the saints to win the divine favor on our behalf. Mary, in particular, has often been presented as "closer" to the faithful believer, in her role of mother, than Christ is. It was precisely this kind of chain of advocates and mediators that early Baptists protested against,[8] and that still provokes a suspicious reaction against any reference to the intercessions of Mary and the saints.

However, setting Hebrews 7:25 into the whole context of the letter alerts us to a different way of reading this picture of the heavenly intercession. No doubt, the metaphor of an "advocate at court" hovers around the edges of the text, but as in the Bible generally, one metaphor about God must be balanced by another, and there is a more resonant image to hand. The High Priest of these chapters is also the "pioneer of our faith" (Heb 11:2) who has gone ahead of us through the sufferings of the cross to "take his seat at the right hand of the throne of God." We then are to "run with perseverance the race that is set before us"—that is, we are to follow Christ, both the "pioneer" and "perfecter" of our faith, into the heavenly sanctuary. Or rather, we are to allow Christ to take us *with him* into the innermost presence of God:

> Since then, we have a great high priest who has *passed through the heavens*, Jesus, the Son of God, let us hold fast to our confession. . . . *Let us therefore* approach the throne of grace with boldness, so that we may receive mercy and find grace to help in time of need. (Heb 4:14-16)

As Charles Wesley memorably paraphrased this thought, "Bold I approach the eternal throne / And claim the crown, through Christ, my own."[9] The prevailing picture of the book of Hebrews is of the believer as entering the divine presence *with* Christ, who has blazed the trail through his own human trust in the compassionate God. Read this way, the heavenly intercession of Christ becomes a prayer to the Father in which we are invited to join, a prayer that enables the praying of those who, as Hebrews 7:25 puts it, "approach God *through* him." We might say that our prayers ride upon the praying of Christ into the most holy place. Christ as High Priest leads the prayers in the heavenly worship; he does not pray alone. While in the temple ritual of ancient

Judaism only the high priest could enter the sanctuary, or the holy of holies, and pray on behalf of the people, the message of early Christianity was that the veil that separated the people from the most holy place had been ripped apart, and that Christ had taken humanity with him into the heart of God.

The image of the high priest entering the sanctuary has been merged here with the image of "sitting at the right hand of God," and the Old Testament text that lies behind the latter picture is Psalm 110:1, "The Lord says to my lord, 'Sit at my right hand until I make your enemies your footstool.'" Indeed, the connection between royal exaltation and appointment to priesthood is already made further on in the same psalm: "You are a priest forever according to the order of Melchizedek" (Ps 110:4; cited in Heb 5:6).[10] As the New Testament scholar W. Loader judges, "No other passage of scripture recurs so frequently in allusion or quotation in the christological expressions of NT times as Ps. cx. i. In this expression we stand in continuity with christological thought from the very early beginnings of its development."[11] In its original context, this saying was no doubt an utterance of a prophet in temple worship, speaking a promise from God to the Davidic king: "The Lord [Yahweh] says to my lord [the king at the time], 'Sit at my right hand.'" As early Christians reflected on the meaning of the death and resurrection of Christ, they found illumination here about the destiny of Christ. Taking the text in a messianic sense, they found confirmation that Christ ("my Lord") had been exalted to share the very life of God. But they then gave the text a twist: unlike the worshippers in the old temple, worshippers of God in the new temple ("in Christ") had been themselves raised to share the exalted position of the King. As the writer of the Letter to the Colossians puts it, "If you have been raised with Christ, seek the things that are above, where Christ is, seated at the right hand of God" (Col 3:1). Or in the words of the writer of the Letter to the Ephesians, "He has raised us up with him and seated us with him in the heavenly places in Christ Jesus" (Eph 2:6).

The intercession of Christ enables us to pray within the very life of God—this is the point of Hebrews 7:25. When Paul makes reference to the intercession of Christ in Romans 8:34, it is in the context of the impossibility of separating us from the love of God in Christ: "Who is to condemn? It is Christ Jesus, who died, yes, who was raised, *who is at*

the right hand of God, who indeed intercedes for us (emphasis added). Who
will separate us from the love of Christ?" Intercession is associated
here with an intimate fellowship of the believer with God; indeed, Paul
has just proposed that when we can only utter wordless groans because
of our sufferings, the Spirit of God "intercedes with sighs too deep for
words. And God . . . knows what is the mind of the Spirit because the
Spirit intercedes for the saints" (Rom 8:26-27). Paul makes clear that
the intercession of the Spirit is to be understood as the Spirit's praying *in us*, not in our absence: "When we cry 'Abba! Father' it is that
very same Spirit bearing witness with our spirit" (Rom 8:15-16). Heavenly intercession, whether of Christ or the Spirit, is thus portrayed as
enabling our praying and approaching God; our prayers are wrapped in
the prayer that is already going on within God. Elsewhere, Paul speaks
of Christ as the supreme "Yes" from God and to God—"in him every
one of God's promises is a Yes"—and then asserts, "For this reason it
is through Christ that we say the Amen [i.e., the 'Yes'] to the glory of
God." Paul immediately adds that God has "given us his Spirit in our
hearts" (2 Cor 1:19-22). We say "Yes" and "Our Father" through the
"Yes" and the "My Father" of Christ. This is what it means to pray, in
the New Testament formula, "to the Father, through the Son and in
the Holy Spirit."

The church father Origen perceived that the heavenly intercession of Christ as our Great High Priest was to be understood in this
way, writing, "For the Son of God is high priest of our offerings and
our pleader with the Father. He prays for [or *with*] those who pray, and
pleads along with those who plead."[12] But early Baptists had the same
insight. The (Particular Baptist) London Confession of 1644 sets out
the threefold office of Christ as Prophet, Priest, and King, in order
to speak of the local congregation as sharing in the privileges of this
office, and so having a freedom over against ecclesial hierarchy because
it exists under the direct rule of Christ. With regard to the priestly
office of Christ, it asserts:

> Christ being consecrated, hath appeared once to put away sinne by the offer-
> ing and sacrifice of himself . . . and having broken downe the partition wall
> . . . is now entred within the Vaile, into the Holy of Holiest, that is, to the
> very Heavens, and presence of God, where he for ever liveth and sitteth at
> the right hand of Majesty, appearing before the face of his Father to make

intercession for such as come to the Throne of Grace by that new and living way; and not that onely, but makes his people a spirituall House, an holy Priesthood, to offer up spirituall sacrifice acceptable to God through him.[13]

Bringing together a number of Scripture references (noted in the margins), including texts from Romans 8:34 and Hebrews, this clause imaginatively links the intercessory priesthood of Christ in Hebrews with the insight in 1 Peter 2:5 about the church as a "holy priesthood" offering spiritual sacrifices. Through his heavenly intercession, Christ makes his people into those who can freely offer their own prayers and intercessions. We notice too that the confession speaks of a corporate priesthood (as does 1 Peter), making clear that the time-honored Baptist appeal to the "priesthood of all believers" must not be understood as the "priesthood of every believer" as an individual. This is a communal priesthood, in which persons share as a priestly community in the priesthood of Christ. As previous chapters in this book have emphasized, believers participate in a Communion of Saints, which together offers up "spiritual sacrifices."

Sharing in the Relationships of God

Both Scripture and the insights of early Baptists make it clear that the prayers of God's people can only be understood as effective in the context of the intercessions of Christ and the Spirit. Of course, the New Testament writers have a cosmological map—of vertical ascent to a spatial location of "heaven" in which the throne of God and a heavenly sanctuary are situated—that is no longer ours. But this does not matter. New Testament writers show, from time to time, that they aware they are using images to express the inexpressible. Metaphors direct us toward a reality that cannot be expressed literally, and which will always need metaphors, although we can allow one to qualify and correct another. Using another metaphor (and one that appears in the New Testament itself, in 2 Pet 1:4), then, we may say that our praying "participates" in the life of God along with the prayers of all God's people. Moreover, there is a reality in the life of God that makes these prayers possible, a movement of loving intercommunication that we might use the metaphor "intercession" to express. There is something like "praying," on which our prayers can ride. Beginning from a firmly christological basis of Christ as High Priest, we have moved now into a vision of God as Trinity.

The ancient formula of the Trinity, created by the church fathers, refers to "three persons (*hypostases*) and one essence (*ousia*)."[14] They did not intend to speak of three "persons" in the modern sense of three self-conscious individuals, as if asserting that these were also, by some paradox, one individual as well. They aimed to speak of a divine life that was rich in relationships and escaped literal description. By *hypostasis*, the fathers meant a "distinct reality" that has being, and the hypostases were entirely characterized by being in relation with each other and the world that God had created. Thus Augustine says, in an experimental (even playful) way, that "the names, Father and Son, do not refer to the substance but to the relation, and the relation is no accident."[15] Thomas Aquinas later gave formality to the notion by creating the term "subsistent relation," stating, "'Divine person' signifies relation as something subsisting. . . . 'Person' signifies relation directly and nature indirectly, yet relation is signified, not as relation, but as hypostasis."[16]

This rather technical discussion means that because God exists eternally in relations, God can open the divine life to receive us as created beings within God's self, to make room for us to move and dwell. The talk about God "in three persons" is not the language of a spectator ("so that's what God looks like!"), but the language of a participant ("this is what it's like to share in God!"). We cannot *observe* three relations in one divine life; we cannot (at least adequately) paint this dynamic interweaving of love on a canvas, or mold it into an image in stone, or etch it onto stained glass. But we can find ourselves *engaged* in it. The doctrine of the Trinity is not a mathematical puzzle, but only makes sense in terms of our participation in the network of relationships in which God happens for us. Jürgen Moltmann speaks of God as "the event of Golgotha," and to the question, "Can one pray to an event?" he rightly answers that one can "pray *in* this event."[17]

Praying "to" the Father, "through" the Son, and "in" the Spirit,[18] we enter into the eternal relations between Father, Son, and Spirit. This means that when we pray to God as Father, we find our address fitting into a movement of love that we can only say is like a speech between a son and a father. When we make the response of saying "yes" ("Amen"), we find ourselves leaning upon a childlike "yes" of humble obedience that is already there, glorifying the Father (2 Cor 1:20).[19] At the same time, we find ourselves involved in a movement of self-giving like that of a father sending forth a son, an eternal movement ("the only-begotten son") that God continues in mission into the world.[20] To pray "in the event of Golgotha" ("under the cross," as Baptists often say) means that these movements of response and mission we find in God are undergirded by movements of suffering, like the painful longing of a forsaken son toward a father and of a desolate father toward a lost son. The heavenly intercession, as Hebrews makes clear, is inseparable from an offering of a sacrifice by the Great High Priest, who in his earthly life "offered up prayers and supplications with loud cries and tears" (Heb 5:7). Simultaneously, these two directions of movement in God are interwoven by a third, as we find that they are continually being opened up to new depths of relationship and to new possibilities of the future by a movement that we can only call "Spirit." For this third movement, the Scriptures give us a whole series of impressionistic images—a wind blowing, breath stirring, oil trickling, wings beating, water flowing, and fire burning—evoking an activity which disturbs, opens, deepens, and provokes. This is a movement that renews all relations between the Father and the Son.

Sharing in these relations, we discover that we are not responding, glorifying, lamenting, and being sent on our own, but being supported by movements of love, pain, and justice that are far deeper and stronger than we can imagine. So far, in describing these relations, I have followed the form of address that Jesus himself taught his disciples, "Abba, Father." But these movements of giving and receiving cannot in themselves be restricted to a particular gender, as is quite clear with the images for the movement of Spirit. The experience of participating in God may require us to say that we are engaging in a flow of relationships like those originating from a mother (cf. Isa 49:14-15), especially in experiences of being spiritually nurtured and fed,[21] or like those that characterize the response of a daughter. We shall be led in prayer to say, "O God you are like a father and a mother to us. . . . We are your daughters and sons."

The Power of Intercession

So far I have set out the christological and Trinitarian basis for praying in the Communion of Saints, or for praying "with Mary and all the saints." Our prayers are in union with the prayers of all God's people, because they all—to be prayer at all—participate in the intercessions of Christ. It is in Christ, in the relations of the Trinity, that our prayers meet. We realize that all saints share in the adoration of God, that we are part of a heavenly worship, of myriads alive and dead (as far as this life is concerned) who cry, "To the one seated on the throne and to the Lamb be blessing and honor and glory and might for ever and ever, Amen!" (Rev 5:13). The prayers of the saints that glorify God ride on the movement in the Trinity that is like a son responding in love and obedience to glorify a father, and our own prayers are supported on this surge of adoration.

But the Communion of Saints has always meant more even than this glorious sense of fellowship in worship. It has indicated that in some way we *need* the prayers of all the saints, and that they need ours. We are praying *for* each other in God. The phrase from the liturgy of St. John Chrysostom with which I began asks God to "make firm our steps" through the intercession of Mary and all the saints. Another eucharistic prayer from the Catholic Mass prays that God will enable us to share in the inheritance of Mary and all the saints, "on whose constant intercession we rely for help."[22] This is where Baptist hackles usually rise. Even Richard Kidd, in writing his prayer at the end of the last chapter, proposes the phrasing "pray *with* me now and in the hour of my death." Can we also ask, "Pray *for* me?"

To approach the question of the intercessions of all the saints, including "all those gathered into God," we need to answer a prior question: why are intercessory prayers needed at all? We rightly ask, if God already intends to act in a certain way, how can our praying make any difference? Surely we cannot instruct God what to do. Or, does God really refuse to help someone because we have neglected to pray? There is the moral problem of whether it is justice that God should help one person because we remembered to ask God, and should leave another in trouble because we failed to ask. Does God really say (in effect), "I would have healed Mary if you had only asked me, but I waited for all eternity to hear your prayer and unfortunately it didn't arrive"? Or, we ask, why do our prayers often apparently go unanswered? We can understand that some requests will not be in line with God's purpose, and God's answer will be "No," but there seem to be many situations where it is the very purposes of God disclosed in Scripture that do not seem to be fulfilled. I suggest that many of these problems are the more acute and baffling because we arc prone to think of God's action as unilateral and coercive, and that we begin to see light when we realize that God acts only in a persuasive way, and always calls for cooperation from created persons. As the Old Testament prophets tell us, God can feel frustration in the short term when people refuse to work with God. Hosea articulates God's painful cry—"the more I called them, the more they went from me" (Hos 11:2)—and the whole of his poem is a lament for rejected love. The kind of "process" thinking to which Richard Kidd referred in chapter 2 has prompted many theologians (who might disagree with other aspects of process thought) to think of God's acts in the world as persuasive, open to being rejected or modified within a complex network of influences.

I suggest that if divine activity takes the form of partnership between God and the world, then as we pray we can add the persuasive power of our love to God's. That is, in praying for others we are expressing our love and concern for them, and God takes that desire into the divine desire for their well-being. God already wants to create a response within persons at every level (conscious and unconscious), to entice them into an openness to new possibilities that will promote healing, to woo them into cooperating with initiatives of grace. God does not have to be moved from reluctance to willingness to help, or have the divine arm twisted by prayer. Our hopes, expectations, and longings for someone are assumed into God's own persuasion, augmenting and amplifying the urgings of God's Spirit, so that together God and the interceders begin to work transformation. Whether we want someone to act justly and generously, or to be comforted, or to be strong in the face of adversity, God is the means of communicating this desire to them, and of making it effective within God's own pressure of grace where on its own our wishes could achieve little. At the same time, of course, the one praying is becoming attuned to the desires of

God, prompted to act appropriately, and where possible, to change the situation with practical deeds of help.

In intercession we find that we are being pulled into a zone of interconnection. This kind of prayer is supremely social. We are being swept into a current in which nothing is separated from anything else, no one from anyone else. We find we are being urged by the Spirit to pray for those far away in the world, some of whom we have never met; we find that we can enter with empathy into the experience of the hungry and needy of the world, and that this opens up an awareness of the hungry and needy parts of ourselves. We who pray for others find that we too are being prayed for as we enter the community of prayer. In intercession we discover the hidden connections between persons and things (explored movingly in the previous chapter by Richard Kidd), which do not appear obviously on the surface of life, and which we often fail to notice. Intercessory prayer is an experience of connectedness and mutuality, because it is praying "in God" who lives in relationships. In intercession we meet others in the *perichoresis*, the divine dance of Father, Son, and Spirit.

Let us clear one misconception out of the way. It would be absurd to suggest that God needs our love to increase the *quantity* of the divine love, in a mathematical way, as if God has only (say) 80 percent of the love necessary and looks to us to supply the extra 20 percent. How could we add anything numerically to the sum of an infinite love? Rather, it is the *kind* of love that is vital: in humility, God has made the world in such a way that God chooses to need the love of *created* persons as well as divine, *uncreated* love in order to carry through creative purposes. As we share in the movements of God's relational life, our love and concerns for others touch them through the mediation of God and are transformed in God. Intercession becomes the enfolding of someone in the interweaving currents of the love of God and encouraging them to find the movements of health and healing that are already there. Our prayer is not needed to get God started, as if God will not act unless we pray: God always draws near to people with persuasive love, with or without us, and God's grace will be the major factor in transforming human life, but our intercessions still make a difference to what God achieves, though we are the minor partner.

Now we can see why the heavenly intercession of Christ (Heb 7:25) is not an attempt to persuade a reluctant God to be forgiving, even through offering the most perfect sacrifice, as some doctrines of the atonement have unfortunately suggested. Not only does the intercession of Christ offer a way into the heart of God for the prayers of created persons, as I have already suggested. Still further, the high priestly work of Christ is the supreme augmenting of uncreated love by human love. In the man Jesus of Nazareth, God has immersed God's self into human existence at its very depths, enduring a death of alienation and forsakenness, identifying with life at rock bottom. Out of that experience, God can now offer human beings a persuasive love that fits into their own situation of forsakenness and loss. The image of the Son "interceding" with the Father points us to the absorption into God of human loves and desires, a receiving of an agonized human concern for those who are lost and straying. This is a more perfect prayer than our intercession can be, and yet God also wants the imperfect, the partial, and the damaged forms of human love and so calls us sisters and brothers with Christ (Heb 2:10-12).

The Finality of Death and
the Hope of New Creation

Thus far I have been describing the power of human intercession, united with the intercession of Christ in God. We may be convinced about this as far as it concerns saints who are still alive, still part of the church on earth. It fits with the Baptist idea of a covenant community and the traditional Baptist aim to find the mind of Christ together. But do we have to draw the line with saints who have died? Can we still pray for each other after death?

Our chapters to this point have, in different ways, wanted to affirm a continuing community of prayer that includes the living and the dead, or all those "gathered into God." However, the authors of these chapters have rightly shown a certain tentativeness in being able to talk about this reality or to conceive what it might be like. There are good reasons for this hesitation—at least three. In the first place, life beyond death is not a matter of empirical observation: it is that "undiscovered country" from which "no traveller returns" to make a report, as Hamlet puts it.[23] In the second place, there is virtually nothing in the Bible about "life after death"—as distinct, that is, from a great deal about a new creation that God promises to bring to the universe following a day of judgment involving all created beings, and that we might (with Bishop Tom Wright) call "life *after* life after death."[24] A universal judgment will bring healing, reconciliation, and disclosure of the truth as a new beginning that will come to those who are both alive and dead. Talk of the "resurrection" and "exaltation" of Christ to God's right hand, including the heavenly intercession, belongs to "new creation" language, as Christ is portrayed not as entering a stage of "life after death," or returning from the dead, but as entering this new creation exceptionally ahead of time, as the "firstfruits" of new life for those who have died (1 Cor 15:20). For this new creation, we have, of course, only metaphors, since it is impossible to speak literally of what is genuinely new from the standpoint of the old creation. It is, in the terms of Jürgen Moltmann, *adventus* (something still to come) and not simply *futurum* (the future of the present, projected out of present conditions).[25] Some will want to interpret "new creation" language as applying simply to a continuous state of life after death (though it will become clear that I do not), and this has often been done in the history of the church; but the fact that the New Testament does not itself identify life after death with "life *after* life after death" (i.e., new creation) is bound to increase vagueness of description of an immediate after-death existence.

In the third place, there is the seriousness or the finality of death within a Christian worldview. This point needs expansion. By "finality," I mean that death is understood within the Jewish-Christian tradition as the event that puts end to the whole human person, not just as the cracking of an outer shell of flesh so that the butterfly of an "eternal" soul can emerge. Here the modern biological view of psychosomatic unity fits in with the Hebrew understanding of the human being as a body *animated* by "life" or "breath" rather than the Greek view of a *soul imprisoned* within a body. The Hebrew view of a human person knows nothing of the dualism between soul and body that Christian tradition has absorbed from Platonism. According to the Old Testament, the *nephesh*,[26] or "life" (often translated "soul"), may certainly be distinguished from the "flesh" (*basar*), but not as an independent entity, or "ghost in the machine" that inhabits the body and could exist outside it as a personal consciousness. At death, the *nephesh* is described as being breathed out, or poured out like water that has been spilt on the ground and cannot be gathered up again (Job 11:20; Isa 53:12; 2 Sam 14:14).

In the face of the seriousness of death, the New Testament stresses that the only hope for created persons is in a new act of God. Hope lies in "resurrection from the dead," or God's re-creating of the whole individual being, body, and personality. This is an event of the new creation, since a resurrected body must have the context of a wholly transfigured physical universe, "new heavens and a new earth." The biblical symbol of the "resurrection of the body" does not indicate a literal reviving of the body with recomposition of its present atoms, but a re-creation of everything that makes us human, as something at least equivalent to being embodied. The image of resurrection thus accepts the psychosomatic unity of the human being; it affirms the goodness of the body and of material existence here and now; and it fits in with our everyday perceptions that a body is necessary for communication with others and orientation to an external environment. By contrast, the idea of immortality of the soul is dualistic, regarding the soul as the essence of the human being that is separable from the body and can exist without it. This makes the body merely accidental, contingent upon the supposedly "really important" component of the soul. Neither the Old Testament nor New Testament supports this idea of a soul. Where the word "soul" is used in Scripture, it refers to the personal life that upholds and energizes the body, and it is not considered to have any survival prospects outside the body.

The finality of death strikes a blow at any attempts we make to justify ourselves. The hope we have in the future cannot be simply the development of our own potential, but hope in God who creates the possible from the impossible. Those who are justified have faced up to the nothingness revealed in the death of Christ, and they trust in the promise of the resurrection that God will bring new possibilities to the world from beyond it.[27] The New Testament understanding of resurrection is not merely, then, about the survival of the individual. It is not about having a survival capsule ("the soul") that outlives the body, but about a new creation. It is a hope for the entire created cosmos, that it will be raised to a new level of being, and that persons will be renewed within this context. Moreover, there is a clue in the resurrection of Jesus that this new creation will be marked by a greater degree of interpersonal existence, a greater participation of each person in the other, a richer dance of life. According to the New Testament, while the resurrection body of Christ is not simply exhausted into the church without remainder, the followers of Jesus may be said in a sense to be his "body," so that here and now the risen Jesus leads a life of deeper participation in others than was possible during his earthly life. God makes room for us in the divine communion of relationships now, and in re-creating us God will "conform us to the image of his Son, Jesus Christ" (Rom 8:29)[28]—that is, our identity will be even more deeply bound up with the resurrection body of Christ and so with other persons than it is at present.

Now, in the light of this form of hope for the conquest of death, we can see why the experience of grief is not only proper but essential. Death has a finality. It *does* put an end to the old creation, all that is familiar to us. It is not a mere flimsy door through which the soul strides and that can be laughed at. In the face of death, we have to trust God to overcome an enemy to life and to re-create, to make again from nothingness. We may trust God that new creation will fulfill all our hopes, but it is a real future that we cannot predict or map, not just an extension of the present; we step out into the unknown. So there is a real loss of the familiar, a loss of the way that relationships have been felt and experienced within *this* creation. We may trust God to remake our relationships with those whom we love, but it will not be just the same, a mere repetition. The dance of life moves on into new and richer measures, into a deeper interweaving of persons. It is right, then, to feel grief for the loss of the old, even though it will be taken up into the new. It is not a lack of faith to feel the awful sense of separation that is so often expressed in bereavement in a period of "searching" for the one who has died.[29] There is loss in the very heart of gain. Indeed, in this experience we enter into the life of God, who also takes a strange journey in the facing of death in the cross of Jesus Christ.

One further point remains in thinking about the finality of death in the present period of the "old creation." I have suggested that the New Testament portrays Christ as the great exception in his experiencing resurrection here and now in the middle of history, and that his "intercession at the right hand of God" is the language of the new creation. If we are to affirm (as I do) that the whole person of Christ was transformed in resurrection, including a transfiguration of his physical body (the tomb was empty), then the question presses as to where his body is now located; this is not a question we have to ask about any other human being who has died, because of the anthropology I have described above. It returns us to an earlier reflection on the symbol of the heavenly sanctuary in which our Great High Priest intercedes. There may just be a mystery here that theology should not presume to resolve, and I offer an answer hesitantly, with no implication that it is the only possible way of conceiving the ongoing bodily life of Christ. We might, for instance, follow some version of John Hick's suggestion that there are parallel universes in which there are cognate physical environments in which resurrection bodies can flourish.[30] I find, however, such speculations to be unnecessary. The clue, as the New Testament scholar John Robinson suggests, may be in the Pauline language of the "body of Christ."[31] Exceptionally, unlike any other human beings who die, Christ has been raised in his body into the physical world that we know, because he has been exalted as Lord of the cosmos. He takes physical form in the many bodies of the world according to the freedom of his will.

The New Testament calls the church the body of Christ because in this community—living in obedience to the word of Christ, telling the story of Christ, celebrating the body of Christ in bread and wine—there is a special encounter with the risen Christ. Here Christ becomes visible and tangible in a particularly clear way, as he intends for the mission of this community. But this does not prevent the risen Christ, in his sovereignty over creation, from allowing people to encounter him in other bodies and communities outside the church; this is the "form of Christ in the world" to which Dietrich Bonhoeffer refers,[32] and on which I intend to reflect in chapter 6. This is how Christ lives the life of the new creation in the midst of the old, though I go beyond the thought of John Robinson and others in affirming that it is not the end of the story of Christ's resurrection. As the New Testament puts it, there will be an "appearance" of Christ when the resurrected Christ, who is at present hidden, will be disclosed to all creation at the time of the renewing of the heavens and the earth and the resurrection of all.

The symbol of the "heavenly sanctuary" of the book of Hebrews thus points to two interwoven realities. As I have already suggested, it is a symbol of participating in God, of living in the space created by the interweaving movements of the relations in the Trinity. But the sanctuary is also in the world, as the space where the interceding of Christ takes place in and through the bodies of the world. The image of the heavenly sanctuary, or a place "at the right hand of God," affirms that God, who is transcendent over the world, is also immanent in the world—or better, that the world is in God, and the "sanctuary" is where the triune God and the world interpenetrate. Many Baptists have traditionally called their worship space a "sanctuary"[33] (as distinct from Anglican, Orthodox, and Catholic churches where "sanctuary" refers properly only to the area around the altar or behind the icon screen); this is appropriate theologically, as the space for worship is where the covenanted community gathers, which is praying "with Christ" and with all the saints. The resonances with older ideas of the church building as a "sanctuary" for those liable to be victims of violence is also appropriate; the church is a space that offers the peace of God over against the conflict of power in our world. The church building is not the only worldly place that can become a "sanctuary" in the sense I have used it—that is, a space in both God and the world where Christ intercedes—but it is a place where this habitually happens.

The Intercession of Saints Who Have Died

If we accept the New Testament account of the finality of death, the question arises as to how we can possibly think of saints who have died as either glorifying God or interceding for the world before a new creation has happened. How can they exist if there is no such thing as an immortal soul that survives the death of the body? How can they "pray" if they are not persons as we know persons to be (even allowing for disembodiment)? What reality does the Communion of Saints have here and now? We might here simply resort to mystery and say no more than that the dead exist "in God." In 2 Corinthians 5, Paul admits to a state of high anxiety; he fears that if he dies before the coming of the new creation, he will not yet have received his resurrection body, and so cannot conceive of how he will go on existing. He does not even consider the Greek option of an immortal, disembodied soul. In the face of this threat, all he can do is throw himself in trust upon God to maintain his identity until the day of judgment comes (v. 10), saying simply that it is better "to be at home with the Lord," without specifying what this might mean. However, I venture—though without any dogmatism—to make a proposal that I have already set out elsewhere:[34] that when we die we continue to exist in something like the "memory" of God.

In chapter 2 above, Richard Kidd has already advanced such an idea, drawing on the notion of "objective immortality" as propounded by the process philosopher A. N. Whitehead.[35] In Whitehead's vision of reality, each actual entity (smallest unit of existence) grows toward its satisfaction by receiving influence from others; when its becoming is complete, it is available in its turn as an object to be "prehended," or grasped, by other entities in their own growth. Charles Hartshorne and others have extended this process into personal relationships; persons who influence us are objectively embedded, and continue to exist, in our own dynamic processes of becoming, and this also applies to God's everlasting reception of what were existents in the world.[36] We might, adapting this kind of view, speak of God's "memory," though this is, of course, scarcely an adequate term for being "in God"; to be remembered by God is a quantum leap forward from being in the memory banks of a computer, or even being remembered by a fellow human being, as Richard Kidd eloquently describes the phenomenon. To be remembered by God would be nothing less than being alive in God. "Memory" is a useful image, but (as Richard Kidd stresses) it must not be taken literally. God is not, after all, a giant monistic mind, but a communion of relationships, and the image of memory only points to being held within the interweaving movement of these relations of self-giving love. The process account of God as a duality of subjective and objective aspects, corresponding to mind and body, fails here—I suggest—to embrace the richness of a Trinitarian vision of God and the sheer "aliveness" of being immersed into such movements of relation, as we catch a glimpse in the Letter to the Hebrews.[37]

We can give no rationalist or literal description of this state, since if we *could* fully conceptualize it, it would no longer challenge present reality, and we would cease to depend on God alone for justification. We can, however, think about it reasonably and imaginatively. Here I want to take a step beyond Richard Kidd's general affirmation that, in some way, persons continue to live in God with their own subjectivity.[38] We might suggest that everything a person is—all her or his memories, habits, attitudes, hopes, fears, and loves—is preserved in God. What characterizes people and makes them lovable is taken into God, and God lives that life in their place—representing them, vicariously standing in for them. After all, we only exist *now* as a person because we exist in God. According to the Christian vision of the Trinity, we share already in the interpersonal life of God as Father, Son, and Holy Spirit; we can trust that "I" will be the same person with the same life story after death because God preserves our *identity* within God's own self. For out of God's memory of us, God will re-create us as a whole person in the resurrection from the dead, in "life *after* life after death."[39]

If we return to the picture of the heavenly intercession of Christ, we recall that all our prayers are held in his prayer. We might then think that the characteristic way in which the saints have glorified and praised God during their lifetime, together with their concerns for others, are kept alive in a God to whom prayer is on-going. The saints' particular ways of self-giving, their love which they expressed for those near to them and those far away—including those they never personally knew—go on living in God and have the potency of prayers, even though the saints themselves are now dead. The human love that they added to the uncreated love of God, and which had a powerful effect on the world, is still enriching the transforming love of God and making a difference. In this sense, the saints who have died are still praying for the world; they are interceding because Christ is interceding. All those who have been gathered into God are praying for us.

As the Catholic and Orthodox liturgies affirm, we depend on the intercessions of the saints, because we share in the life of God. This does not mean, however, that we depend on their "merits" to win us any favor with God, as sometimes the liturgies express it.[40] Such a concept, as we have seen, is not even appropriate for the high priesthood of Christ; atonement is not a transaction in which merits are transferred. Further, if my account can stand as at least an imaginative exploration of what it means for the saints to be "at home with the Lord," there can be no question of praying "to" the saints or asking them to do things for us, such as—at the lowest level—finding lost keys and parking spaces or—at the highest level—being our advocates with God. That kind of direct, earth-bound relation is just not available in the face of the finality of death.

By contrast, the agreed statement of the Anglican-Roman Catholic International Commission, *Mary: Grace and Hope in Christ*, does make room for asking Mary and the saints to intercede for us, despite the rejection of invocation of the saints in the *Thirty-Nine Articles* of the Church of England (article 32). The statement insists that the mediation of Mary and the saints is always subject and subordinate to the unique mediation of salvation by Christ (as testified by Hebrews 7:25 among other texts),[41] and points out that "the Scriptures invite Christians to ask their brothers and sisters to pray for them, in and through Christ," citing James 5:13-15.[42] Moreover, with regard especially to Mary, the statement echoes many Roman Catholic sources in appealing (twice) to the story of the wedding at Cana (John 2:1-12), where Mary "mediates" between the guests and Jesus, drawing Jesus' attention to the needs of the guests (their lack of wine) and bidding the guests "do whatever he tells you."[43] When the wine is understood symbolically as the new wine of the kingdom, Mary is said to be portrayed as bringing to Jesus the needs of the guests for salvation. In the next section, I am going to urge Baptists to give more honor to Mary than we have often given in the past, and to acknowledge the special place of her prayers among the intercessions of the saints; but asking Mary or any other of the saints to pray for us, or to take our prayers to Jesus, fails—I am afraid—to recognize the seriousness of death in putting an end to the kind of personal and social activity that the story of Cana portrays. Nevertheless, while we cannot *ask* the saints to pray for us, we can be confident that their prayers for the world, and so for us, still go on being *effective* in God. As Brian Haymes writes in chapter 1, "They pray, not because we ask for their help, but unbidden in the bonds of love as those who share the life of God in Trinity."[44]

Correspondingly, we can certainly go on praying for those who have died. As C. S. Lewis once wrote, the fact of a person's death can hardly stop us from continuing to love him or her; he asks, "What sort of intercourse with God could I have if what I love best were unmentionable to Him?"[45] Intercession is, as I have described it, a loving concern that enriches God's transformative actions, and there is no reason why death should put an end to this. The abuses of the church in the Middle Ages, such as charging huge sums of money for prayers and masses for the dead in order supposedly to shorten their time in purgatory, ought not to prevent us from simply praying for each other. We pray then "with" Mary and all the saints, not "to" them; we can also say that the saints are praying "for" us and we "for" them. In the light of these principles, I suggest that we can indeed pray the prayer offered at the end of the last chapter—"All you, gathered into God, pray with me"—as long as we understand the invocation "all you" as having a poetic and rhetorical form, being actually addressed to God *in whom* all are gathered, rather than being a direct conversation with the saints. We can, moreover, certainly say "pray with me," while being confident that they are also—in the way I have proposed—praying *for* us.

My account of God's "standing in" for those who have died in faith and love, and of their intercessions continuing through the intercessions of Christ, depends on the hope that God will re-create those whom God holds vicariously alive at present. Divine representation of them requires, I suggest, the concreteness of the assurance that they will be re-created as whole persons who can again pray in new situations, joining in the songs of heavenly worship, though in a more corporate and communal life. Those who "represent" others do so on the basis that those represented *can*, in the right circumstances, finally appear in their own persons.[46] I suggest that it is only tolerable for created persons to exist in the memory of God their Representative if this is their penultimate life and they will finally "appear" when Christ is disclosed to all creation as Lord of the cosmos (*parousia*). For the universe as we know it to be the creation of a good, just, and living God (i.e., for a theodicy), several factors call for those remembered to be remade as whole persons.

First, creation is about God's going out of God's self to create diversity, in which God takes pleasure; if all created things return only to the memory of God, this seems a denial of the extravagant generosity of God in creating multiple things of beauty that glorify the rich life of God. Second, and related to this, others have spent their love and care in enabling "me" to be myself; "my" survival with some unique identity, though in deeper community, is not because of my own worth but because my total loss would waste the love of others. Third, the fact of suffering calls for a consummation of all things; there are too many for whom we pray whose potential was stunted and never came to fulfillment, and whom justice requires should have the opportunity of growth, adventure, and greater completion. Finally, communion with God is such a blessing that a loving God would surely not allow this relation to fail; if there is just a hint of eternal life in the Psalms,[47] it develops in the context of continual worship that the worshipper cannot conceive being terminated.

It can readily be seen how each of these reasons is integral to the experience of prayer—glorifying God, enjoying fellowship with God, and interceding for others. The phenomenon of prayer itself calls for the renewal of creation. There does not seem to be any scientific reason why the physical universe, in which energy takes a whole variety of forms, should not be raised through the creative spirit of God to a new level of complexity. This would not be the replacing of the universe but its transformation. As the scientist-theologian John Polkinghorne writes, "A credible eschatology, which takes account of the eventual death of the universe and looks beyond it to God's new creation, is surely an indispensable component in realistic Christian thinking."[48]

As a biblical symbol of expectation of a new act of God (though continuous with present reality), there is not only the colorful and mythological picture of the saints under the altar of the heavenly sanctuary crying "how long will it be?" (Rev 6:10). There is also the very image of Christ as the intercessory High Priest in Hebrews 7:25. As we have already seen, the picture of the High Priest seated "at the right hand of the throne of the Majesty in the heavens" is dependent on Psalm 110:1, and this contains the essential element of an "until":

> The LORD says to my lord:
> "sit at my right hand
> until I make your enemies your footstool."

When applied in a messianic interpretation to Christ, this introduces an eschatological aspect into the heavenly session, though in early Christian thinking the rather vindictive and nationalistic note about the "enemies" is generally transformed into a peaceful coming of the kingdom of God. As Moltmann notes, the New Testament theme of the exaltation of Christ contains a promise of something not yet complete: Christ is "on the way" to his final destiny, and the story has not come to an end.[49] When merged with the picture of the High Priest, an element of tension enters into the heavenly intercession; as New Testament scholars have suggested, intercession is seen as an interim activity of Christ, occupying the time of history before the end.[50] This prayer is forward looking and time limited, like the Lord's Supper itself, which is to be celebrated "until he comes." The tensions inherent in the Communion of Saints are not, then, to be resolved by an appeal to a supposedly timeless nature of eternity. The conundrum I have mentioned, that we enjoy fellowship with the saints *before* a general resurrection and a new creation, cannot be solved by the proposal that eternal life breaks into the present moment "here and now" on the basis of eternity's being one simultaneous moment. This would be to undermine the commitment of God to human history; while God cannot be the slave of time as we are, God can commit God's self freely to tread the path of time, or the many timescales of the universe at once.

Praying with Mary and All the Saints

Throughout this chapter I have been referring to praying "with Mary and all the saints," though so far this has mostly been an expanded version of the phrase "with all the saints." Now I want to consider why we might single out Mary by name even when we do not always name other saints—though we might well do so on suitable occasions. This question, of course, depends on the larger one of what persons we mean when we use the term "saint." Our chapters so far have used "saint" to refer to *both* all Christian people who have been made holy by Christ—a typical Baptist use—and some whose lives seem to stand out as particular disclosures of the grace and glory of God. Our authors have argued that both uses are appropriate: all Christian disciples are saints, and yet some are remembered more than others.

If we ask *why* some lives draw our attention as manifesting the grace of God in a more vivid way than others, we might offer several reasons (and here I expand on some reflections in chapter 1).[51] First, we might say that this is not due to their own individual virtues, but simply because the church corporately has *found* them to be a focal point for reflecting on the generosity of God in human life. It is a matter of the mind of church, not individual heroism. This is a contrast that Brian Haymes is going to develop helpfully in the next chapter, telling the story of a quiet and humble life that exemplifies it. But we might add some other considerations too. God always acts intentionally in the world, with a purpose directed toward a particular time and place, rather than in a vague and general way; so we may say that God *intends* some human lives, regardless of their personal virtues, to display the divine glory in a particularly striking way (see John 9:3). But, if I am right about the cooperative way in which God works in the world, we must also say that God's intention needs human response to be actualized, and so the way that a person responds to God's invitation is also part (though not the whole story) of his or her standing out as manifestations of grace, remembering always that the human response of faith is itself enabled mysteriously by the grace of God. Finally, the circumstances surrounding a person's life also play a part in whether the church remembers him or her as a "particular saint"; the same kind of life in another setting might not lay the same claims on memory, and so once again we are not concerned with personal exceptional merit. Contingent circumstances, such as persecution or special opportunities for mission, might occasion a life to "shine."

Now, all these factors seem to converge in an exceptional way in Mary, the mother of our Lord. She has a unique place in salvation history, as the one chosen and *intended* by God to be the mother of the Redeemer. She has a crucial role in the mystery of the incarnation, as the Apostle Paul witnesses: "But when the fullness of time had come, God sent his Son, born of a woman, born under the law, in order to redeem those who were under the law, so that we might receive adoption as children" (Gal 4:4-5). Mary also made a *response* to the invitation of God that is a model for all disciples, saying "yes" in humble obedience when the purpose of God was announced to her: "Here I am, the servant of the Lord; let it be with me according to your word" (Luke 2:38). As Karl Barth puts it, Mary represents the whole of humanity in being the definitive hearer and receiver of the word of God.[52] She not only obeyed the word when it came at the annunciation, but she "treasured" and pondered the word in her heart (Luke 1:29, 2:19, 2:51). She went on modeling faithful discipleship in her life, growing in faith as a pilgrim disciple; she was faithful along with a few at the cross when others forsook Jesus, and she was in the upper room with a small company after his death; she was overshadowed by the Holy Spirit before the birth of Christ, and she received the gift of the Spirit at Pentecost. *Circumstances* too play a part in the special witness of her life: according to the Gospel record, she was the first disciple of Christ, being a unique witness to his saving acts, from his conception and birth to his death and the giving of the Holy Spirit after his resurrection. If some object that a critical reading of the Gospels is always liable to undermine the strict historicity of these features of her life, we may respond that it is undisputed that the church has *corporately found* her life to be a special manifestation of God's grace, beginning from the very writing of the stories of the events surrounding the birth of Jesus, and ascribing to her the prayer called "Magnificat" (to which we shall return below).

In two recent significant theological conversations between Baptists and Roman Catholics, the Baptist participants have agreed that it is right to honor Mary as Elizabeth does in the Gospel, greeting her as "blessed among women" (Luke 1:42), and that the title *Theotokos* is fitting for her.[53] This term—"God-bearer" or "Mother of God"—does not of course mean that Mary is divine or the source of Christ's divine nature, and it certainly does not mean that she is mother of God the Father or of God the Holy Trinity. The title has a basis in Scripture ("the mother of my Lord" [Luke 1:43]) and safeguards the confession that Jesus Christ is "truly God" as well as "truly man," since Mary is the mother of the eternal Son of God according to his humanity. As Karl Barth again affirms, Mary is Theotokos because she not only received the word, but gave birth to Christ who *is* the very Word of God,[54] or "the Person of God speaking."[55] In recent conversations Baptists and Catholics have agreed that, while Mary has a special calling in the plan of salvation, like every Christian she too was elected, justified, and sanctified by God's grace (Rom 8:29-30), and was redeemed by Christ her Savior (Luke 1:47).[56] Baptists, however, have not agreed with Catholics that this redemption was effected before her conception (preserving her from original sin—"immaculate conception"), that she consequently led a sinless life, and that her redemption was completed in an assumption to heaven. If Mary is to be a model disciple for us, Baptists think, it is appropriate that she had to grow in faith and trust through normal human conditions and through making the mistakes that we all make.[57] There are indications of this, they think, in the Gospel records.

It is precisely as such a faithful disciple, I suggest, that we remember Mary and affirm that we pray "with Mary and all the saints." Her life shines out as a manifestation of the grace of God for the reasons I have given, and her prayers have a special place within the heavenly intercessions of Christ. The Gospel of Luke witnesses to this by assigning to her the great prayer that the church goes on praying as second only to the greater prayer of Christ, the "Our Father." Her prayer, beginning "My soul magnifies the Lord," reveals her to be a social prophet, declaring that God has a bias for the poor and oppressed: "He has brought down the powerful from their thrones, and lifted up the lowly." Praying with Mary means adopting the same vision of society, in which God yearns to "fill the hungry with good things" and to "send the rich empty away" (Luke 1:52-53). Biblical critics suggest that the prayer may in earlier traditions have been attributed to Elizabeth, and note that it has strong parallels with the prayer of Hannah, in 1 Samuel 2:1-10, at the birth and dedication to God of the infant Samuel (as well as containing a catena of other Old Testament texts).[58] However, the fact that Luke has chosen to give the prayer to Mary, whether or not this is strictly "historical" in the modern sense,[59] is itself highly significant: at this early period, Mary is being seen as representative of all faithful disciples, and her prayers are regarded as having a place that should be marked and commemorated among *their* prayers.

Other saints have left us prayers that they offered in their earthly lives, and having these to use is one of the gifts of the Communion of Saints and one of the dimensions of "praying with the saints." But as I have suggested above, these are tangible signs of the *ongoing* prayers and intercessions of the saints that are held alive in God, and this we may believe is true of Mary. Uniquely, among disciples in the New Testament, she is portrayed explicitly as saying "yes" ("Amen, let it be so") to God, and so it is helpful to say that we pray "with Mary and all the saints" in that the name Mary constantly reminds us that "we say Amen to the glory of God" through Christ (2 Cor 1:20). In the phrase "praying with Mary and all the saints," the name "Mary" evokes the story of a human "Amen," which is carried on the "Amen" of Christ into the most holy place.

I want to expand on this idea by reference to the agreed Anglican-Roman Catholic statement, *Mary: Grace and Hope in Christ*, which I have already mentioned above. The virtue of this agreed text is that it sets the person of Mary in the context of her sharing, with all disciples, in the life of the triune God through prayer. It links the "yes" of Luke 1:38 with the "yes" in Christ of 2 Corinthians 1:20. But, unfortunately, while it identifies the "yes" of Mary as a human "yes" to God, it confines the "yes" of Christ to the "yes" of God's promises spoken *to humanity*. Mary's "yes" is directed to God, in response to God's "yes" to her (and to us) in Christ. The report asserts that "Mary's 'Amen' to God's 'Yes' in Christ to her is both unique and a model for every disciple and for the life of the Church."[60]

While, of course, this is good theology, it is a limited theology. It aligns our praying to God only with the model prayer of Mary, and not with the intercession of Christ himself on which Mary's prayer relies. What it misses is the "yes" spoken by Christ *to God*, the obedient "yes" of the Son to the Father within the Trinity. I have already suggested that 2 Corinthians 1:20-21 depicts the "yes" in Christ as being both from and *to* the glory of God. This is why "it is through him that we say 'Amen' to the glory of God." Losing the obedient "yes" of the Son means that we miss the movement within the triune life of God on which we can lean our own "yes." Instead, there may be a tendency to look for support for our "yes" only from the "yes" of Mary, and so to some kind of mediation of Mary between us and Christ. We lose the dramatic image of the book of Hebrews, a movement in which disciples enter the most holy place with Christ, supported on his intercessions. We are no longer praying with the Mary who prays with Christ.

The author of Hebrews in fact lays constant stress on the obedient "yes" of Christ, which lies behind the portrayal of his heavenly intercession. Referring to his Gethsemane experience, the author explains that "although he was a Son, he learned obedience through what he suffered" (5:8). The "prayers and supplications, with loud cries and tears" (5:7) recall the prayer of Christ in Gethsemane, the model instance of saying "yes" to God: "Not my will but yours be done" (Luke 22:42). The book of Hebrews opens with three prayers of Christ to God, three instances of a "yes" to God discerned spiritually from texts in the Old Testament:

"I will proclaim your name to my brothers and sisters
In the midst of the congregation I will praise you."
And again, "I will put my trust in him."
And again, "Here am I and the children whom God has given me."
(Heb 2:12-13)[61]

These prayers are introduced by the statement that God is bringing many children to glory, by making "the pioneer of their salvation perfect through sufferings" (Heb 2:10). The image is one of movement, led by Christ. Many are to be brought "to glory," into the most holy place; so the writer can say, "*You have come* . . . to Mount Zion, to the city of the living God, the heavenly Jerusalem and to innumerable angels in festal gathering and to the assembly of the first-born" (12:22). This fellowship of saints is to be brought "to glory" through Christ, "the mediator of a new covenant" (12:23). In the words of our key text, Hebrews 7:25, he is "able to save those who *approach* God through him, *because he always lives to make intercessions for them*" (emphasis added).

If we lose this movement of saying "yes" within the triune God ("I will put my trust in him," "Here am I"), which is already there ahead of us, then we lose the theological foundation for praying "with Mary and all the saints." We also lose the possibility of expanding our horizons about the members of this "festal gathering" and "assembly of the first-born," or "the great cloud of witnesses" by whom we are surrounded. Are they really only members of the Christian church? Brian Haymes drops us an important hint in chapter 1 when he writes, "The only God we know is one who has a fundamental relationship with creation, and the only humanity we know is one inseparably related to God, needing a salvation it cannot of itself supply."[62] This "inseparable relation" is, I suggest, a being held within the interweaving relationships of the triune God. Because there is already a movement within God of a Son responding in obedience to a Father, then it is possible to discern many in our world who are leaning on that movement to say "yes," in their own way, to the purpose of God.

The church has its own place within the fellowship of the divine life, an indispensable task given it to tell the story of the Christ who is sent by the Father and who says "yes" to the Father. It has no excuse for not witnessing to this story and for not allowing its own life to be stamped with its patterns. But it is surely possible for others, who do not know or tell the story, also to live and act in the rhythm of the one who says "I have come to do your will, O God" (Heb 10:7)—since "in him [God] we live and move and have our being" (Acts 17:28). Wherever the poor are fed, or the rich and powerful are put down from their thrones, or the oppressed are freed, or victims of violence are given refuge, or the natural world is preserved from destruction, or witness is made to good things of the spirit that transcend materialism, we can discern a movement in harmony with "the pioneer of our salvation." We can be sure too that this loving concern for the world is taken up into God, and into a great reservoir of intercession for the world, so that the Communion of Saints includes those who never shared the table of the Lord on earth, but have come to the "festal gathering" in God. This is what we can, and must, have in mind as we pray the great prayer of thanksgiving at the Eucharist "with Mary and *all* the saints."

5

The Fellowship of Faces

Brian Haymes

In the chapters of this book, we have been developing the theological theme of "covenant," which is so illuminating as a central concept of Baptist thought and practice. This has inevitably led to a stress on the communal, corporate, relational aspect of Christian life and existence that begins and ends in God. We cannot be in covenant with ourselves alone, as if covenant might be some private aspect of our being. Neither does the Christian tradition know of any private covenants between God and discrete individuals that are apart from the great story of God's purposes for all humankind. Therefore, even where the story seems to tell of a personal covenant that God initiates, for example with Abraham, the context and purpose is always social and corporate, catholic and cosmic (Gen 12:2-3).

It is a theology of covenant that underlines the significance of the church in the purposes of God. Since the initiative in biblical covenants is always with God, then we assert that the church is the people of God by God's gracious calling, an affirmation in sharp distinction to any suggestion that it is a collection of individuals who have chosen a particular religious option. The church is the firstfruits of the new humanity, participating by grace in the covenant life and love of God in Trinity. We wish to recall any contemporary Christians who can sometimes make so much of finding "a church" to their liking to the strong biblical affirmation that God chose us before we chose God. The corporate nature of the church is an essential affirmation about the church of God, gathered in Christ.

Early Baptists possibly understood this better than later generations. The stress in their confessions was more on the initiative of
God, the God who makes covenant, than upon any individual right to
choose and respond.[1] In some respects, therefore, the emphasis in this
book is to call into question more recent affirmations and practices—
in particular, those understandings among Baptists that overemphasize
the importance of individual decision before God. We are not denying
the significance of this theology of call and response—indeed we could
hardly do so and remain Baptists—but we are suggesting that we have
been in danger of overemphasizing the individual in our theology of
the church and the practices of Christian living, thereby distorting the
faith at the heart of the Scripture's proclamation.

That such a development should happen among us in the last two
centuries is understandable because philosophically and socially we
have experienced the influence of the Enlightenment with its stress
upon the autonomous individual's rights, reason, and decisions. The
marginalizing of ancient traditions, the emphasis on human rationality and reason, the cry to be free of all "authorities" to follow our own
decisions of conscience and understanding—these have been part of
the air any person in the modern Western world has breathed. It has
led to ways of thinking and speaking that suggest that my becoming
and being a Christian is essentially an individual matter, my own decision. Sometimes, indeed, some forms of proclamation can suggest that
my salvation basically depends upon my making a decision to accept
Christ in order to "be saved" in such a way that the emphasis falls
upon the human act of deciding and not upon the fundamental gracious work of God. This is, of course, a half-truth, but then half-truths
can veil half-lies. An excessive stress on individual decision can lead to
distortions in gospel life and proclamation. It can imply that we can
live in the salvation of God in Christ without the church, its story,
traditions, and common life. It can turn baptism into a personal act
of witness alone, thus ignoring or underplaying the corporate and sacramental work of God in both the proclamation and response to the
divine call.

This cultural stress on the individual has other consequences.
Our reading of history can become a record of "great persons" as we
stress the heroic nature of special people in the faith. So preachers

can become more significant than the story of their congregations, independent evangelists more significant than local congregations and their pastors. In the worst forms of recollection, some lives may virtually be abstracted from their social context, which is reduced to a mere backdrop to their apparently significant and inspiring living. This is not to deny the particular significance in history of special individuals. It is only to suggest that this can be a distortion in the story of the faith, which leads to a price being paid in failing to recognize the significance of other less glamorous or interesting persons and groups in and through whom God has forwarded the divine purposes. Sometimes, later and more careful historical studies reveal something of the human frailty of those lives that once so impressed. The ability to discern true holiness and faithfulness in the purposes of God in particular lives and congregations requires a community grounded in a tradition through which the Spirit extends, as it were, the love and grace of God into the lives of disciples.

We have already noted in this book that although Baptists in the manner of the New Testament have assigned the word "saint" to *all* those baptized into the new humanity in Christ, we have been ready to recognize and rejoice in the fact that some lives have had a particular quality of disclosure of the ways and grace of God. This has been not a matter of individual or partisan claim so much as a communal recognition and discernment, in the light of the Spirit's leading and the appreciating of scriptural tradition. Other Christians often reserve the title "saint" for such people as these. These "saints" are recalled in the church memories not because they were experts, or particularly effective in "their ministry," but because they exemplified the character of one who shared the life of Christ and so became a faithful witness to Christ in the world. For such people the whole church is ready to give thanks to God, rejoicing in what the covenant-making God accomplished in and through their living.

Baptists have sometimes been ready to talk about "heroes" who made history.[2] This has been an important and not unhelpful way of telling the story of what God has done. But it can lead to a stress on individual accomplishments and the praises of achievement-orientated congregations. It is noticeable that conference occasions and national assemblies may carry advertisements stressing who is speaking rather than any subject matter, the celebrity rather than the content being judged to be really significant and attractive. In this respect we simply echo our age of celebrities. But these cultural influences stressing individualism can lead to distortions in the church by neglecting the importance of our corporate life in Christ and those traditional practices by which such life is sustained and nurtured. As Samuel Wells puts it, it is by the church's constant *improvisation* of the word proclaimed that it embodies and extends the drama of God's purposes for all the world through time.[3] He draws important distinctions between heroes and saints. Heroes are usually the center of the story told about them, as their heroic deeds are described and saluted. By contrast, the saint only has significance in the story of God. As an individual the saint may be anonymous, invisible, unheralded, one whose presence in the story is not necessarily crucial. Saints may indeed be hidden on the periphery of the public world. They are not noted for their daring sacrificial interventions into situations of danger, throwing themselves into the conflict. They are, however, faithful to their calling, which may bring them into unsought conflict with the powers. Saints do not intentionally compete for worldly power and influence, since they know that such matters belong fundamentally to God alone. In consequence, their lives make no sense apart from the God they serve.

Likewise, the martyrs do not seek deliberately to give their lives as suicide bombers might. They have their lives taken from them because of their faithfulness to Christ. They are first and foremost members of the church, the body of Christ, for the sake of the world. In summary, as Michael Pasquarello puts it: "To be a saint does not require one to have outstanding gifts or talents. All that is required is that one employ all the resources of the church's tradition . . . rather than create them for oneself, and that one long for the glory of the church's destiny . . . rather than assuming one must achieve it oneself. In the present . . . one must seek in all ways to cooperate with the other members of the company, the communion of saints, rather than stand out from them as an isolated hero."[4]

The overaffirmation of the individual has been a distorting feature of some Baptist theology that has led to the neglect of the Communion of Saints. By contrast, the earlier emphasis on God's covenant-making desire meant that more attention was paid to the church, its life, and its worship as a participation in the life and ways of God. The point is well illustrated in the 1606 church covenant of the group of worshippers meeting in Scrooby Manor, Gainsborough—a Separatist group associated with John Smyth and Thomas Helwys that, "as the Lord's free people, joined themselves (by a covenant of the Lord) into a church estate, in the fellowship of the Gospel, to walk in all his ways, made known or to be made known unto them (according to their best endeavors) whatsoever it should cost, the Lord assisting them."[5] Membership of such churches could be described as a matter of "walking together and watching over one another,"[6] a deeply relational understanding of being church. In *A Declaration of Faith*, the newly Baptist company gathered around their pastor John Smyth (who remained in Amsterdam after the return of part of the congregation to England with Thomas Helwys) and expressed one important aspect of their conviction about the nature of the church:

> That the members off everie Church or Congregacion ought to knowe one another, so that they may performe all the duties of love one towards another both to soule and bodie. Mat. 18.15. 1 Thes. 5.14. 1 Cor. 12.25. And especiallie the Elders ought to knowe the whole flock, whereof the HOLIE GHOST hath made them overseers. Acts 20.28. 1 Pet. 5.2, 3. And therefore a Church ought not to consist off such a multitude as cannot have particuler knowledg one off another.[7]

The strong emphasis on interpersonal relationships is obvious in these historical references. Those who formed the confessions argued that they were only reflecting the teaching of the Scriptures. The "saints"— that is, the church members—are baptized into Christ, into a company that no one can number, bounded by neither space nor time, where each is related to the other in Christ. The Church is a fellowship in Christ by the Holy Spirit. It is a fellowship at once both human and divine, a fellowship of faces, and at once both catholic and personal in relating, a fact recognized in the ways Baptists celebrate the sacraments of baptism and the Lord's Supper.

The candidate for baptism is almost certainly already known to the congregation, among whom he or she has been nurtured and "examined" in preparation for this great step of faith and commitment. Baptism is no private or individual event but is received in the presence of the congregation assembled by God in worship. The candidate is named. The candidate is asked whether she or he is turning to Christ in repentance and faith. The face no longer looks predominantly inward but looks to Christ along with Christ's people. The whole community is a living witness to the grace and call of God. They are present to one another and to Christ, face-to-face. It is assumed that baptism implies church membership, the sharing of a local congregation's life and love. The solitary individual Christian is an abstraction because at the heart of Christian existence in Christ is relating and belonging in the church. Practicing believers' baptism without reference to church membership is a serious theological aberration that inevitably weakens the church's life.

Again, when the congregation is gathered around the table, Baptist practice has been not to "go forward" to a communion rail in order to "make our communion," but rather to serve one another, passing on the gifts of God as we receive them from member and deacon. Often we affirm and celebrate the peace of Christ in greeting one another, face-to-face, proclaiming to one another the gracious word, "The peace of the Lord be with you," an activity much more significant than merely greeting friend or stranger. Allowing Christ to speak the word of peace through us to another (John 20:19-21), we acknowledge that Christ is our peace, he who has made us one, breaking down any dividing walls of hostility, creating in himself a new humanity, thus making peace (Eph 2:14-16). Sharing bread and wine is something we do together.

Gathered at the table to share the Lord's Supper, the congregation in many places stands in thanksgiving and remembrance of one who has died since last the church gathered at the table. The person's life is recalled briefly, and God is praised for the love shared and the hope in which the members stand. We picture their face and affirm our continued oneness in Christ our life. Should any service of worship have an impersonal character, then it will feel cold, lacking that evangelical warmth which is the gift of the Spirit.

We live and pray in the fellowship of faces, a theological affirmation we need to probe deeper. Both literally and metaphorically, the Bible often speaks of the face. In moments of worship, people "fall on their faces" before God or another in an act of obeisance (Num 20:6; Ruth 2:10; Dan 2:46; Ezek 9:8). Psalm 42:2 in its longing for God asks,

"When shall I come and behold the face of God?" Moses commands the people to gather regularly to "appear before" the Lord their God to hear the reading of Torah (Deut 31:10-11). To seek God's face is to seek God (Ps 24:6). The heavenly beings bow their faces before God (Rev 7:11). Thus, *face* is often used in the Bible as a metonym to refer to the person or the person's presence in relation to God. Although God may be remote and mysterious, Baptists have trusted the biblical story that implies that we always live before God. Fifty years ago Martin Buber explored what he called "the eclipse of God," which he took to be the loss of awareness that all our life was *coram deo*, in the presence of God.[8] More recently, George W. Stroup has argued, "A God who is a remote mystery or impersonal transcendence may exist and in some sense may or may not be present in the world, but Christian faith presupposes not only God's existence and transcendence but also that people live before God and are accountable to one another because they are first accountable to God."[9] Is there a connection between the face of God and what the philosopher Emmanuel Levinas calls the "face of our neighbour"?[10] And might such a connection help us in growing into the Communion of Saints?

These two questions surely require an affirmative answer. There is little doubt that in the biblical story there is the closest of connections between God and humankind; notwithstanding, the two are not the same. The following four brief points indicate the force of this claim.

First, the God of the Christian faith is creative. All that was, is, and has yet to come to be is dependent on the divine creativity. Particularly in the biblical story, God creates humankind "in God's own image" (Gen 1:27), essentially a relational concept. The breath of life breathed into human beings is the divine breath, as the dust of the earth is given new life and humankind comes to be in the purposes of God. Liturgically, this is celebrated, for example, in the regular reading of many of the Psalms and on harvest festival occasions, and even more decisively in those acts of worship when parents bring a newborn child into the assembly in order to give thanks for the gift of life. In every newborn child there comes the divine affirmation that God is staying with the project of creation and new creation. It includes new creation, for the faith proclaims that even from the dust of our death God is able to bring forth the new creation, the new heaven and earth in which our humanity finds its fulfillment in sharing the life of God in Trinity in ways presently beyond our expressing.

Second, a further feature of this fundamental relationship between God and humankind is found in stories such as that in Genesis 3 when God comes searching for Adam and Eve. "Where are you?" is God's question to the two who now seem to be in hiding, resisting the relationship that means so much to God, hiding their faces. The God of the Scripture story is one who comes searching, calling, seeking the lost. The other side of this relationship is there in those Psalms where the worshipper calls out to God in longing and trust—for example, Psalm 42 where the cry is of deep longing for God, or Psalm 51 where the request is for forgiveness and renewal of life after transgression. That humankind finds life and love in the service and worship of God is a fundamental presupposition of human existence in the Bible. It is therefore no surprise when the connection between deep human relations and those with God are linked, as when Jacob, finding that the brother he has seriously wronged in the past is now receiving him with warmth and love, declares that "to see your face is like seeing the face of God" (Gen 33:10). Earlier, in the struggle at Peniel, Jacob, perhaps in some relief, says, "I have seen God face to face and yet my life is preserved" (Gen 32:30). In such passages, the connection between human faces and the face of God is assumed even though the "faces" are not the same.

Third, and most obviously, the Bible tells the story of incarnation. The Word that was in the beginning—by whom all things were made, the Word that was God—took flesh and became a human being, and so the glory of God is seen in one full of grace and truth (John 1:1-14). Paul puts it in terms that directly speak of seeing God's face: "For it is the God who said, 'Let light shine out of darkness' who has shone in our hearts to give the light of the knowledge of God in the face of Jesus Christ" (2 Cor 4:6). Here the doctrines of creation and incarnation are inseparably linked. God takes human flesh for the salvation of the world, which remains the object of God's love. Christ is the image (*eikon*) of the invisible God (Col 1:15), the human face of God, the one in whom all things hold together. Christ's human face is at the same time like any other human face, and yet is the face of God. To see any human face is therefore to be confronted by an "other." It is to see something of the Other.

Here we underline again the importance of Trinitarian convictions. God is the creator, the author of all life and love. The image of God is the defining theological description of humankind in Scripture, so that to see an other is potentially to see something of the Other. The face of God is recognized in other humans but most decisively in the face of Jesus Christ, the incarnate Word.

Although the Spirit is often represented in Scripture in nonpersonal terms, such as wind and fire, it is by the Spirit that the divine presence is recognized in human faces, dramatically in a covenant context when Moses' face glows because he has been with God (Exod 34:29). Christ's disciples are those who have seen the glory of God in the face of Jesus and now face toward God in him, enabled by the life-giving Spirit by whom God's work of transformation goes on. Repentance is turning toward the face of the Other, an action made possible by the Spirit. The Spirit does not have a face in Christian theology but fulfills the task of enabling recognition, of connecting, of being face-to-face.

There are practical implications to all this that become the fourth point about human faces and the face of God. If God has taken human flesh, then human flesh is important. Every person shares the flesh that Christ shared. So, if any people say they love God but hate their brothers or sisters, they are liars, for to love God is to love others (1 John 4:16-21). This is the form practical knowledge of God takes. Knowing of God is a way of life in which we share a fellowship of faces, responding in love to the claims of the other. Worship that does not issue in a life of love only suggests that what has been called worship has not engaged with the face of God, has not been faced by the face of God, and has not had the faces of worshippers turned toward others.[11] Thus the prophet Jeremiah reminds disobedient Shallum of his father Josiah: "'He judged the cause of the poor and needy; then it was well. Is this not to know me?' declares the Lord" (Jer 22:16). At worship, in the reading of Scripture, in the offering of praise and prayer reciting the works of God, in bread and wine, in making peace, in one another, in friend and stranger, and by the Spirit, we find ourselves before the face of God. We are "looked at." "All of us, with unveiled faces, seeing the glory of the Lord as though reflected in a mirror, are being transformed into the same image from one degree of glory to another; for this comes from the Lord, the Spirit" (2 Cor 3:18). In particular, we see and are seen at the baptismal pool and the Lord's table, where all faces both conceal and reveal the gracious presence of God.

This world (which we sometimes divide into nature and spirit), then, is shot through with the work and life of God. Bushes may burn, the heavens declare the glory of God, and all human beings bear the likeness of God. We live in a world of persons, and what it is to be truly a person is revealed in Jesus Christ, truly God and truly human.

This is not to say that every face is the face of God. News comes of a gunman shooting down an American congresswoman and others attending an informal political rally. In other parts of the world, terrorists plant bombs or deliver them in suicide acts designed only to kill and maim. This is not the face of God. It is the face of the evil of which we are capable. Sometimes we can see something of ourselves we would rather hide. So a process of discernment is at work in perceiving the face of God, such that two realities are held together; both of them depend upon the work of the Spirit in us, opening our eyes to the truth focused in Jesus. On the one hand, we are given to see the face of God, and especially in the vulnerable, needy, poor, and dying. A striking example of this is in the work of Mother Teresa of Calcutta, who saw, in the faces of the destitute and discarded, the face of Christ. In serving them, she served him, echoing Jesus' parable (Matt 25:31-46). Living before the face of God in worship and prayer, we are transformed and enabled to see differently. We move from worship before the face of God to discerning that face in others and even to being that face for them. On the other hand, it is before God that we see something of the truth of ourselves and our share in the evil of the world. It is only the saints who are really conscious of their sin, and that happens as they, in sincerity, face God through the days of their life. They are not morally perfect, and they know it. But they have turned toward God in trust, in faith, in hope, and in love, and by grace they are given to see God and know themselves forgiven, healed, and called to share the saving purposes of God for all the world.

"Saints" see and live this truth, whether we mean either all church members or the particular few whose lives disclose the grace of God to the world in a startling way that calls for attention. One of the great advantages of knowing our history is to find ourselves facing those whose lives have been glorious in the service and honor of God. In some parts of the church, this has been emphasized more than perhaps Baptists are given to doing. Consider the vision of God and the people at worship in the Syrian Liturgy of St. James from the sixth century. It is here in the form of a hymn in translation by Percy Dearmer and Gerard Moultrie, and can be found in several Baptist hymnbooks.[12]

1. Let all mortal flesh keep silence,
and with awe and welcome stand;
harbour nothing earthy-minded;
for, with blessing in his hand,
Christ our Lord with us dwelling,
loving homage to demand.

2. King of Kings, yet born of Mary,
as of old on earth he stood,
Lord, of Lords, in human vesture,
in the body and the blood:
he will give to all the faithful
his own self for human food.

3. Rank on rank the hosts immortal
sweep in joy before your face,
shining in the light exalted,
friends and loved ones in embrace,
as the dark dissolves before you,
light of all the human race.

4. At your feet the seraphs cluster,
veil their faces in that light,
spirits of the just made perfect,
now in timeless splendour bright,
saints and angels, all adore you,
serve and praise you in the height.

The great themes expressed in this hymn reflect—if not in contemporary Baptist praise—basic Baptist understandings of being church, as we pray "facing" one another before God, the living, and the dead. Our experience has been that we have found that others reflect for us the face of God, and not only members of our denomination—indeed not only Christians. Living the Christian life as being a face-to-face encounter, in the fellowship of faces, is distinctive of our history and present life, in spite of our relative neglect of the doctrine of the Communion of Saints.

The rest of this chapter will take an unusual course among Baptists. It will focus on the life and thought of St. Thérèse of Lisieux, one who practiced and taught the importance of "facing" others. Can she help us Baptists in exploring these aspects about being the church? I must confess that there is a personal reason for this study. I and my wife, Jenny, were invited by two family members, both priests of the Anglican Church, to share a "pilgrimage" to Lisieux organized by the Anglican Fellowship of St. Thérèse. This proved to be such a compelling experience that we made further retreat visits, staying at the Carmel in Lisieux and opening ourselves to the practices and understandings of those who spoke about St. Thérèse as one of their closest friends.

In many ways Thérèse is an excellent example of a point made earlier about sainthood and lack of obvious merit. There is little that is heroic about her life, but her living has no meaning apart from the story of God she inhabited and expressed. It may seem almost self-contradictory to focus on an individual in the light of what has been asserted about the importance of the corporate life of the church for Baptists, but Baptists have always known, along with the whole church, that some lives do disclose the divine presence and grace in a specially striking way, and that such persons—"the saints"—can be unnerving in their holiness. While concentrating on Thérèse, we shall not forget that her story only has its deep significance because it is part of the story of God, a disclosure of God. Her story has little or no meaning apart from the story of God and is primarily set, of course, within a community context.

Thérèse was born in Alençon, Normandy, in 1873, into an intensely religious Catholic family. Both her parents had, in earlier life, sought to enter a monastery and a convent but had been refused. Later, they developed careers, her mother Zelie-Marie as a lacemaker and her father Louis Martin a watchmaker. Each morning they went to Mass at 5:30 a.m. and maintained strict observances and prayers in their household. Thérèse was the youngest of nine children, among whom only five daughters survived childhood. Marie was the oldest, then Pauline, Leonie, Celine, and lastly Thérèse. When Thérèse was four years old, her mother died of cancer. Before this, because of her mother's illness, she had spent fourteen months at another household in the care of a nurse. Thérèse chose Pauline to be her new "mother," but increasingly she became very close to her father and he to her. Her own observations of those days show a contentment: "My first recollections are of loving smiles and tender caresses; but if God made others love me so much, He made me love them too, for I was of an affectionate nature."[13]

The family then moved to Lisieux. Pauline had long cherished the ambition of becoming a nun and entering Carmel, and when Thérèse was eight years old, Pauline fulfilled her ambition. Five years later Marie also entered the Lisieux Carmel. In these ways Thérèse suffered serious family losses in her life, as familiar faces were gone from her either by death or vocation. Her health proved to be poor, and she became very delicate as a consequence. Certainly, after her mother died, she changed from being a lively happy child to a shy inhibited girl. However, throughout this time, she was also intensely religious and soon desired that she too would become a nun and enter Carmel with her two sisters. She was told that she would have to wait until she was at least sixteen years of age before she could think of doing so. After much deliberation with the bishop—and even, somewhat precociously, addressing the pope on a visit to Rome with her father—combined with her undoubted zeal, she was allowed by special dispensation to enter Carmel when she was only fifteen. Her love for God, although childlike in expression, proved nonetheless to be profound. On the one hand, she longed to be a saint, but on comparing herself to their stories, she observed how unworthy, powerless, and little she was. However, this did not stifle her desire to be someone whose life would serve and honor God.

Two years before she died, during recreation time with the other nuns, she recalled some incidents about her childhood, and her sister Pauline suggested that she should write these stories down. The mother prioress, who happened at the time to be her sister Marie, agreed and ordered her to write her spiritual autobiography. Obediently, she did this and in consequence produced a remarkable spiritual testimony to her life. It was published soon after her death and became an extraordinary success under the title *Story of a Soul*. It remains a bestseller of its kind all over the world. It is comprised of three manuscripts, the first one covering her childhood and the other two her life at Carmel and her own journey of faith.

In many ways, her unremarkable story is simply told. Given her consequent fame, it is surprising that she brought nothing novel to her teaching—neither did she institute any new works of mission or community life. Her very simplicity raises questions as to why she has had such a deep influence. On entering Carmel, Thérèse was still a child with all the difficulties that growing up entails. Undoubtedly, she consequently brought a lot of emotional baggage with her that she would need to work through. She was stubborn by nature and had always been indulged and spoiled, especially by her father. This did not help her settle into the rigors of the religious life, and the difficult attitude of some of the nuns toward her, especially that of the mother prioress, made her life very uncomfortable at times. But already she had a deep sense of relationships in God, and particularly with Jesus, and she believed that she would at last have time to get to know God even better, to deepen the love she felt, as well as to pray for the conversion of more souls, which was her particular passion. All the trials of her early experiences in Carmel in retrospect proved to be the catalyst for evolving her way of life and loving. In time, her desire for God, her dream of being holy and saintly (even a martyr), and her longing to make a difference to the world overcame much of her loneliness. She was convinced that God would not have put these longings and desires within her in the first place if God did not want them to come to fulfillment.

Once, while reading about St. Paul, she came upon the famous hymn in 1 Corinthians 13 asserting that the goal and purpose of life is love, and suddenly, she believed, it was as if Jesus himself had spoken to her, telling her that her vocation would be love and that this calling could be realized here and now:

> I finally had rest. Considering the mystical body of the Church, I had not recognized myself in any of the members described by St. Paul, or rather I desired to see myself in the *all*. *Charity* gave me the key to my *vocation*. I understood that if the church had a body composed of different members, the most necessary and most noble of all could not be lacking to it, and so I understood that the church *had a Heart and that this Heart was BURNING*

WITH LOVE. I understood it was Love alone that made the Church's members act, that if *Love* ever became extinct, apostles would not preach the Gospel and martyrs would not shed their blood. I understood that LOVE COMPRISED ALL VOCATIONS, THAT LOVE WAS EVERYTHING, THAT IT EMBRACED ALL TIMES AND PLACES . . . IN A WORD, THAT IT WAS ETERNAL!

Then, in the excess of my delirious joy, I cried out: O Jesus, my love . . . My *vocation*, at last I have found it . . . MY VOCATION IS LOVE![14]

With this new understanding and the careful working out what it would mean for her living, she evolved what she was to call her "Little Way" of discipleship. For her it meant trying to get on with life as it actually was, living it with kindness, unselfishness, detailed care—doing it all for love of neighbor and God. She accepted that she was powerless and unworthy but still knew that she was loved by God and called to love others. She began to look on everything that happened to her as a gifted opportunity from God, constantly asking what this task or encounter demanded from her. She writes, "It is no longer a question of loving one's neighbour as oneself but of loving him as *He, Jesus, has loved him and will love him to the consummation of the ages*."[15] Whether making a bed, reading, gardening, praying, washing, encouraging, listening, or paying attention to colleagues, especially the difficult ones, her life of discipleship was offered to God. In her understanding, Jesus waits for us especially in our weakness, asking us to make friends of the things we run away from, our failures (often in the form of relationships with difficult people), disappointments, inadequacies, and sin. Repentance then makes our sin no longer a stumbling block but a stepping-stone, with God revealing more of God's grace to us little by little. So her littleness became very important to her, and she believed that because she continued to be regarded as nothing, she set holiness free to transform it into trust and transpose it into the practice of self-abandonment.

So hers was a simple way of life, a desire for poverty, hiddenness, and self-sacrifice, in love, in quiet trust of God. She was able to say with total conviction that she was loved and forgiven, and that enabled her to love and forgive all others and to see them as she believed God sees them. So the commandment of Jesus—to love God and your neighbor as yourself—took on a special meaning and was to be practiced directly. She believed God loved everyone else as much as God loved her, and she wanted everyone else to know how much God loved them and to love in return. Her vocation, she claimed, was love, love for the whole world. However, predictably enough, her littleness was no easy way. She encountered trials and temptations but accepted them and gradually grew through them, making them offerings to God, in keeping with her life of submissive obedience. Each discovery about herself she saw as a new beginning, while at the same time realizing that it had been there already waiting to be discovered and now could be experienced and used in a deeper way. So these discoveries were not in the end simply a self-fulfillment but enabled her to go beyond herself to God and learn where and how God wanted her to be herself. It was again a form of self-abandonment. No longer was it just some self-enclosed seeking for God but rather the realization and faith that God with Christ's face was in all the events of her life and that she lived *coram deo* (before God).

In all this, she had many periods of darkness where she found no consolation from God, not even at the Eucharist. At one particular time when she was very ill, she even contemplated suicide, but she clung to the thought that God was, and would be, present in the suffering however bad it was. In the heart of the suffering, she believed, was a core of peace, as if the suffering and joy were, on some deeply mysterious level, the same thing, as two faces of love. So she could still say that in the darkness she enjoyed profound peace because she believed and trusted that her darkness, her nothingness, would become the means of reaching God. Only from the bottom of the pit can one look up in hope and trust of being raised up by God. For her, at times, discipleship was a participation in the darkness of faith, learning to see things as God sees them, trusting that what seemed too far away might become within reach.

All through the nine years she was at Carmel, she learned that developing her personal attitudes to others was an important aspect of discipleship, involving an accepting of the changing circumstances of life and transforming any "hindrances" into character-forming virtues. In all things it was essential to live the truth, always refusing to allow there to be a gap between what she said and what she did, but also being willing to be disturbed by another.

She had at one time longed to be a missionary, and that was denied to her, but in time she saw herself, through prayer, as a missionary to the whole world. She was to touch many lives with her Little Way, including two missionary monks with whom she was asked to correspond. It was in the silence of prayer she felt she was sharing in the work of redemption and that in some mysterious way God was even making the salvation of others dependent on her and those like her. So she realized it was not just choosing our own way to live but decisively preferring to live in a certain way with and for others. Her conviction was that the emphasis should be placed more on the way you live than the way you think, but that nevertheless if you transform the way you think, you will live differently.

She was diagnosed with tuberculosis, and this became a great test of her faith and trust in God. The decline in her health coincided yet again with the desolating experience of the absence of God. Yet she still saw all this to be yet another means to enable her to learn to bear it all and say nothing about her trials and pain, only to respond to others with love. She pictured herself travelling with Jesus in the garden of Gethsemane, in the darkness of his abandonment and the agony of the cross. At the very end of her life, she said that she would spend her heaven doing good on earth. This is one of the reasons why so many Catholics find consolation in praying to St. Thérèse for her help. She died on September 30, 1897, at the aged of twenty-four. She was canonized in 1925 and is one of the few women to be declared a Doctor of the Church.

When anyone enters Carmel to begin the life of prayer and devotion in the Carmelite tradition, they are given a name. So, initially, Thérèse was known as Thérèse of the Child Jesus. Veneration of the Child Jesus was important within the Carmelite tradition going back into the seventeenth century of French mysticism. In giving the name, there was no intention to load a person with any sentimental baggage about childhood, but rather there was a concentration on the humility, vulnerability, and humiliation of the divine majesty in weakness and helplessness. The childhood of Christ was divinity disguised, quiet and hidden, as befits a sister's existence in a Carmelite community of prayer and devotion. There is little evidence, however, that Thérèse learned of this tradition at Lisieux. It would be interesting to find links between "the imitation of Christ" in his childhood within the French mystical tradition and Thérèse's Little Way, the way of spiritual child-hood, and that study has scarcely been done. This name, however, had nothing like the significance of the name given at the receiving of the veil when she was sixteen years old.

She asked for the name "Thérèse of the Child Jesus and of the Holy Face." It is said that it was her sister Pauline who guided her to this devotion, but there was a family incident that too is impor-tant. Thérèse and her father were very close. Although he was far from well, he managed to attend her profession of vows. We cannot imag-ine what feelings were present in his life, of what it meant to this very devout Catholic to have yet another child enter Carmel. Soon after Thérèse was professed, he became seriously ill, deprived of his sanity, such that his face lost all vitality and became closer to a death mask. It evoked a strange childhood vision of Thérèse, one that disturbed her deeply: Her father was away at the time. In the vision, she saw a man who looked like her father, only older in years and with more of a stoop. His face could not be seen because his whole head was covered by a cloth. Thérèse called out but there was no response and the fig-ure disappeared.[16] She never forgot the incident and came to believe it prefigured the family tragedy when her father, suffering from frequent paralysis, lost his mind and had to be committed to special hospital care. Here was a faithful servant of God in some desolation and grief, whose face was to become barely recognizable.

The veneration of the Holy Face had been a particular feature of the Lisieux Carmel. Mother Geneviève, founder of the community, had placed in the chapel an image of the "Veil of Veronica" with its alleged imprint of the face of Jesus on the way to Calvary. Thérèse came to address the Holy Face in prayer. She painted it on vestments. She carried a copy in her breviary so that it was always before her in choir. At the end, she had the picture fixed to the curtain on her bed so that it was always in her view. Hans Urs von Balthasar is surely right when he asserts that "her whole life in Christ is concentrated into her *devotion to the Holy Face.*"[17] How might this help Baptists and others appreciate the depth of meaning in the doctrine of the Communion of Saints, the fellowship of faces?

The material in *Story of a Soul* is very rich. Upon its publication it sold thousands of copies, and it remains an inspiring spiritual classic for many today. It contains more than enough for a full theological study, but for the purposes of this chapter, let the following serve as points of focus for our reflections.[18]

We have already stressed the importance of the church as community, the fellowship of the Holy Spirit, those called to share the life in Christ. Within that fellowship, faces are always crucial but not without ambiguity, for faces can conceal and reveal. In consequence, fellowship in the church can sometimes be reduced to attempts to get along together, hiding important differences under a superficiality of good nature. Congregations, as we know, can become moral and spiritual mixtures. That has always been the case. Baptists can be said to have been born in separation and to have lived by that doctrine. We have developed ways of justifying our manner of separated being. But can we imagine it is the way of the saints in glory? Their communion is deep in Christ. There is no other. Thérèse lived focused on the face of Christ in order that she might live a life of love toward all faces. For her, the broken and compassionate face of Christ was at the heart of the world's salvation. It calls into question all our ways of power and domination over others. But, to be dominated by this face is to be loved in a way that transforms our conception of what it is to be loved.[19] It is for this reason that Thérèse urged a concentration on the face of Christ for novices.

It might be judged, however, that Thérèse appears at first artificial and superficial in her manner of life. She did not always find living in the community easy, and indeed some of the sisters seemed to have given her a hard time. One in particular annoyed her by making unhelpful noises during service in choir. Thérèse learned to pray for her sisters and smile. She took with much seriousness the instructions in Matthew 6:16-18, as she saw her gift of a smile as a part of her vocation. The face has a hiddenness about it. Smiles may be expressions of warm love or cold derisive pity. What Thérèse was trying to live by was a delight in the *imago dei* before her eyes in every face she encountered. In many ways she was trying to evoke love from another by looking on the face and affirming its value. Toward the end of her life she writes, "I feel that my mission is about to begin, my mission of making others love God as I love him.[20] There is nothing superficial or artificial about that kind of smile, even if its depth of meaning is not always apparent in the face. She saw this response as being essential if the church really is to share the life in Christ. She prayed for her sisters, all of them in communion.

The Holy Face she saw in chapel was the face of the wounded and dead Jesus. The scars were obvious. Thérèse linked this with the repulsiveness of the servant of the Lord:

> Who has believed what we have heard?
>> And to whom has the arm of the LORD been revealed?
> [2] For he grew up before him like a young plant,
>> and like a root out of dry ground;
> he had no form or majesty that we should look at him,
>> nothing in his appearance that we should desire him.
> [3] He was despised and rejected by others;
>> a man of suffering and acquainted with infirmity;
> and as one from whom others hide their faces
>> he was despised, and we held him of no account. (Isa 53:1-3)

Was this a face that could be loved? The servant goes on in silence, accepting what is done to him. Sin is focused in this body whose face bears the scars. For the servant, living *coram deo* is costly and bitter. It is a matter of trust, of hope in God. Two things seem to have struck Thérèse. One is that the dead face, brought down to death by reason of obedient trust in God's purposes and ways, is a thorough sacrifice. The servant has given everything that can be given, even to life itself. Exhausted and broken in body, the face with closed eyes awaits whatever God wills and offers all. Everything has been sacrificed, completely. Thérèse links all this with the cross of Jesus and the life of faithful obedience and discipleship. In the Holy Face, she sees the sacrificial victim, the one who in life and death has lived *coram deo*. The cross is iconic, challenging all political and religious powers. David Ford suggests the metaphor of the cross as a "black hole" that sucks in all other relativities and pretenders.[21] A second conclusion is that there is no easy consolation to be seen in this face, something Thérèse knew in her several, and long-lasting, times of pain and darkness. Living before this Holy Face, one can only trust as the servant trusted. Jesus has completed the life of worship and service at the cross, waiting God's response and being utterly dependent on it. The response is resurrection, but Thérèse will not hurry there. The Holy Face bears scars but not beauty. Here, love for God and God's people is lived out even unto death. How can we help one another to love this unlovely face?

"To make Love loved." It is important for us to recall that these reflections from Thérèse have their home in a small Carmel community of sisters. Together they were often at prayer, singing the psalms and so drawing on the deep metaphor within the Scriptures of "facing." There they watched over one another, making their offering and waiting for God's response, as did Jesus, dead and buried, his offering complete. They lived before the face of God. For Thérèse, personally, her life was marked by mortification, often without any apparent consolation, but she nonetheless lived in solidarity with the one of the Holy Face, the dead Jesus. This was her focus of veneration. The dead face stood for the sacrificial victim, the one who in life and death lived as she wished to live, *coram deo*. It is not easy for us to see ourselves as we are, or as we are seen by others, and as we are seen by God. Thérèse's sustained devotion to the Holy Face enabled her to appreciate the faces around her, all made in the image of God, all reflecting that image. So she lived and prayed in the fellowship of faces, but, in her Catholic tradition and teaching, what she received and gave could never be reduced to the visible faces around her. In her own theological terms, she prayed for souls—past, present, and to come—as she knew herself to be part of the mystical body of the living Christ, the church. And she lived in the hope of the beatific vision when no longer shall we see through a glass darkly but will come face-to-face at that place where nothing accursed will be found any more, for this will be before the throne of God and of the Lamb, where God's servants will worship and serve and see God's face (Rev 22:3-4). This will not be a totally new experience for anyone who has sought and affirmed the fellowship of faces among those who bear and have born the *imago dei*. But it will be glory almost unimaginable, even as God's response to the one with the Holy Face is resurrection.

Thérèse learned that at the center of this life before God is the necessary facing of others, of otherness, in God. She had known the joy of those who have known the light of God shining upon them in the face of Jesus, as she had also known the dark abyss of God's turning away the divine face. The dynamic of love and worship goes on within the life of the triune God, for Jesus—the one for all others—is at the heart of this worship, enabling the church in every age, even though it is beset by selfishness and struggles with power, to know the remaking and restoring of facing. So he is the savior who invites us to look and enter into God's salvation—but only with the others.

A prayer attributed to Thérèse runs:

> O Jesus, who in Thy bitter Passion didst become "the most abject of men, a man of sorrows," I venerate Thy Sacred Face whereon there once did shine the beauty and sweetness of the Godhead; but now it has become for me as if it were the face of a leper! Nevertheless, under those disfigured features, I recognize Thy infinite Love and I am consumed with the desire to love Thee and make Thee loved by all men. The tears which well up abundantly in Thy sacred eyes appear to me as so many precious pearls that I love to gather up, in order to purchase the souls of poor sinners by means of their infinite value. O Jesus, whose adorable Face ravishes my heart, I implore Thee to fix deep within me Thy divine image and to set me on fire with Thy Love, that I may be found worthy to come to the contemplation of Thy glorious Face in Heaven. Amen.[22]

It is possible that I have "stretched" Thérèse's thought, taking it further than she actually meant. However, in the story of her life, the reader senses that holiness—that loving that belongs to God and saintliness—and finds expression in the fellowship of faces. Earlier in this chapter, reference was made to Mother Teresa of Calcutta and her way of life. In both her living and that of Thérèse, something fundamental, foundational, about the life of faith is disclosed. They meant what they said, and they lived what they said. Their words and deeds were usually one, and in that we sense disclosure, the Word becoming flesh among us. Miroslav Volf puts the point this way:

> Charles Taylor tells the story of hearing Mother Teresa speak about her motivation for working with the abandoned and the dying of Calcutta. She explained that she did her work on tending them because they were created in the image of God. Being a Catholic philosopher, Taylor thought to himself, "I could have said that too!" And then, being an introspective person and a fine philosopher, he asked himself, "But could I have *meant* it?"

Volf goes on to reflect:

> *That*, I think, is today's most fundamental challenge for theologians, priests and ministers, and Christian laypeople: to *really mean* that the presence and activity of the God of love, who can make us love our neighbours as ourselves, is our hope and the hope of the world—that this God is the secret of our flourishing as persons, cultures, and interdependent inhabitants of a single globe.[23]

It is certainly a challenge to any local congregation, in its worship and church meetings, that it becomes—in the deep costly theological sense as set out in this chapter—a fellowship of faces, living *coram deo*, as do all the saints.

6

COMMUNION AND COVENANT

Paul S. Fiddes

"The Tie That Binds"

In *Our Town*, one of the best-known plays by the American novelist and playwright Thornton Wilder, the hymn "Blest Be the Tie That Binds" appears at a central point in each of the three acts. It is sung in act 1 as the "Stage Manager" introduces us to the varied inhabitants of Grover's Corners, a small town in New Hampshire in 1901. We hear it first just after he comments, "This is the way we were: in our growing up and in our marrying and in our living and our dying."[1] It is sung in act 2 at the wedding of the young George and Emily as the bride whispers in panic, "I never felt so alone in my life," and begs her husband-to-be, "If you love me, help me. All I want is someone to love me . . . and I mean for *ever*."[2] It is sung in act 3 at the funeral of Emily, who has died in childbirth just nine years after her wedding; in a dialogue among the dead, during the ceremony up in the hill cemetery, Emily recalls, "It seems thousands and thousands of years since I . . . Papa remembered that that was my favourite hymn."[3] The hymn marks the stages—as the Stage Manager suggests—of growing up, marrying, and dying.

> Blest be the tie that binds
> our hearts in Christian love;
> the fellowship of kindred minds
> is like to that above.

Before our Father's throne
we pour our ardent prayers;
our fears, our hopes, our aims are one
our comforts and our cares.

We share our mutual woes,
our mutual burdens bear,
and often for each other flows
the sympathizing tear.

When we asunder part,
it gives us inward pain,
but we shall still be joined in heart,
and hope to meet again.[4]

This glorious hope revives
our courage by the way,
while each in expectation lives,
and longs to see the day.

From sorrow, toil, and pain,
and sin we shall be free;
and perfect love and friendship reign
through all eternity.[5]

This hymn has been dubbed "the Baptist anthem," and it is sung in Baptist congregations throughout the world (though I have experienced it rarely in the United Kingdom since more charismatic hymnody has become popular among Baptists). It was written by Baptist minister John Fawcett (1740–1817) while he was minister at Wainsgate near Bradford, and it may well have been composed in the wake of strong emotions. The story as told by one of his biographers states that in 1772 he accepted a call to a large and fashionable London church (Carter's Lane, as successor to Dr. John Gill), but after the farewell service had been held and the wagons had been loaded with his furniture, he was so moved by the grief of the people that he decided to remain with his poor but devoted congregation.[6] In "emotion recollected in tranquillity," it is said, he composed this hymn. Whether the story is apocryphal or not, emotion does run through the lines; but it is not a merely sentimental ditty, as one would expect from a man who was a considerable theologian, earned a degree of Doctor of Divinity, declined an invitation to be principal of Bristol Baptist College, and founded the Northern Education Society (later Rawdon Baptist College). At the heart of the hymn, there is a theology of covenant, "the tie that binds," and this covenant is set in the context of the Communion of Saints ("a fellowship of kindred minds . . . like to that above") and an eschatological hope ("each . . . longs to see the day"). We notice that the mention of an ongoing "fellowship above" leads immediately to the thought of prayer ("before our Father's throne"), hinting subtly that there is a communion of intercession unbroken by death as well as undisturbed by distance ("still joined in heart"). Eternal life is described in corporate terms, not individualistic reward, as "perfect love and friendship." Fawcett, in an accessible and popular way, strikes many of the same notes that we have sounded in our book.

This hymn is not a religious version of "Auld lang syne," a nostalgic remembrance of past friends no longer present, but is about the reality of a covenant that persists through the ages, among the people of God in the past, present, and future. This quintessentially Baptist hymn prompts the question of this chapter: what dimension might a Baptist theology of covenant offer to belief in the Communion of Saints? Previous chapters have affirmed that a theology of the covenanted community is *congruent* with a theology of the eternal communion of the living and the dead, but what distinctive *contribution* might "covenant" bring? In answering this question, I intend to return now and then to Wilder's play, written by an artist who was strongly influenced by the narrative tradition of Puritans in America[7] (which is perhaps why he portrays the hymn as being sung by the choir of the Congregationalist church, rather than by the Baptist chapel "down in the holla" by the river).[8]

The idea among early Baptists that a church was formed by its members entering into a covenant together was rooted deeply in the ecclesiology of English Separatists, Christian believers who separated themselves from the newly formed Church of England in the late sixteenth and early seventeenth centuries. Significant for Baptists was the congregation of such Separatists at Gainsborough near Lincoln in 1606 or 1607, who—as we have already mentioned—"joined themselves by a covenant of the Lord into a church estate, in the fellowship of the Gospel, to walk in all his ways."[9] This company was not yet a Baptist church, but within a year a part of the congregation would be in exile in Amsterdam with its pastor, John Smyth, and within a further year it would have adopted the practice of believers' baptism. The language of the covenant as recalled here reflects the Separatist heritage of conceiving covenant in two dimensions at once, vertical and horizontal; that is, the church was gathered by the members' making a covenant or solemn agreement *both* with God *and* with each other. Here is the characteristic pledge "to walk in the Lord's ways," which reaches back to the earlier congregational covenant of the Separatist church led by Francis Johnson,[10] and forward to the many covenants of local General and Particular Baptist churches from the mid-seventeenth century onward.

Covenant always resists autonomy, not only of single members within the local covenanted congregation, but also of separate congregations joined together in association. The *London Confession* of 1644 depicts the associating together of churches in the body of Christ, and while it does not explicitly use the word "covenant," it follows the Separatist *A True Confession* of 1596 in applying to congregations the covenant language of "walking together":

> And although the particular Congregations be distinct and severall Bodies, every one a compact and knit Citie in it selfe; yet are they all to walk by one and the same Rule, and by all meanes convenient to have the counsell and help of one another in all needfull affaires of the Church, as members of one body in the common faith under Christ their onely head.[11]

In historic Baptist understanding, the local church does not have "autonomy," which means "self-rule" or "making a law for oneself," because it stands under the rule of Christ, who is the covenant maker. It does have "freedom" or "liberty" from external ecclesiastical constraint in its life and mission; this is not based in Enlightenment concepts of autonomous individuality, or in the self-regulation of a voluntary society, but in the lordship of Christ. Because the risen Christ who calls into covenant stands in the midst of the congregation, it cannot be *imposed* upon from outside in its obedience to him. But since Christ also calls churches together into fellowship and rules in the midst of their assembly, the local congregation has a *responsibility* to seek the mind of Christ in interdependence with others as well as in its own meeting. It is characteristic of Baptist life not to regulate the relation between the authority of the local congregation and the authority of the association of churches, but to leave freedom for churches to "walk together" in the bonds of covenant trust.

A venturous covenant like this is the story that lies behind Fawcett's opening reference to "the tie that binds," often too quickly dismissed as a merely sentimental feeling.

Four Dimensions of Covenant

If we are to understand why this theological idea of the covenantal "tie" might make a distinct contribution to belief in the Communion of Saints, we need to observe by way of preparation that the notion of covenant, as it developed among Baptists in the seventeenth century, came to have four strands or dimensions.

In the first place, "covenant" referred to an eternal "covenant of grace" that God has made with human beings and angels, for their salvation in Jesus Christ. Calvin was influential in developing this idea,[12] and again from Calvin is the belief that there is only one eternal covenant but that it takes a different form of application or dispensation in the two eras of the Old Testament and the New Testament. Under either Testament, the covenant is made through Christ as mediator, but under the old, Christ is present in shadowy types, whereas he is fully manifested in the new.[13]

Second, the divine covenant could refer to an agreement between the persons of the triune God, in which the Son is envisaged as consenting to the will of the Father to undertake the work of salvation. This idea is embodied in the Westminster Confession, and its influence is seen in the Baptist Second London Confession of 1677, which specifies the eternal covenant as being "a transaction between the Father and the Son about the Redemption of the Elect."[14] In his treatise on the covenant, *The Display of Glorious Grace* (1698), the Baptist pastor Benjamin Keach regards the "federal" agreement between the Father and the Son as the primary meaning of the covenant of grace.[15] In the "Holy Covenant" between the Father and Son, "Jesus Christ struck hands with God the Father, in behalfe of all God's Elect."[16]

Third, the term "covenant" could refer to an agreement that God makes corporately with God's church, or with particular churches, and here writers tend to appeal to the covenant formula of God with Israel—"I will be their God and they shall be my people"—together with forms of the formula in the New Testament referring to the church (2 Cor 6:16-18; Heb 8:10).[17]

Fourth and finally, covenant had a special meaning among Separatists and—later on—Baptists; it referred to the kind of agreement I have already mentioned as being made at Gainsborough in 1606–1607, a pact undertaken and signed by church members when a particular local church was founded, and subsequently by new members on entering it. Smyth defines a church by this way of gathering it: "A visible communion of Saincts is of two, three or more Saincts joyned together by covenant with God & themselves."[18] That he is envisaging a literal act of covenant making is clear from his assertion that "the outward part of the true forme of the true visible church is a vowe, promise, oath, or covenant betwixt God and the Saints."[19] During the course of the seventeenth century, it seems that the actual act of covenant making dropped out of practice in some congregations as receiving baptism as a believer was deemed sufficient for church membership,[20] but the theology of the church as a covenant community persisted. The covenantal language of "walking together" regularly appears in early Baptist confessions,[21] including the *Second London Confession* of 1677 that echoes the wording of covenant promises when it states that members of the church "do willingly consent to walk together according to the appointment of Christ, giving up themselves, to the Lord & one to another."[22] In the last years of the seventeenth century, the publication of their church covenants by both Benjamin and Elias Keach (father and son) exercised a considerable influence on the revival of covenant making among Baptists. These covenants were often copied or modified, and the popularity of making church covenants among both General and Particular Baptists increased to the extent that when the church at Downton, Wiltshire, was reestablished in 1793, it assumed that the making of a covenant was "the usage of all organized Churches of the faith of Jesus Christ."[23]

For two centuries, then, Baptists clearly thought of the gathering of the local church in covenant terms, even if they did not always have the outward form. As John Fawcett, writer of "Blest Be the Tie That Binds," put his understanding of the "tie" in 1797:

> It is the custom in many of our churches to express this [covenant or mutual compact] in writing . . . though this circumstance cannot be thought essentially necessary to the constitution of a church.[24]

Although the theology and practice of covenant has been widely lost among Baptists during the past two centuries, the increasing use of the language of covenant today, especially in the United Kingdom and the United States, shows that it is being recovered and being understood as central to Baptist identity. The richness of the idea lies in the weaving together of the four strands I have identified, although their interaction will properly take new forms for new times.

For instance, it is no accident of words that the very same term "covenant" is used for the mutual agreement of church members (meaning 4) and the eternal gracious decree of God for human salvation (meaning 1)—that is, both for a local and an eternal covenant. It was a creative move of the early Baptists to fuse these meanings together, so that B. R. White judges, of the thought of John Smyth, that "it seems that for him, in the covenant promise of the local congregation the eternal covenant of grace became contemporary and human acceptance of it was actualized in history."[25] Moreover, God's making of covenant with the church (meaning 3) is simultaneous with the making of covenant *by* the church (meaning 4). For Baptists, the act of local covenant making is not simply a human enterprise, a promise by believers to be faithful; a covenant community is not merely a voluntary association that has come to certain resolutions about the members' common interests. Baptist confessions of faith have usually held together a voluntary "gathering" of the church, with its being "gathered" or called together by Christ as the covenant mediator (revealed in this office, as Calvin insisted, in both Old and New Testaments). The *Second London Confession* of 1677, for example, describes believers as "consent[ing] to walk together *according to the appointment of Christ*"; churches, it affirms, are "gathered by special grace . . . according to His mind."[26] The modern English statement *The Baptist Doctrine of the Church* (1948) declares that "churches are gathered by the will of Christ and live by the indwelling of his Spirit. They do not have their origin, primarily, in human resolution."[27]

Covenant in the Church and in God

Perhaps most pertinent to our present inquiry about the relation between covenant and the Communion of Saints is the weaving of the second strand of covenant into the whole weft of the meaning of covenant. That is, there is an eternal covenant within the life of the Trinity (meaning 2). This dimension seems to present most difficulty to the modern mind, and we must release the idea from the rather narrow confines of seventeenth-century Calvinistic thinking, in which a covenant within God is a kind of legal bargain or transaction between God the Father and the Son about atonement for the elect.[28]

A first step is to affirm that the *relations* within the triune life of God are irrevocably bound up with the covenant that God makes with human beings. This is the move made by Karl Barth, developing the biblical and Reformation themes of covenant.[29] Taking up the idea of the "eternal covenant of grace" (meaning 1), Barth envisages a "primal decree" in which God's making of covenant with created sons and daughters eternally shapes the relationships of love within God's own triune being. The covenant of grace is thus *integral* to communion between Father, Son, and Holy Spirit; in the primary decision for the covenant with humanity, God determines God's own being throughout eternity, ordaining "who God is" as "God for us."[30] This for Barth is not speculation; we know this because the human person of Jesus of Nazareth is inseparable, by God's free choice, from the person of the eternal Son or Logos. The election of Jesus Christ, representative for all human beings, is a "double decree" at the "beginning of all God's ways and works," in which God has chosen all *humanity* for divine fellowship, and has chosen *God's own self* as covenant partner with humanity.[31] "What a risk God ran!" marvels Barth, in which only God could lose and creatures could only gain.[32]

A logical, second step in this uniting of covenant with Trinity in the "election" of Jesus Christ would be to say that the eternal relationships within the Trinity may themselves be envisaged as a kind of covenant relationship. Then, just as there is a human communion that participates in the "communion" of the Trinity, there would be a human covenant within the "covenant" of the Trinity. Recent ecumenical theology has developed a rich "communio ecclesiology." *Koinonia*, or communion, can describe the relation of an individual believer to a local congregation; the relating of churches together on various levels of human society; the relation between churches and their leaders (pastors and bishops) and leaders with each other; the communal life created by sharing in the Eucharist; the relation of the local to the universal church; the relation of the church on earth to the church "in heaven" (the Communion of Saints); and the participation of all these relations in the loving fellowship of Father, Son, and Holy Spirit.[33] It seems, then, from our discussion so far that the same participation might also be described as "covenant."

Barth, however, avoids explicitly speaking of the inner Trinitarian relations as a covenant. This is because he objects to the traditional picture, characteristic of Calvinistic "federal theology,"[34] of two subjects having legal dealings with each other in a transaction about atonement. Perhaps the kind of portrayal he has in mind is that offered by the Baptist theologian John Gill, who writes of the eternal covenant as if it were a church meeting voting on an issue: "In the eternal council [Jehovah] moved it, and proposed it to his Son, as the most advisable step that could be taken to bring about the designed salvation, who readily agreed to it . . . and the Holy Spirit expressed his approbation of him to be the fittest person to be the Saviour by joining with the Father in the mission."[35] Barth's objection to this kind of heavenly council (which he calls a "mythological scene") is that God would not in actuality be God *without* making an eternal covenant of grace with human beings in Christ. From all eternity, God has determined God's own *being* by this covenant of grace.[36] There is then no need for any further covenant making, on the subject of salvation, at some later point within the persons of the Trinity.[37]

But there are advantages in bringing together the language of "communion" and "covenant," as we shall shortly see, especially with regard to the Communion of Saints. We can actually take Barth's critique and use it as a way of *redefining* an inner divine covenant, improving on Gill's rather absurd scenario. In Barth's own spirit, we can do what Barth refrains from doing. We might say that *as* God the Father makes a covenant of love eternally with the Son in the fellowship of the Spirit, so simultaneously God makes a covenant in history with human beings. In one movement of utter self-giving, God the Father "chooses" both the divine Son and human children as covenant partners. In fact, the divine covenant is not a matter of transaction at all, but a flowing of love, a movement of infinitely generous giving and receiving within God.

This is the kind of theological depth to the concept of covenant that is particularly congenial to the Baptist tradition of a church gathered by covenant. It draws attention to the "ontological" element in covenant—that is, the dimension of sheer being that underlies any doing. Thus, for instance, our mission to the world is not a matter of mere human strategy but shares in the mission of the Father who eternally "sends forth" the Son. Our covenant with God, freely given in grace, is bound up with that "covenant" in God's own communion of life in which God freely determines to be God. If we think of the covenant in Christ like this, then it becomes even more astonishing that the "horizontal" human dynamic of covenant making should be taken into the "vertical" dimension of God's covenant. We are participating not only in God's covenant with us, but in an inner covenant making in God. Church is what happens when these vectors intersect, and God in humility opens God's own self to the richness of the intercourse. This might incline us to read the lines in Fawcett's hymn with an even deeper meaning:

> The fellowship of kindred minds
> is like to that above.

The "fellowship" that is "above" is certainly that of the Communion of Saints, but there is perhaps a hint that it is also the fellowship that is the life of the triune God. This, at any rate, is how the Baptist theologian Stanley Grenz reads these lines, commenting that "as the hymn suggests, the indwelling Spirit shapes the fellowship of Christ's followers after the pattern of the love that preexists in the triune life."[38]

Covenant, Purpose, and an Open Future

Now we have arrived at the point where we can discern positive advantages in interpreting the "Communion of Saints" as the "Covenant of Saints," and I am going to suggest three gains in the remainder of this chapter. The first is that "covenant" involves ideas of will and purpose that are not necessarily implied by "communion." Covenant is about making promises and being faithful to them, and this has implications for the interweaving of covenant in church and Trinity.

In chapter 4 I suggested that as we pray "to" the Father, "through" the Son, and "in" the Spirit, we are entering into the eternal relations between Father, Son, and Spirit. This means that when we pray to God, we find our address fitting into a movement of love that is already there and that we can only say is like a speech between a son and a father—or indeed between a daughter and a mother. Based on the picture of the intercession of Jesus in the book of Hebrews, I proposed that whether we are alive or dead, we are praying for each other *in God*. Everything persons have been—all their memories, habits, attitudes, hopes, fears, and loves—is preserved in God, and God lives that life in their place, representing them, vicariously standing in for them. The human love that they added to the uncreated love of God, and which had a powerful effect on the world, is still enriching the transforming love of God and making a difference. In this sense, the saints who have died are still praying for the world; they are interceding because Christ is interceding. All those who have been gathered into God are praying for us. Now, this must mean that God, in humility, allows the relations within the triune life to be *shaped* by the human lives they represent. The way that God knows God's self is going to be affected by the hopes, joys, and sufferings of that human community. It is not just—as Bonhoeffer puts it—that in the Communion of Saints Christ stands between each member of the human community, making the relations between them, enabling them to communicate with each other.[39] In the *perichoresis* of God with the world, human persons also stand between the movements of divine love that we identify as being like a Father, Son, and Spirit. God will not represent us without sympathetically entering into lives that are being represented. God relates to God's self through human relations.

Much of this vision can be expressed in terms of an interweaving "communion." The language of "covenant" makes clear that God's own *purposes* are being reshaped by the entering of human community into God with its own purposes, aims, and intentions. To be concrete, God's will for the future of history is being formed through holding covenant promises made by local churches in all their everyday circumstances within the very covenant between Father, Son, and Spirit. One aspect of the Communion of Saints we have been exploring is its orientation toward the new creation. To pray within this communion means—as Fawcett puts it—that a person "longs to see the day." The prayers of the saints in which we share are for the kingdom of justice to come "as in heaven, so on earth," and I have been suggesting that God has promised to re-create those whom God holds vicariously alive at present. Now, if the Communion of Saints is really interweaving with the communion of God, as covenant within covenant, this must mean that God also has a future for which God longs, a fulfillment that is yet to come. In some sense, God shares in our prayers and "longs to see the day."

We might think of this in terms of new possibilities that lie in the future, the surprise of the new, which cannot just be contained in present reality.[40] In the first place, we may be sure that God, in God's own self from all eternity, envisages possibilities for the world to which we are blind. But we should surely go on to add a further understanding of possibility in God: that God can also conceive *new possibilities* from the divine imagination as the creative work proceeds. As Keith Ward suggests, this can be conceived as a kind of divine desire, in which God continually aims to "realize new and imaginative forms of beauty and intellectual complexity," limited only by "God's character as wise, good and loving."[41] Such freedom in God means that the end of all things must have a kind of openness. The end will have a surprising quality to it because, as one Old Testament scholar puts it, "God fulfills his promises in unexpected ways."[42] The picture of God this assumes is not one who has a blueprint for the future, but one whose promises are elastic enough to be adapted.

In making promises rather than exact predictions, God thus leaves room for the new and the yet unknown, but we must ask whether this space *only* comes from the possibilities in God's own creativity. To take the love of God seriously implies that God allows those who are loved to make a contribution to the mutual relationship, and so to share in God's creative project. As soon as love is understood to be more than a "doing good" to the other, and to involve mutuality and passions, space must be made for genuine human response to the purpose of God. The reality of human freedom also points, of course, in the same direction.

So we may envisage yet a further kind of possibility that constitutes the future: new possibilities are not only conceived by God eternally, but emerge from the *interaction between the creator and the created* in the course of history.[43] They emerge from the engagement of God in the Communion and Covenant of Saints.

We can imagine, for instance, a painter beginning her work with a vision of what she wants to portray, but then finding that her materials themselves—the texture of the canvas, the swirling density of the oils, the impact made by the brushstrokes, the way that color and shape actually look when laid on a flat surface rather than simply conceived in abstract—all make their own contribution. So the potter finds that he has to take account of the pliancy of the clay, the carpenter the grain of the wood, the sculptor the lines of resistance in the marble. Adapting a phrase from W. H. Vanstone, we may say that "the activity of creating includes the passivity of waiting—of waiting upon one's workmanship to see what emerges from it."[44] It is not only the creatures who wait for the end, but also God. In the interaction of God with the world within the Communion of Saints, God waits.

The end of all things is certain, not because God will coerce creation into it, but because the persuasive love of God, calling created things and persons into partnership, is the strongest power in the universe. Out of the possibilities that God eternally envisages in the face of human despair, God is able to offer *particular* aims and possibilities that always take the initiative. Without this initiative, God could offer no guidance, inspiration, challenge, and consolation in the midst of the actual experiences of life, joyful and painful. As Israelite thinkers in the Old Testament reflect on their experience covenant, they find that when Yahweh's unfaithful people have broken the covenant, Yahweh can always offer a specific new beginning,[45] and life need not be a weary repetition of "more of the same." But although the end, with an overcoming of evil and death, is thus certain, the *content* of what this will be like is open, depending on the kind of cooperation that creatures offer to God. This means their work for peace and justice within history, and it also means the service ("liturgy") of prayer in which the living share with the dead in the Communion of Saints.

We expect an end that is open, a coming of Christ to his glory, which is certain and yet surprising. This challenges the view of a monarchial

God whose power is shown in determining the lives of creatures. It suggests a vulnerable God, whose power is shown in loving persuasion and not coercion. I have been advocating the concept of a God who always makes new possibilities, working humbly in partnership with us. Such a God makes waiting worthwhile, since such a God has a real future.

Some who read this will be concerned about what this might mean for the traditional attribute of divine omniscience. Can God *know everything* if the end is not totally fixed in advance? Can God be omniscient if the end is not determined but is open both to God's creative freedom and to the results of human response? Clearly, in this case, God cannot know the future in detail. For those who wish to resolve this issue, I suggest that we do not have to abandon the notion of God's omniscience, but we have to rethink it. We might follow a number of modern philosophers of religion (including H. P. Owen, Richard Swinburne, and Keith Ward) in defining omniscience in the sense that "God knows everything there is to be known."[46] God knows all the actualities and all the possibilities that there are, but does not know possibility *as* actuality until it actually happens in the world. As process thinkers such as Charles Hartshorne have pointed out, classical theism has been wrong to insist that God cannot be pure act (*actus purus*) unless God knows all possibilities *as* actualities, so that God knows all time in an instantaneous flash; rather, God can be perfectly active as all actuality and all possibility without confusing one with the other.[47] God cannot know the details of the future, because these events have not yet come into being through God's own creativity and the cocreative response of the world; by God's own choice in creation, they are just not there *to be known*, and so not knowing them cannot limit divine omniscience. When they *are* actual, God will know them perfectly. God also knows that the overall possibility of new creation will be actualized, while not knowing particular possibilities until they emerge.[48]

So God knows the future in a way that we do not. God is related to all reality, as we are not; God knows the *particular* possibilities that are present or emerging within the world *here and now*, as we know them not; and most of all, God knows the power of divine persuasive love to bring about the fulfillment of God's purposes. So God, who freely chooses to walk the path of time, will walk it in a different way from us, with an infinitely greater hope and certainty, though there will still be something open about the future, even for God. This is the implication of God's commitment to covenant with humanity and of God's engagement with a Communion of Saints that includes the living, who respond to God's purposes now, and the dead, whose response God has kept alive within God's self.

To return for a moment to Wilder's play, we see he certainly does not explore theological issues in this theological way. But he uses the hymn "Blest Be the Tie That Binds" in the context of a providential understanding of history derived from his Puritan heritage, setting the story of this town and its inhabitants in the wider narrative of God's purposes. At the wedding when the hymn is sung, the Stage Manager, who has taken on the persona of the minister, reflects:

> Every child born into the world is nature's attempt to make a perfect human being. Well, we've seen nature pushing and contriving for some time now. We know that nature's interested in quantity; but she's interested in quality, too—that's why I'm in the ministry. And don't forget all the other witnesses at this wedding—the ancestors. Millions of them.[49]

While the talk here is of "nature" and not a God of love, the Stage Manager (or minister) relates his ministry to an overarching purpose of creating persons in the fullest sense. When the hymn is sung at the funeral, he reflects on the state of the dead: "They're waitin'. They're waitin' for something that they feel is coming. Something important and great. Aren't they waitin' for the eternal part in them to come out clear?"[50] One of the dead speaks of the need to be "ready for what's ahead."[51] Within the community of the living and the dead, there is an orientation to the future, a forward momentum, a "pushing and contriving" toward "quality," an expectation of something to come that will mean fulfillment, and a confidence that it *will* come. But at the same time, there is a strong awareness that lack of human response to love is inhibiting what "they feel is coming." It will not come entirely, regardless of human response and cooperation. In the dialogue among the dead, the dead conclude that "live people don't understand."[52] Emily cries out, "O earth, you're too wonderful for anyone to realize you," and asks, "Do any human beings ever realize life while they live it?—every, every minute?" The Stage Manager replies, "The saints and poets, maybe—they do some."[53]

Covenant, Saints, and Singularity

The idea of covenant thus, first, makes explicit the element of purpose within the Communion of Saints, holding the present and the future in tension. It also holds together individuality and community. Each person for himself or herself makes covenant with others and with God, each making a promise and taking responsibility for the other. Yet the covenant is not an individual possession; the community as a whole is also in covenant with God. Covenant embodies the truth that a "person" is not confined to individuality, exceeding the boundaries of the individual self by existing only in relation to others. Throughout this book we have lamented an individualism that neglects community, and proposed that this can be remedied by recatching the vision of a Communion of Saints. Yet stressing "communion" on its own has the danger of lapsing into a mere collectivity and even into the disaster of totalitarianism. It is a second advantage of "covenant" language to retain a place for the individual, or perhaps we should better say for the personal reality indicated by a cluster of words like "character," "identity," "self," "worth," "integrity," and especially (as we shall see) "singularity."

The Enlightenment reinforced the idea of an individual rational mind existing over against the world, maintaining its identity through independence from others and attempting to exercise domination over nature in a claim for uniqueness among living things. During most of the modern period, the Christian church has been strongly influenced by this mood of individualism, and perhaps Baptists have been influenced more than most, with their concern for "personal faith," expressed in the practice of baptism only of believers who can profess faith for themselves. Too often, "personal" has been equated with "individual," and the setting of baptism in the midst of the church has been forgotten. On the American Baptist scene, an influential voice promoting a spiritual individualism was the Southern Baptist theologian E. Y. Mullins in the 1920s, propounding what he termed "soul competence," or a stress on the ability and responsibility of the individual soul before God.[54] While some contemporary Baptist voices still celebrate this principle as safeguarding "fragile freedoms" that are seen to be under threat,[55] others have become suspicious of it, from several streams of Baptist life. One conservative Southern Baptist theologian believes it leads to an introspective theological method that amounts to "solipsistic Christianity,"[56] while a group of "moderate" Baptists associated with the Cooperative Baptist Fellowship similarly find that Mullins' theory of soul competency defines freedom "in terms of the Enlightenment notions of autonomous moral agency and objective rationality."[57] In their "Manifesto," these latter theologians advocate communal reading of the Bible and emphasize "shared discipleship," proposing (very much in the spirit of this present book) that true freedom is "something we encounter through the divine community of the triune God and with the Christian fellowship that shares in this holy communion (1 Jn 1:3)."

Nevertheless, in a postmodern (or late modern) period, the balance seems to have shifted the opposite way from Enlightenment individualism; the individual subject has been under threat from philosophies that emphasize the vulnerability of the conscious self to the hidden forces of unconscious desires, and that emphasize the "construction" of the self through systems of language and social structures. Practically, individuals live in an environment of multinational corporations, global banking, and intrusive communications, where the subject no longer appears in control of its own destiny. The crisis in the financing of housing in recent years (2009–2013), prompted by unwise loans and borrowing by international banks, has especially left individuals feeling at the mercy of forces larger than themselves. There seems a desperate need to rebalance self and community, individual and society.

In this context, the American Jewish philosopher Edith Wyschogrod has reflected on "saints and postmodernism" in a book of that title. Her question is this: can there be an account of the saintly life that convinces in the postmodern age? At a time when there seem only to be "forces" of existence in endless permutations and the responsible self seems to be disappearing, can we make intelligible a life that has the power to change the behavior of others?[58] She is arguing for "narrative ethics," for the shaping of ethical choices and behavior by the impact of stories rather than by a set of rules. It seems that the people we call "Saints" might offer us such stories, and our previous chapter has offered us an outstanding example in Thérèse of Lisieux. The stories of the saints seem to presuppose the integrity of the individual. But, Wyschogrod asks, can we have any confidence in the effect of an individual life to influence whole structures of power? This is an especially poignant question for a Jewish philosopher who spent much of her professional life reflecting on the phenomenon of the death camps established by the powers of the Nazi state. She also asks, can we pay attention to particular stories without being drawn back into the modernist exaltation of the individual consciousness above an engagement with the world and other persons?[59]

First, Wyschogrod points out that many of the thinkers called "postmodern" are deeply concerned for the respecting of "difference" and the relation of the self to the "other" (and here she distinguishes "differential postmodernism" from "ecstatic postmodernism" in which the self is dissolved into mere currents of desire, floating free of any identity).[60] Indeed, this otherness is to be taken so seriously that we cannot regard the human subject as simply reflecting upon itself without its making a detour by way of the other's reality and the other's demand upon the self. Although the radical character of this alterity might seem to deny the reality of the subject altogether, there can be no "other" unless there is a self to be held responsible to it.[61] There cannot just be "disseminated drops" of compassion for others; there must be selves that are compassionate. At the same time, to suppose that the relation of the self to others *originates* in the consciousness is to fail to grasp the infrastructures of language and culture within which the conscious self exists. She urges then that a "naive individualism" needs to be replaced by a "singularity" that takes account of difference and relation.[62] "Saints" stand out as "singular beings," unique in their experiencing of compassion and their initiation of action to relieve suffering.

Second, this "singularity" means that "saints" cannot be classified within some overall category. "Saints" are not particular exemplifications of a universal virtuous class of compassion and generosity, members of some ideal social whole. Nor is the "other" to whom they sacrifice themselves to be construed as a particular part of a larger whole characterized by suffering and privation.[63] To think in this way (the "saintly," the "needy") is to subjugate persons to a totality that we construct for ourselves, out of our own consciousness, as a way of coping with the world, and which is just a larger version of ourselves ("more of the same").[64] There is something "excessive" or "wild" about someone who appears to be a saint, urges Wyschogrod. For the saint, the "other" is the object of a desire that exceeds any expectation of fulfillment; from the viewpoint of the saint, the suffering and need of the other is always insatiable, always impinging upon the self, always vaster than the intention of the one who relieves it. The saint desires, says Wyschogrod, "not only the welfare of the Other, but the Other's beatitude—not only to sit at the right hand of God oneself but to desire the elevation of the Other."[65] The desire of the saint is excessive, transgressing all attempts to limit and define it. This is a desire that seems to be released from the bonds of any unifying consciousness—unconstrained, absurd in its generosity, yet "always guided by the suffering of the Other."[66]

Now, can we make sense of this "singularity"? Wyschogrod is wanting to say more with this term than that we are never merely individuals, but always individuals in relation. She is wanting to resist the view that the particularity or individuality of the saints is to be understood by reference to a generic universal of saintliness, an "essence" that is created by our consciousness in order to give us a sense of controlling the world. In that case, we could compare a saint with some reality "out there," and test a saint by seeing how well he or she represents a reality we have already established in our minds. This not only runs into the problem, stressed by postmodern philosophers, that representation is an unstable process (a matter we will not pursue further now),[67] but means that the saintly life would cease to shock and disturb us in the way that it evidently does, with power to shape our own behavior. The life of Thérèse of Lisieux for example, as described in our previous chapter, has features in it that do not conform to a conventional view of what it means to be a saint. Reading it, we might at times ask why she was canonized at all, let alone recognized as one of only thirty-three Doctors of the Church. The Catholic theologian Karl Rahner confessed that "many things about Thérèse of Lisieux and her writings only irritated or quite simply bored me."[68] Yet, as Rahner himself perceived, there is "something about" her life and her story that undeniably has the power to impress itself upon us, and which causes us to seek to live before the face of others and the face of Christ.

From the standpoint of a Baptist theology of covenant, Wyscho-grod's account of the "singularity" of saints, valuable as it is, has some deficiencies. First, it is clear that Wyschogrod does not want to con-fuse singularity with mere individuality, but there is a tendency in her account to deny any individuality to persons *at all*, and so the identity of persons seems to be left hanging in the air. The problem then is how to establish the worth of every person, made in the image of God, as proper recipients of movements for justice and equality. A Baptist stress that all are (or can be) saints draws attention to individual worth, and consistent Baptist support for the notion of "natural rights," in the eighteenth and nineteenth centuries, and "human rights," today, moves in the same direction.[69] Although Wyschogrod stresses "differential postmodernism," the implications for the general nature of the self in a postmodern context remain unclear. She really only seems inter-ested in the exceptional, highly eccentric personality who has made an impact on human memory. Might it be possible to retain a core of individual identity—although never existing without relation to oth-ers—that still has the *character* of "singularity"? We shall return to this question in the next section.

A second point is that Wyschogrod does not relate this "singular-ity" of the saints to the God whom they themselves confess, and who for them is an inalienable part of their story. Surely we must respect the fact that they themselves could not tell their stories without God at the center of the narrative. The Baptist scholar James McClendon is, like Wyschogrod, interested in a narrative ethics, or the shaping of ethical behavior by story, but unlike Wyschogrod he finds the impact of the story in "biography as theology." He finds a "character ethics" supe-rior to a "decisional ethics,"[70] and emphasizes that the formation of character is always situated in community.[71] Indeed, communities have their own kind of corporate character. But communities also have their own "convictions," and so certain persons have "singular and striking lives" that have the power to mold the character of others because they embody the convictions of their community about God in new ways. Such people share the convictions of their community but give them new scope, correcting or enlarging the community's moral vision, so that their stories "compel" us to consider them and form our own moral outlook.[72] Probing more deeply, McClendon suggests that the convictions of such singular persons are expressed in certain "dominant images" under which they live out their lives, which are religious insofar as the images that form them are related to a vision of God.[73] Thus, their stories, shaped by these images, continue to challenge us and to create ethical attitudes in us. Further, Christian doctrine must be brought into interaction with their stories and their images, not only to validate it, but to allow it to be modified and developed in this context.[74] So biography becomes theology as well as ethics.

In an appendix, McClendon relates his discussion to the notion of saints as singular personalities and gives as an example the potential for celebrating in worship the story of the American composer Charles Ives,[75] of which McClendon has made a study earlier in the book. A dominant image, which McClendon identifies in the music of Ives, is that of "Beulah Land," taken from a camp-meeting hymn, expressing the conviction of the evangelical Christian community about the hope for a future, perfected, and blessed community, when "Angels, with the white-robed throng, join in the sweet redemption song."[76] Ives, shows McClendon, is "singular and striking" in that he not only affirms this image, but exposes the way that contemporary American society, while supposedly sharing this vision of an ideal society, is actually trampling it underfoot with its own values of nationalism, financial greed, and white supremacy.[77] This critique emerges, suggests McClendon, in much of Ives' music and especially in the clashing and apparent cacophony of musical motifs in the second movement of the Fourth Symphony, at the heart of which the melody of "Beulah Land" is sustained. This example, I suggest, stands aptly alongside my own appeal to John Fawcett's hymn, with its similar vision of a fulfilled society of love.

Another contribution to the place of a vision of God in narrative ethics is made by the Baptist patristics scholar Henk Bakker, who has made a special study of martyrdom and sainthood in the early church. There, he maintains, the telling of martyr stories was intended to form Christian personality and character in a kind of "rhetorical mystagogy."[78] The last words of a martyr, preserved in the story, would (in the words of the Christian poet Prudentius) "introduce God to the inner being" of the hearer,[79] and open up the boundaries of everyday experience to the divine mystery, since the saint in his or her suffering would be identified with Christ. Stories would have the power of consolation, admonition, and instruction, and were intended to create a frame of mind that would prepare the hearer for his or her own final journey. Stories of the martyrs, stresses Bakker, are thus "formative texts," in being able to shape attitudes of life and in opening to the hearer to the glory of the transcendent divine presence.

In different ways, McClendon and Bakker add to Wyschogrod's notion that the "singularity" of the saints is inseparable from their openness to God. Narrative ethics requires some kind of integrity or core of the self—there has to be the story of "someone" to make an impact on others—and this is underlined by their relation to God and the worth that God bestows on them. For McClendon, a particular image held by the saint opens up a sense of God, challenging the convention of society around; Bakker notes that a particular experience of suffering by the martyr opens up a vision of God for that person and others. A theology of covenant, I suggest, moves us toward an understanding of human singularity that does not neglect a proper kind of individuality (far from "individualism") in all who are saints in the sense of living a life open to others in self-giving. By covenant I mean the interweaving of the four dimensions of covenant I outlined in an earlier section, which means that any human community only exists within the communion of the Trinity, and that the triune God only exists (by God's own desire) in *perichoresis* with human individuals and communities in covenant.

It does not at all follow that God also must be an individual as well as "singular." The priority of God as the supreme singularity, the one to whom all others are in debt for their existence, lies precisely in the fact that God cannot be conceptualized either as an individual subject or three individual subjects. This is the point of the image of the Trinity, which can only be imaged (and imagined) as movements of relation. God can never be classified under a universal concept, as one instance of a group: "To whom will you compare me that I should be like him, says the Lord?" (Isa 40:25). The desire of this triune God for the world is so excessive that God has determined only to exist in relation to a covenant with the world, in relation to the Communion of Saints. God alone is "singular" without being an individual; as infinite, God cannot be "a being" with edges, limits, and boundaries. The idea of "Trinity" stretches our imagination to conceive of an ultimate reality that is truly personal but is neither one individual nor three. Human persons, as finite, are bound to be individuals, although this individuality is always being constituted by relation with others.

It is only out of God's own singularity, then, that saints have the power to be singular, and only out of the excess of divine grace that saints have the ability to give themselves so excessively that—like God—they escape any categorization and elude all typecasting. It is, moreover, because of the boundless self-giving of God that the saints who have died and who are now represented by God are not just bundles of memories, characteristics, and emotions, but are "singularities" whose uniqueness we experience within the community of saints. It is because they are "singular" (not merely individual) that we can be confident that God will re-create them, and us with them, to exist in a new creation in new relations.

The man, Jesus Christ, in whom God is incarnate is, of course, an individual as well as a singularity. Jesus stands out, above and beyond all saints, as the preeminent singular individual in covenant relationship with God his Father, but only because he is exceptionally open to others, to God, and to the future, not because he safeguards his selfhood. Jesus appears unclassifiable in his singularity. As John Milbank points out, there is an elusiveness about the person of Jesus in the gospel records, and the narratives have to resort to a whole multiplicity of metaphors in order to identify him: "Jesus is the way, the word, the truth, life, water, bread, the seed of a tree and the fully grown tree, the foundation stone of a new temple and at the same time the whole edifice."[80] Asking "Who do people say that I am?" Jesus escapes all labels (Mark 8:27-30). According to the earliest records, the title he most often uses of himself is "Son of Man," and this is altogether ambiguous. The name could mean the glorious figure of the book of Daniel who "comes with the clouds of heaven" and represents the whole of Israel before God (Dan 7:13-14),[81] or it could simply mean "mortal man," "Everyman," or "I" in the third person (Ezek 2:1, 2:3, 3:1, 3:4, 3:17, 4:1).[82]

Jesus Christ cannot be pinned down by a name. He is singular, unique, because the pattern of his words and actions fits exactly into the movement of God's triune life, which is like a father relating to a son in a spirit of love and hope. Notably, as we have already explored it,[83] as our Great High Priest his praying to the Father fits exactly into the movement within the Trinity, which is like a son responding in love and obedience to a father. Jesus of Nazareth is thus inseparable from the relation of eternal "Sonship" in God; we cannot think of one without the other.[84] While our lives do not fit as well as his, we can share in the divine movements of love and justice with Christ, so that we are carried as communities and as "singularities," each in our own way, into the most holy place of the presence of God.

Covenant, Identity, and Communication

A third advantage of interpreting the "Communion" of Saints as a "Covenant" of Saints is the implication of communication between persons. Of course, this may be thought to be involved in "communion" as well, but it is not made as explicit as in the idea of "covenant," and "communion" might slip into formless feeling. Philip Sheldrake has made the observation that the doctrine of the Communion of Saints is "one of the least developed of theological themes in the west," and that the situation was not helped in the Reformation when the argument centered on "the validity or invalidity of devotion to discrete saints and particularly their power as intercessors or mediators."[85] That is, the meaning of "communion" itself was hardly explored, and I suggest that it is precisely an attention to Baptist ideas of "covenant" and its element of intercommunication that begins to remedy this deficiency.

Complementing the pledge to "walk together," historic covenant making among Baptists usually included the promise to "watch over one another." Alongside the office of "oversight" (*episkope*, or—in older English—"watching over") given by Christ to spiritual leaders in the community, it has been the covenantal responsibility of all members to watch over each other—as expressed in the London Confession of 1644:

> And as Christ for the keeping of this Church in holy and orderly Communion, placeth some special men [*sic*] over the Church, who by their office are to govern, oversee, visit, watch; so likewise for the better keeping thereof in all places, by all the members, he hath given authority, and laid duty upon all, to watch over one another.[86]

"Watching over" would certainly have meant praying for each other, and the pastoral care of "watching out" for each other, but it would also have included offering words of praise and encouragement when people's courage failed and—sometimes—included speaking a word of warning. When warning was thought to be appropriate, this was not communicated as an individual act but in the company of another member; in serious matters the mind of the whole congregation in a church meeting would be sought, and in contentious issues the association of churches would be consulted.[87] This practice of "church discipline" has dropped out of use in modern times, or it has degenerated into the abuse by powerful personalities of weaker people. But, whatever new forms intercommunication should take in a new age, supportive speech, mutual prayer, sympathetic conversation, spiritual discourse,[88] and appropriate exhortation are at the heart of covenant.

It is impossible, for instance, to think of a "Communion" of Saints without a fellowship of prayer. Further, a "Covenant" of Saints evokes the vision of saints in glory praying not only for the world but also in some sense for each other, maintaining an intercommunication between themselves. Given our theological perspective of the continuing life of the saints in God only through God's "representation" of them ahead of a resurrection, we cannot think of heavenly conversations along the lines that we know them here on earth, although the Christian imagination has often projected ideas of ideal dinner parties in heaven, sometimes accompanied by the party game of asking who would be on the list of guests. (The poet William Blake imagined himself dining with Isaiah and Ezekiel).[89] But the concept of "covenant" still invites us to think of some kind of intercommunication of saints in God. While aware that we are reaching the limits of speech here, we might say that since the God who represents or "stands in" for persons who have died is triune, their ongoing life is bound up with the interweaving relations within the life of God, so that they share in the intercommunication of God's own self. Prayer is the expression and articulation of love,[90] and God can maintain that expressiveness. Just as they only live in God, and only relate to us in God, so they relate *to each other* in God.

Returning to the concerns of the last section, the idea of communication has been significant in our late modern age for trying to conceive an individuality that is not individualism. Everyday situations of life constantly raise questions of a balance between the integrity of the self (or "singularity") and openness to others. We might call it being "uniquely centered" without being "self-centered." Postmodern thinkers are surely right to oppose the Enlightenment view of the person, in which what matters is the ego reflecting upon itself; rather, the person lives from openness beyond itself to others. In line with covenantal discourse, the person may be said to be a center in the sense of being a center of *communication*. For the philosopher Emmanuel Levinas, discourse with others pays attention to them and recognizes their ethical demand on us, so that "in its expressive function, language maintains the other," and "conversation is not a pathetic confrontation of two beings absenting themselves from others."[91]

As Calvin Schrag puts it, reacting against the Enlightenment self, the subject does not exist independently in itself, but is *implied* by a network of communication, emerging along with the self-disclosing of other subjects. For this role of the self, he uses the phrase "space of subjectivity," indicating that the subject is "not an entity at all, but rather an event or happening that continues the conversation."[92] What is primary is not self-reflection, but a "happening" in relationships. Nevertheless, wholeness requires a certain kind of personal centering, an individual integrity. We may agree that the person is not a *ready-made* entity, a kind of core of existing identity, but it still develops an identity as a *consequence* of relations with others.

Using a geological image, Alistair McFadyen speaks of the person being "sedimented" from the flow of communication between subjects; individuality is a "structured, continuous identity sedimented from significant moments" of acts of communication in which there is exchange.[93] McFadyen appears to be using the metaphor of "sedimentation" in the sense in which a layer of rock is laid down over eons. David Cunningham, in an exhilarating book on Trinitarian theology, suggests that a more appropriate image is the "sediment" that collects on a riverbed, which is always being composed and recomposed in a dynamic way by the movement of the current.[94] Whether geological or fluvial, the metaphor of sediment does imply that unless there is some centered subject maintaining a spirit of communication, we cannot be there for others at all.[95] As McFadyen points out, personal relationships may sometimes only be served if the personal subject has enough integrity and character to *resist* the demands of others that proceed from a distortion of the self in the other. It does not help another if one accedes to a demand for drugs, for instance, or for financing a style of life that is self-destructive. Respect for others, of course, means that we must also be ready to be resisted by *them* in what *we* want.

We need to be aware of this tension within ourselves, between integrity of the self and openness to the other. In order to care for others, we need a new discovery of the inner self, to understand our own needs and fears. Otherwise, we will fail to notice the self-interest in our offers of care, which are really a kind of exploitation.[96] The person who fears the threat of illness and death will often seek out the disabled and the dying and anxiously try to support and comfort them; the person haunted by doubts about belief will demand a religious certainty from others. A desire to help can be a cry for help, and unless this is acknowledged, the relationship will actually become depersonalized.

We might read Wyschogrod, then, as suggesting that a saintly "singularity" can prompt us to find the relation between self and the other, between self-enclosure and self-openness. A narrative of wild, excessive love and desire has the power to shock us into finding a story for ourselves that is not based on the momentum of our consciousness toward control of the world and others. A theology of covenant places this human story within the context of God's triune life. The self can find itself aligned with a relationship that is already there, a willing response of a Son to a Father, and so can participate in the movement of the Son's will in saying "Yes, Amen" to the Father's purpose. Openness to others then means neither conformity to the *other*, which would be a loss of one's own will, nor an expression of our own will in a desire to dominate, but conformity to *Christ* whom we meet in and through the other. The self is properly centered by being directed outward to others and having its own will conformed to a perfect relation of life. This might then mean either yielding to what another wants, or resisting it, according to whether this is in harmony with the Son-Father movement of will that we experience in God. The relationship is covenantal, with elements of purpose, singularity, and expressive discourse.

In the logic of covenant, this very movement of the will of Christ by which we are to be shaped is thus itself shaped and colored by *many* human situations in which there has been worked out not a will to power, but a will toward the good of others. All these situations are held alive within the "memory" of God, as God "represents" the saints; the relations of the Trinity cannot be separated from them. We find our will shaped, then, within a movement that is a whole community, nothing less than a Communion and Covenant of Saints held in the intercommunication of love. In this way, there can be what Alastair McFadyen calls a "mutual formation of the will in society" that does not simply swamp the individual's ethical responsibility, even though McFadyen himself does not appeal to the Communion of Saints.[97]

Here, an insight from African traditional religion may be helpful, when placed in the context of Christian theology. Joe Kapolyo, a New Testament scholar from Zambia who is also a minister in the Baptist Union of Great Britain, draws attention to the belief of the Zambian Bembe people that a person can "inherit" the person or spirit of a dead relative, who henceforth "inhabits" them, opening up a hope for survival and influence after death in the midst of community. Noting that such a hope is bound to be finally disappointed, Kapolyo suggests that as Christians, by contrast, we "inherit" Christ, who is our "inheritance kept in heaven" (1 Pet 1:1-3).[98] Perhaps we might integrate this Christian reformulation more closely with the original Bembe belief, by proposing that we *do* "inherit" those who have gone before us, but only because of their union with Christ in God, not as a direct or private relationship. We are in no way possessed by their spirits. I have laid stress on the way that God "represents" the saints who have died, standing in for them and maintaining their personalities and gifts until the resurrection. This is why we can have a covenant relationship with the saints in light. Surely we can say that in covenant God also allows us to share that representation with God's own self, so that we can inherit something of the character, gifts, and virtues of the saints, and carry on their mission of love to the world.[99] Through us, they can thus form part of a "mutual will-formation" in society,[100] on earth as in heaven.

Thus, a healthy relation of self to other is always part of a wider sphere, a network of relationships whose edges we can never calculate. What threaten to be claustrophobic and stifling relations are liberated when they are set within a wider communion and a more comprehensive covenant. The engagement of a community in the triune God places its members in a context of relations that is as wide as the world, as God opens the divine life to include all creation. The Trinity is—in a phrase used by Wolfhart Pannenberg—a "field of force."[101] Moreover, the width of this force field of relations is not just spatial but temporal. The Spirit of hope is continually opening it up toward the future, giving our relations a place in the movement of God toward a new creation. This is what it means for the church not only to *understand* itself theologically but to *live* in God.

Here we might return for the last time to Wilder's play. As the choir sings, three times, "Blest Be the Tie That Binds," Wilder widens our vision beyond the domestic relations of the people of this small town, who he has been lovingly observing in their journey of life. The wedding, in which a bond is to be tied, is in the presence of many others who have loved in relationship, as the minister asserts: "Don't forget all the other witnesses at this wedding—the ancestors. Millions of them. Most of them set out to live two-by-two, also. Millions of them."[102] The play ends with the cemetery scene, with the Stage Manager looking up at the night sky, setting the efforts of people on this planet in the context of the multitude of stars "doing their old, crisscross journeys in the sky." Though "scholars . . . seem to think that there are no living beings up there," the stars symbolize human lives, which can be told "all by name."[103] While the embittered, dead organist Simon Stimpson complains of the "ignorance and blindness" of human beings, Mrs. Gibbs replies, "That ain't the whole truth, and you know it . . . look at that star."[104] Millions of stars, millions of ancestors—unless we understand our context in a larger story and a boundless community, we shall fail to "realize life while [we] live it."[105]

The Difference the Doctrine Makes

Paul S. Fiddes, Brian Haymes, Richard Kidd

> Come on! Come on! This hillock hides the spire,
> Now that one and now none. As winds about
> The burnished path through lady's-finger, thyme,
> And bright varieties of saxifrage,
> So grows the tinny tenor faint or loud
> All all things draw towards St. Enodoc.
> Come on! come on! and it is five to three.[1]

This is the first verse of John Betjeman's poem, "Sunday Afternoon Service in St. Enodoc Church, Cornwall," written about the church where he now lies buried in the churchyard. The church stands, almost buried itself, among the sand dunes above Daymer Bay in North Cornwall. In the nineteenth century, before its restoration, it was literally buried, and the vicar had to be lowered through a hatch in the roof once a year to read the service and keep the church open. Worshippers today, as Betjeman describes them, respond to the "tinny tenor" of the bell hung in a bent and stumpy tower and wend their way through the dunes strewed with wild flowers, making their way carefully over the fairways of the St. Enodoc golf course that now surrounds the church. It is, without doubt, an ancient place of worship, seeming to reach back into the lives of the Celtic saints who are commemorated in the several medieval churches around, perhaps missionaries from Wales or their children—St. Enodoc, St. Manfreda,

St. Endelienta, St. Doghow (or Docco), St. Kew. The air is full of a sense of the Communion of Saints, not only those named but the many people who have worshipped in these places for the last thousand years. Truly, "all things draw to St. Enodoc."

The neighborhood is not inhabited only, or chiefly, by the retired. There are many young people around, especially at the thriving surfing center of Polzeath nearby. The group of churches to which St. Enodoc belongs has recently appointed a youth worker to meet this challenge, in partnership with the Methodist Church. The church of St. Endelienta nearby is becoming a center for contemporary spirituality and the arts, and draws dozens of young people from all over the United Kingdom twice a year to play and sing in two music festivals. The question then arises: what relevance does the rich history of the saints in this area have for such modern issues? The same kind of question has perhaps has been prompted in the reader's mind by the chapters in this book: what practical difference could belief in the Communion of Saints make for life in the church today? Hints have been dropped for the alert throughout the book, but now the authors want to apply themselves specifically to this question. St. Enodoc is a parish church of the Church of England, but the same issue arises for Baptists wherever they are, once they have become sensitive to the reality of the Communion of Saints.[2]

The Doctrine and the Nature of the Church

There is a strong streak of pragmatism in Baptist life and history that makes the asking of this question virtually inevitable: what practical difference does believing in the Communion of Saints actually make to a local congregation of disciples? Our answer is essentially that believing the doctrine *enlarges* the meaning and practice of faith. It results in taking a longer view of history, being liberated from the immediate moment, and participating in a community whose placing is in the eternal purposes of God. It also results in the enlargement of our experience of prayer; we find ourselves in a fellowship that exceeds the boundaries of that group of disciples whom we can know only in our own locality, or in this life. This larger view and experience is there in the apostolic affirmation and prayer that it is only with "all the saints" that we can know "the length, breadth, height and depth" of the love of God (Eph 3:18).

The consistent Baptist emphasis on the theological significance of the local congregation, the church gathered by the triune God, has strengths and weaknesses. Among the strengths is the focus on God—calling, making covenant, guiding, disciplining, inspiring those through whom the divine purposes are being worked out for all people. Such a community, living under the rule of Christ, is the church by gracious calling. Being together in Christ, it is already an expression of the divine purpose when Christ will be all in all. But this emphasis on the gathered congregation can lead to distortions, among which is the temptation to act as if this local congregation is virtually all that the church is and that its immediate concerns are those to which the church is primarily called to respond. Thus, the divine mission becomes contracted to the immediate and local. Among such powerful and demanding concerns may be the congregation's budget, or any denominational program's call for loyalty and support, or social and political issues of the moment, be they local, national, or international. For any number of reasons, the church may become reactive to these matters as they claim their place at the top of the agenda, determining the shape and goal of church life. Such issues are not unimportant and may even have their place in the *missio dei*, but in the immediate freezing moment, the calling of the kingdom may be reduced to the financing of the new boiler. For such a purpose, the saints may well be judged to be of no great worth, certainly nothing like the significance and immediate value of heating engineers and financiers (who may nonetheless be saints, of course).

In such ways, the horizons of the church may be redrawn and the life, identity, and calling of the church redefined in seriously limited ways. The horizon has shrunk. Vision is restricted by the immediate and local. This does not happen without consequences for the understanding of God and God's mission purposes. There are all manner of temptations of this kind that beset local congregations, but the overall result may be the active guiding conviction that the main reason for what they do is the maintenance of their own survival. This may be highly desirable in all sorts of ways, but it does not of itself express the life of the kingdom. Those who seek to save their life may well lose it.

In these and other ways, the doctrine of the Communion of Saints invites us to take a larger, longer view of the Christian calling in the purposes of God. The history of the saints and martyrs of the faith is illustration of the fact that—whatever the immediate pressures and claims of changing days for the local congregation—the church lives by the calling of God, and the saints are those who have responded to that call and so have been living expressions of grace in the world. They are testimony to the faithfulness of God, the God who keeps promises and does not leave the divine purposes without witnesses. The longer, larger story of the church tells of the God who takes up human failures and misunderstandings into the purposes of the kingdom, the restoring and renewing of all things in and through Christ. This does not happen without the saints. So, the congregation that recalls the saints of the church is enriched by the story of God and God's ways in human lives. Recalling the saints illustrates the risks and diverse meanings of discipleship, the wide variety of forms of life following Christ may take. Such may relate to immediate issues before the congregation but draw the members into the larger purposes of God for the world. This is not to limit the contribution of the saints to being only illustrations and examples of discipleship, however valuable that is. Recalling the saints sets the local congregation itself in the larger context of divine purpose, liberating it from the imperial claims of the potentially demanding immediate moment.

This longer, larger view of the Christian calling underlines the essentially ecumenical nature of the church. Whatever schemes of union are proposed, explored, enacted, or rejected by synods, councils, or assemblies, no one seriously doubts but that God has been at work in lives beyond the denominational limits. "Saints" are to be found in all the denominations and, many will acknowledge, beyond the bounds of the Christian community. Thus, Mahatma Gandhi and Nelson Mandela are more than freedom fighters who become wise creative political leaders and peacemakers. They are among a huge company of those in whom many discern the activity of God. The long and large story of the saints and martyrs is a constant cause for thankfulness by the whole church. Recognizing this in our prayer and praise enlarges the understanding of the God who calls us to be witnesses in our time. Believing in the Communion of Saints takes us way beyond our carefully drawn denominational boundaries into an ecumenical world of God's creating and gift.

Recalling the saints and martyrs often has political implications. Take, for example, the case of Archbishop Oscar Romero. The Roman Catholic Church has not yet come to declare him to be a saint, but there are many way beyond El Salvador who see—in his life and ministry, his stand against an oppressive regime, and his affirmation of the poor and vulnerable—the signs of holiness and faithful witness. His life became countercultural. He challenged the accepted ways and heroes of the nation and church. Like Martin Luther King, Dietrich Bonhoeffer, and many others, he stood against the cultural norm and was killed because of it. Baptists will be glad to recall such lives and sacrifices, and along with them those of us in the English tradition of Baptists will remember such ones as William Carey, William Knibb, Dorothy Hazzard, and Hannah Marshman. Recalling the memory of the saints and martyrs is inspiring and disturbing at the same time, but the church is enlarged and enriched by such memory. Affirming the Communion of Saints blesses the church with a great treasury of prayer and practice to be explored.

Recognizing the great diversity of membership within the Communion of Saints and embracing differences of gender, nationality, education, and social standing may help us recover the one world in which we are called today to be the church. Saintliness is not reserved for our own church, our own denomination, or our own nation. God's love and grace find expression all over the face of the world as human lives become places of divine disclosure. Growing in the knowledge that this is so is part of God's work of reconciliation. The Communion of Saints speaks of the healing of the nations, overcoming those ancient painful divisions, the cultures of death that confine us still. Visions of that great company that no one can number, from all the tribes and nations on earth, inspire and affirm our international gatherings, such as the Baptist World Alliance, the World Council of Churches, and the United Nations. These sometimes all-too-human organizations carry a hope the Communion of Saints inspires. They are a foretaste of what will be when Christ is all in all.

Believing in the Communion of Saints brings us a longer, larger view of the church, the gospel, and the future of the world than is normally found among us. The doctrine enlarges our sense of being the church, reaching now beyond "just us" in our locality, out into different times—past and future—and different places, with different people united in Christ. We who can worry about declining smallness are part of a great company beyond our numbering.

Moreover, enlargement of faith is not only a matter of a viewpoint. It is the very stuff of spiritual experience. We have argued in this book that because we are united in Christ, we *are* one with all saints, those alive in Christ and those dead and alive in Christ—"one church on earth and in heaven," as the traditional saying puts it. This means, we have proposed, that we are one with them in prayer. All Christian praying is offered to God, through Christ our one High Priest. In consequence, Baptists, along with many other Christians, have resisted prayers to the saints, in the sense of asking for their help. But here we have affirmed our conviction that we pray *with* the saints. We have argued that in the bonds of Christ, they pray for us, unbidden, in a fundamental living relationship of love in Christ. They long for the coming of the kingdom. By God's calling and grace, we engage with the saints and participate with them in the praise and prayer of God, though only *in God*. We are united in the searching, saving love of God, united by gracious covenant mercies. Further, this fellowship of prayer has implications for a doctrine of the church. Baptists have affirmed that the church is "called together" or "gathered" by God, to offer acceptable worship and service. Thus, when we join together in prayer with the saints, we are already gathered into one by grace; this is what is reflected in our prayers to the Father, through the Son, inspired and enabled by the one Spirit. We are united in God, participants in the divine love and life. With the saints we share God's company; they are part of God's ever-present communion with the world. Confessing faith in the triune God, we find saints among us in *our* fellowship of believers. The congregation, gathered for worship, is larger than we thought or than appears to the eye.

So the doctrine enlarges our hope. Hope becomes more than something individual such as "my" personal survival after death. It is a hope that includes our life now, the death we all shall die, and the life beyond death that remains the gift of the gracious God. The hope is of a new heaven and a new earth, impossible for us to picture but glimpsed even now in remarkable new ways of being human, sharing a hope that goes way beyond any easy optimism. And the doctrine leads us into a larger understanding of God and God's relationship with us and all creation—God whose work extends beyond the limitations of even the best of our thought. It is the one God in Trinity who called, sustained, enabled, and gave us the amazing company of the saints. This is the God of our beginning and our end, the beginning and end of all that was, is, and ever will be—God our hope and salvation.

The doctrine finds its own place in the great creedal statements of the church. In the Creed of Nicaea-Constantinople, it follows the affirmations about belief in the Holy Spirit and the holy Catholic church; then comes the Communion of Saints, the forgiveness of sins, the resurrection of the body, and the life everlasting. These articles speak of holiness, hope, and praise. Every time they are confessed, the church utters a prophetic word, a call to a deeper communion with God, between the churches and with each other around one table. On this table God has placed, and goes on placing, the holy food for a holy people living in hope of God's work begun in Christ Jesus that will surely come to completion when all things cry glory in God's new creation.

The Doctrine and Our Worship

While we live still amid the old creation, what practical difference would it make if we came to worship here and now aware that we come not as isolated individuals, but to "the assembly of the firstborn who are enrolled in heaven . . . to the spirits of the righteous made perfect, and to Jesus the mediator of a new covenant" (Heb 12:23-24)?

At the very beginning of worship, this might cause us to move away from customary phrases centered on ourselves—like "*we* come to worship," or "*we* come tired from the week past," or even "*we* build a throne"—and to listen instead to voices of many saints who *call* us to worship God with them, remembering that covenant is not a voluntary agreement but a being summoned into relationship. They may be the voices of saints whose witness we have in the Old and New Testaments. In many texts, they bid us: "Come! Let us raise a joyful song to the Lord, a shout of triumph to the rock of our safety"; "How good the Lord is! Only taste and see"; "Let all who hear say 'Come.' Come, you who are thirsty—take the water of life as a free gift to all who long for it"; "Come close to God and he will come close to you; humble yourselves before the Lord and he will raise you high"; "The Lord is near; have no anxiety, but in everything make your requests known to God"; "You have not come to . . . darkness, gloom and whirlwind—you have come to the City of the living God"; "Surely you have tasted that the Lord is good: so come to offer spiritual sacrifices, acceptable to God through Jesus Christ"; "Show yourselves eager to make firm the unity which the Spirit gives, by the peace that binds you together."³

Or the voices that summon us may be from the history of the church: "This is Christ's thirst, a love-longing to have us all together, wholly in himself for his delight" (Julian of Norwich); "Cleanse your eyes, and the bright sun shall shine upon you, and you shall see clearly" (John of the Cross); "Know this, that as we pray the holy angels encourage us and stand at our side, full of joy" (Evagrius). Such invitations are to be read aloud at the beginning of worship, by one or many voices, not as a text from a book, but as living voices that are addressing us here and now, speaking into the covenant assembly as present members of it.

With regard to intercessory prayer, we might take our cue from John Fawcett's hymn that was a motif of our previous chapter:

> Before our Father's throne
> we pour our ardent prayers. . . .
> We share our mutual woes,
> our mutual burdens bear. . . .

In intercession, we are praying "in God," taking part in a vast and mutual network of relationships and ongoing prayer offered by the living and the dead. This certainly means that we will want to draw on a treasury of prayers that we inherit from the saints. Many Baptists will know a prayer of St. Augustine ("You made us for Yourself, and our heart is restless until it finds its rest in you"), of St. Patrick (beginning, "Christ be with me, Christ before me, Christ behind me, Christ in me"), of St. Francis of Assisi (beginning, "Lord, make me an instrument of your peace"), of St. Ignatius Loyola (beginning, "Teach me to serve Thee as thou deservest"), and of John Wesley (beginning, "I am no longer my own, but thine"). Others they might get to know include Dietrich

Bonhoeffer, awaiting execution in a Nazi prison ("Lord, whatever this day may bring, Your name be praised"), and many of the prayers of Martin Luther King, including this one, which turns into intercession the content of his speeches during the civil rights movement:

> We thank thee, O God, for the spiritual nature of man. We are in nature but we live above nature. Help us never to let anybody or any condition to pull us so low as to cause us to hate. Give us strength to love our enemies and to do good to those who despitefully use us and persecute us. We thank thee for thy Church, founded upon thy Word, that challenges us to do more than sing and pray, but go out and work as though the very answer to our prayers depended on us and not upon thee. Then, finally, help us to realize that man was created to shine like stars and live on through all eternity. Keep us, we pray, in perfect peace; help us to walk together, pray together, sing together, and live together until that day when all God's children, Black, White, Red, and Yellow will rejoice in our common band of humanity in the kingdom of our Lord and of our God, we pray. Amen.[5]

Prayers left by the saints are not just useful "liturgical material"; they enable us to pray *with* the saints here and now, as they live in God.

As we remember saints from the past of the church universal, we shall also want to draw on the memory of the congregation for the "saints" who have influenced them in their particular past. On Mother's Day, for instance, we might invite the congregation, of all ages, to speak out loud the names of their mothers, or those who have been like mothers to them. So the church will fill with the sound of names, leading all into a greater company. One Baptist minister recently celebrated All Saints Day with a service to which he issued this invitation: "On Thursday, November 1, at the church there will be a short service at 3:00 p.m. to mark All Saints Day.[6] It will be an opportunity to remember those who have died and the great crowd of witnesses that have gone before us, and to bring our grief, whether recent or long standing, in prayer to God." The liturgy of prayers and Scripture readings offered opportunity to speak names out loud, to listen to music, to reflect, and to light a candle.

Another significant example of this practice of remembering stands in the liturgy for the Lord's Supper of the Evangelical Baptist Church of the Republic of Georgia, which follows the shape and much of the content of the Orthodox Divine Liturgy of St. John Chrysostom.[7] As in that "Divine Liturgy," after the words of consecration over the bread and wine, and before the prayer before Communion (including the Lord's Prayer), there is a moment for the commemoration of the saints. In the Baptist liturgy, those sharing in the Lord's Supper also remember their own "spiritual guides":

> *Celebrant:* As we celebrate this Holy Communion, we remember those who have gone to their peace in faith: our forefathers, fathers, mothers, patriarchs, prophets, apostles, Mary the Theotokos [God-bearer], preachers, evangelists, martyrs, confessors, and every righteous spirit made perfect in faith.
> *(At this point congregants are invited to utter the names of those departed who have played a significant role in their spiritual journey by saying: Remember Lord . . . [my spiritual guide's name])*
> *Congregation:* Grant us boldness, courage, endurance, heart for service, and ministry after their example.

The Evangelical Baptist Church of the Republic of Georgia has also, in recent years, adopted the practice of displaying icons of the saints in worship, including icons of Martin Luther King and its own founders from the nineteenth century. As in Orthodox practice, icons are censed at the beginning of worship (that is, the smoke of the burning incense is directed toward them) at the same time as the congregation is censed. In the words of Malkhaz Songulashvili, archbishop of the church, "In the worship setting when both icons (representing the invisible church) and the faithful (representing the visible) are censed by clergy a symbolic connection is being made with relational character of the Trinity who lets visible cultures participate in the mission of his invisible, yet most beautiful self."[8]

In other Baptist churches, there may be a resistance to installing permanent icons of the saints or using painted images, but few congregations object to projecting visual images on a screen during prayers. Artists in the congregation might be asked to depict past saints as they might be envisaged to be present in this particular congregation (remembering that their presence is always through being in God, as represented by God, not as ghosts or wandering spirits). Painted crosses in El Salvador portray these kinds of scenes. And photographs of "saints" known by the congregation in its time can also be projected on the walls of the church so that worship takes place in the midst of many witnesses.

As we read Scripture in worship, we shall recall how a particular passage has spoken to a saint of the past with a force that cannot be ignored. For example, reading Romans 1:17—"The just shall live by faith"—we will remember how Martin Luther's reading of this text fired the renewal of the Christian church. Reading Matthew 28:18—"Go into the world and preach the gospel"—we will recall how this text inspired William Carey to leave his familiar Northampton village for the strange land of India. Reading Matthew 6:24—"No one can serve two masters"—we may remember how this verse inspired the Jamaican Baptist deacon, and enslaved person, Sam Sharpe to organize a sit-down strike, an act of passive resistance that initiated the Great Jamaican Slave Revolt of 1831–1832 and cost him his life. Reading Mark 2:14—"And Jesus said to him, 'Follow me,'"—we shall recall Dietrich Bonhoeffer's comment, "When Christ calls a man, he bids him come and die,"[9] and his own obedience as a disciple that took him finally into a Nazi prison and to execution. Many texts in the Bible have an afterlife in the lives of the saints, and they come to us colored with the deep hues of the Communion of Saints. We do not just *remember* the way a past Christian read these texts, but in the communion of God, we can read the texts *with* the saints, sharing the impact the Scripture made on them in their time.

When considering the range of contemporary forms of worship and spirituality among Baptists, talk of "pilgrimage" is an increasingly constant feature. Rather than a continuation of the enormously popular medieval practice of visiting the relics of saints and martyrs, among Baptists and evangelicals generally "pilgrimage" tends to be an extension of the metaphor of the Christian life as a pilgrim way into some actual physical journeying or physical activity. The label of "pilgrimage" may be no more than a mere sanctification of tourism—for instance, to the Holy Land. But "pilgrimages" often take a more local form of a journey—perhaps a walk—to a site where a notable Christian has lived or died, or where there has been a formative act of Christian witness or a Christian protest against injustice. In some way, a place is connected with "the saints," whether these be recent or further back in the past, whether well known or nameless. Many Baptist Christians, for example, have made a "pilgrimage" to Birmingham, Alabama, where Martin Luther King was imprisoned and many African American Baptist Christians suffered and even died at the hands of a white racist government. The museum containing Dr. King's prison door has become a kind of shrine. It was in fact with Birmingham, Alabama, that we began this volume.[10]

Now, since the saints are present in every place of worship, through the presence of the triune God, is there any reason to make pilgrimage to "sacred places" associated with the saints? Was Gregory of Nyssa right in criticizing the visiting of sacred places with the comment, "The changing of one's place does not bring about any greater nearness to God. No, *God will come to you* (cf. Ex. 20.24) wherever you are. . . ."[11] Might a proper doctrine of the Communion of Saints help with this question and throw light on what is a growing form of spirituality among Baptists?

In the history of the Christian church, places became sacred, and so became the goal of pilgrimages, because they were closely linked to a person or persons considered "sacred" or "holy"—that is, the *hagioi*, or the saints. The place acquired its attraction through holy *people*, not on its own account. As Augustine expressed it, "the wonderful tabernacle" of God is "the faithful people."[12] But it was thought that the place mediated the presence of the saint who had lived there, especially when he or she was buried there and the tomb could be visited. And because the saint had lived in the presence of God, perhaps becoming intensely close to God in the moment of a martyr's death—even being identified with Christ in his sufferings—he or she was believed to be able to bring the presence of God to the worshippers. Presence meant power, and so the possibility of miracles. The logic ran that the place mediated the saint who mediated God to the pilgrims who came.[13]

Our argument in this book has been almost the reverse. We have not begun with a physical place but with *God* as the place where the saints gather. As Philip Sheldrake puts it in his book *Spaces for the Sacred*, "We may think of God as the one truly catholic place."[14] The triune God makes space in God's self for all the saints, and God is universally present in the world. Our thought then is this: God is the place of the saints who therefore enables them to be present with us in any place of worship. Far from our being dependent on a saint for the presence of God, the saint depends on God for his or her presence with worshippers today. Moreover, the worshippers too can "represent" the saint and so make manifest his or her values and virtues in the world today. In the light of all this, there would seem to be no basis for pilgrimages to places felt to be sacred. We may have sympathy with the theologian Rudolf Bultmann, who wrote, "Luther has taught us that there are no holy places in the world."[15]

Yet for all that, we do instinctively feel places to be "holy" and feel their attraction as a goal of pilgrimage. One of our authors, Brian Haymes, has given testimony to this in his chapter about his visits to the Carmel community of St. Thérèse of Lisieux. Many Baptists in the United Kingdom today have been influenced by the Celtic spirituality of the "new monasticism" of the Northumbria Community, in whose leadership several Baptists have been involved;[16] the website of the community explains that its identity is "rooted in the history and spiritual heritage of Celtic Northumbria," that visitors are attracted by "the Celtic saints and the Northumbrian landscape" and that its original mother house was "located close to Cuthbert's Cave in North Northumberland."[17] Clearly, a sense of place is important for this spiritual movement. Similarly, a good number of United Kingdom Baptists have made retreat on the Isle of Iona, whose ancient abbey was founded by St. Columba, or they have used the worship resources produced by the ecumenical Iona Community. Here is where a doctrine of the Communion of Saints, as we have been developing it, can make a difference, giving theological grounding to what may be sometimes a vague feeling about the significance of place, and encouraging those folk who long "to go on pilgrimage" and "to seek strange shores,"[18] to do so in the right frame of mind.

First, the act of journeying is itself a spiritual exercise, expressing outwardly in physical form such journeys as every human passage through life, the pilgrim path of Christian discipleship, and inner voyages of the spirit in prayer and meditation. For Baptists, the physical act of walking in company can be an expression of the covenant pledge to "walk together and watch over each other," and if we follow the identification of "Communion of Saints" with "Covenant of Saints" as has been suggested in earlier chapters, we can truly believe that saints of past and present are companions, walking with us. Saints of the past are as much on the journey as at the destination, and realizing this can give a depth and richness to our own journey. Second, since God "stands in" for the saints and makes them present in any place, this will certainly be true for places especially associated with their life, ministry, and death. We meet with the saints there because we meet in the space of the triune God; they do not mediate *God* to us, but God mediates *them* to us, and so enlarges our fellowship of prayer.

According to the doctrine of the Communion of Saints, we do not need to travel to a particular place to have our vision enlarged by the presence and prayers of the saints. But we may think that, as David Brown puts it, "any and every place that has a human imprint on it may actually have the potential to function sacramentally. What makes the difference, though, is not the human being as such but whether God can be experienced in speaking . . . through the place."[19] Just as God is present and speaking to us in all times and places—but we may still know a special focus of God's presence and word in the sacraments of baptism and Eucharist[20]—so a place might, by extension from these church sacraments, be "sacramental." As the physical elements of bread, wine, and water become means for a special encounter with God, so may the physical elements of a place—its rocks, water, grass, trees, and buildings—when it has been the location for the faithful witness and worship of God's people through the ages. A place can open us up toward God, and entering into God means entering into the Communion of Saints within God. There is thus an intimate binding together of place, saints, and God. It is the covenantal gathering of the saints in a place that gives it the potential to be sacramental, and it is this sacramentality that gives us a doorway into the wider life of the saints within the infinite space that God opens up in God's own self, within the interweaving relationships of the Trinity.

Practically, this means that we can enjoy the spiritual benefits of the "sacred places" we visit without becoming anxious about whether we are in exactly the right location, whether we have said the right prayers, or whether we have seen and touched venerated objects. On medieval pilgrimages this anxiety took the form of wanting to be as close as possible to "relics" of the saints, or even acquiring them at crippling cost, in order to have as much presence of God as possible.

On modern pilgrimages, there is often the anxiety of the tourist, wanting to take exactly the right photograph that proves one has "been there," or acquiring just the right souvenirs that will somehow perpetuate the presence of the place when one is back home. There may also be the anxiety of the scholar about the historical accuracy of the story attached to the saint and the place. There is an undeniably "fictive" aspect (to use a term from Paul Ricoeur)[21] about the narratives of saints' lives, mixing fact and fiction with the aim of producing a story that will inspire. As Sheldrake points out, saints' lives, or hagiographies, often present a world of what "*ought* to have happened" and "what it is possible *can* happen," rather than what actually happened.[22]

Pilgrims who have a vision of the Communion of Saints will not be troubled by these anxieties. They will be grateful for the way that a particular place can open up a deeper immersion into that communion, but will have the calm assurance that what matters in the end is entering there into the triune fellowship of God "with Mary and all the saints." It is not the saint, the relic, the right place, the best photograph, or even the accurate story that brings us to God. It is God who brings us into a wider space of life and love than we could ever imagine.

The Doctrine and Pastoral Care in Dying and Bereavement

The doctrine of the Communion of Saints, we have proposed, enlarges our vision of the church and its worship. It also widens the possibilities of its pastoral care. One of our several aims in this book has been to articulate something of the variety and complexity of experiences to which people give testimony in connection with dying, death, and bereavement. These experiences are often painful and in many ways highly undesirable, but they can also occasion some of life's most profound moments, tinged with what we identified as a quality of "strangeness." Such strangeness, as the word itself suggests, remains elusive; it is not a shortcut into proof or the explanations of things. For some, however, it can provide a point of entry into the hinterland of religion and even a gentle introduction to a way of faith.

Experiences associated with death make us extremely vulnerable. They often herald the times when we are most in need of pastoral care, when our vulnerability might well be further intensified if we lack appropriate frameworks within which to think about and deal with our needs in the broader context of a faith tradition. In exploring the core theme of this book, we have sometimes wondered if a relative silence around talk about the Communion of Saints leaves Baptists especially open to such vulnerability—in contrast, for example, with traditions that provide their followers with well-developed patterns for thinking about, caring for, and praying with those they love, and not least those they are losing or have already lost into death.

It is not that we are expecting to find definitive explanations for life's most intense encounters with the hiddenness that surrounds human death; that, as we have said, would betray a fundamental misunderstanding of the mystery that is integral to faith.[23] One of the great challenges for all human cultures, however, is to develop a coherent pattern of metaphorical discourse, sufficient to enable us to negotiate our way through these complex and disturbing experiences around the boundaries between life and death. From earliest times, not least in the Greek and Roman cultures of the ancient world, this wisdom has been gathered in sacred texts, including stories of the heroes and the saints, and its absence leaves us dangerously unprepared and, at times, open to misleading superstitions and to easy manipulation by unscrupulous peddlers of uncritical religion. One way or another, we still need maps that chart our way through these turbulent waters.

An example of just how important it can be to have tested ways of speaking about these issues around life and death is well illustrated by the much-loved book from an earlier generation, *A Grief Observed*.[24] In 1961 there appeared in print a groundbreaking text that reproduced in journal form the intense and personal experiences of a widower recently bereaved. It charted, with previously rare openness and honesty, some disturbing experiences of disorientation and tormented faith associated with the loss of a much-loved partner. It might have remained largely unknown had it not soon come to light that the author was not "N. W. Clerk," as first appeared on the cover, but none other than the highly respected Christian writer and broadcaster, C. S. Lewis. His journal recorded some of the intense and frightening experiences now recognized as common to many who are recently bereaved, which leave them feeling, as many have testified with hindsight, near the edge of madness and fearing that they might never again be able to live what they had previously thought to be "normal" lives.

Lewis' journal testifies to an extended process within which he found quite distinct moments of transition. More recent research has confirmed the importance of understanding grief as a process,[25] and has come to a broad consensus that, while its stages and transitions can vary significantly from individual to individual, the process unfolds within broadly recognizable patterns. Initially, Lewis described an overwhelming sense of numbness, absence, and frustration:

> It feels like being mildly drunk, or concussed. There is a sort of invisible blanket between the world and me. I find it hard to take in what anyone says. Or perhaps, hard to want to take it in. It is so uninteresting. Yet I want others to be about me. I dread the moments when the house is empty. If only they would talk to one another and not to me.[26]

These are feelings that have burdened generations of Christians with guilt. If I really believe God's promises of resurrection, they have asked, what right have I to indulge such apathy and hopelessness? This is very much what Lewis also said of himself, as his numbness shifted toward desperation and frustration. Soon he was writing not only about the painful absence of his partner but about God's absence too, God's silence at the moment of greatest need. "Where is God now?" is a cry that echoes through human history and even, as Lewis noted, on the lips of the dying Jesus.

How important it is to be affirmed in the normality of these experiences, to be handed a map from a wise and trusted Christian companion. That is the role that *A Grief Observed* has played for so many who have experienced bereavement in the years since its true authorship came to light. It was enormously significant that such a respected orthodox Christian believer should testify to sharing precisely these experiences following the loss of his own partner. This disclosure gave many faithful Christians real hope that their own experiences were much more "normal" than at first they had feared and that they, like Lewis, might again still hope for a future at peace with God and with themselves.

The pastoral importance of the publication of Lewis' journal is relevant here because there are such strong parallels to the way in which narratives we have referred to in our own book, experiences and life stories clustered around the Communion of Saints, can also become a significant pastoral resource—fundamentally, enabling us to live more easily with some of the extraordinariness of what is, in fact, ordinary life. To live in a community starved of these narratives is to be cut off from the comforting knowledge that there are respected Christian companions who share our experience and have already made enough sense of its strangeness to discover genuine peace with themselves, with others, and with God. Such knowledge, then, is crucially important not just for ourselves but for those for whom we have a pastoral responsibility.

Lewis' unfolding experience is relevant too. In the final of his book's four chapters, he wrote about of the beginning of a new phase:

> Turned to God, my mind no longer meets a locked door, turned to H., it no longer meets that vacuum—nor all that fuss about my mental image of her.[27]

This was progress indeed, both with respect to H. and with respect to God. In a way that could not have been imagined in the earliest days of grief, the desperate sense of the loss of God had eased; and H. was accessible too, free from the anxiety of trying to hold on to the fading mental images that had so tormented him soon after his loss. He continued:

> There was no sudden, striking and emotional transition. Like the warming of a room or the coming of daylight. When you first notice them they have already been going on for some time.[28]

Nor did Lewis rush to exaggerate his increasingly positive experience into what he called "evidence for anything." His confidence remained fragile:

> That impression which I can't describe except by saying that it's like the sound of a chuckle in the darkness. The sense that some shattering and disarming simplicity is the real answer.[29]

The return to meaningful life was a slow and hesitant process. It is the fact, however, that Lewis found elements of hope that became enormously encouraging for others who found themselves on a similar track.

It probably does not matter that our individual journeys will not always take the same form. Lewis increasingly found satisfaction in the idea that H. was still present to him as a "meeting of minds."[30] Attempting to describe his continuing relationship with H., Lewis wrote:

> It's the *quality* of last night's experience—not what it proves but what it was—that makes it worth putting down. It was quite incredibly unemotional. Just the impression of her *mind* momentarily facing my own. Mind, not "soul" as we tend to think of a soul. Certainly the reverse of what is called "soulful." Not at all like a rapturous re-union of lovers. Much more like getting a telephone call or a wire from her about some practical arrangement. Not that there was any "message"—just intelligence and attention.[31]

The central idea in this passage, a meeting of pure intelligence, will certainly not satisfy everyone who is grappling with bereavement—but the fact that Lewis had found a way through from near despair to a new kind of hope has been enough to inspire many. Lewis himself ended his account of observed grief on an appropriately humble and humbling note:

> But I mustn't, because I have come to misunderstand a little less completely what a pure intelligence might be, lean over too far. There is also, whatever it means, the resurrection of the body. We cannot understand. The best is perhaps what we understand least.[32]

This tentative but hopeful spirit is very much in line with the tone of much of our own writing about the Communion of Saints. We too have tried in places to describe something of the strangeness that accompanies our awareness of those now departed from us, but we too know it would be foolish to push our own preferred metaphors too far.

Some of our own encounters as pastoral visitors resonate well with Lewis' experience. As pastors, we have often found ourselves working with people who—rather like Lewis in the early stages of his grief—simply do not know what to make of their experience at this critical stage of their life. This makes them very gullible to the clutches of anyone with advice to offer, much of it reaching too far beyond the reasonable evidence. Our experience is that some Baptists and other evangelicals can be especially vulnerable at this point. One of us remembers, for example, a very nervous church member sharing her deep fearfulness in advance of a wedding. She had been widowed quite tragically some years before and had continued to carry a very strong sense of her husband's presence long after his death. For many years, this had been a source of great comfort, something that she had found very supportive and helpful, but suddenly it had begun to generate a new feeling of anxiety. With increasing discomfort she was confronted with the prospect of dealing with her powerful feeling of her first husband's presence in the new marriage bed. Suddenly, the narratives that had enabled her to safeguard and value her earlier relationship, something enormously positive, were in danger of turning against her and inhibiting her potentially new life. Her received ways of understanding her first husband's presence were quite different from Lewis' "meeting of minds," being something more akin to a "ghostly presence" that was watching intently "from above."

Perhaps, more serious attention by Baptist preachers and teachers, to the Communion of Saints—which need not be about "minds" and is certainly not about "ghosts"—might be one way to help people such as this woman in churches like ours understand how we, the living, might relate appropriately to our dead. It has been a persistent theme of this book that we do not relate to them in any other way than living for ever "in God." It seems that this particular woman, sadly, had an understanding of a relation *exactly* like that of relations in life, only extended beyond the grave.

We also remember numerous pastoral encounters when it became clear that people needed to know—as the lasting impact of Lewis' book has illustrated—that their seemingly distorted perceptions around times of intense grief were properly within the range of the acceptably "normal." They needed to know, for example, that a sudden and intense feeling of a lost partner's presence and touch is not a sign of impending insanity, and that a numbness about God is not a sign that faith has totally collapsed. Again the pastoral challenge is to provide a supportive narrative—nothing too cleverly philosophical, but something with enough intellectual integrity to hold life together through desperate times.

Pastors know that people need to find ways to begin to speak about their own impending deaths. Good practice suggests that this is not something that can or should be forced on anyone, but a caring pastor will be listening carefully for the moment when a clue, perhaps something quite small, is given that the time is right. The sadness is that many people leave all this so very late on their journey into death, causing untold, but at least in part avoidable, pain both to themselves and to their loved ones. The problem is that if we are not accustomed to speaking freely about life and death—while the living is still good, drawing on models that feed the imagination with significant metaphors of hope—then it is not surprising that many find it hard to begin under the pressure of rapidly declining health.

We have stressed, in several of our contributions to this book, the place that uncertainty and provisionality holds in thinking about death and beyond. We are in no doubt, however, of our need to be immersed in strong narratives of hope at these times—well aware that the language of such hope does not come easily to modern minds. Our own society's truth questions have tended to become too mechanical, too calculating. We have lost the ability to hear and live with truth encoded in narratives, and to allow it to wrestle with our fears and build our hopes. A deathbed is no place to try to reverse the habits of a lifetime and to learn how to be fed by the language of metaphor. This puts, therefore, the onus on pastor-preacher-teachers to work gently over time in their faith communities building resources for people to grapple with death in the midst of life, and exploring how our understanding of the Communion of Saints might be a significant point of entry.

We suggest that living in life's midst with a growing understanding and appreciation of the Communion of Saints can provide a significant resource as we journey toward the goal of dying well in the faith of Christ. It is unlikely that many of us, faced with a terminal prognosis, will escape the need to move through a variety of painful stages in preparation for death. Perhaps, however, wise preparation can contribute to enabling the journey. Pastors find themselves listening to all manner of clichés at these difficult times—many of them little more than desperate attempts to avoid reality, and many of them bearing little connection with the mainstream of our Christian inheritance. We commend the search for healthy and helpful ways to think about and to enact a lasting relationship with all those who have been instrumental in shaping who we are and have become. Most obviously this means appropriate and meaningful relationships with parents, partners, children, and other intimate companions, long after they can be a visible part of our daily lives. As Lewis recorded so well, beyond the intensity of early bereavement, there is the real possibility of a return to another place of stability in communion with all God's people, a place that can be, long term, peaceful and life giving.

The Doctrine and Baptists at the Table and the Pool

Central to the practices of the Christian faith are the Lord's Supper and baptism, and it is here above all that we would expect a belief in the Communion of Saints to make a difference. In fact, we have been relating this doctrine to the Lord's Supper and baptism throughout our book, evoking a picture of sitting around the table with the memory, and in the company, of the saints and of entering the baptismal pool not alone but surrounded by a great host of witnesses. Baptists— gratefully—share much of the practice and meaning of these two sacraments with the rest of the Christian church, and yet it is possible to identify distinctive contributions they have made to the richness of the whole. Here in conclusion we would like to identify some of these characteristic Baptist elements and to ask what difference the enlarging vision of the Communion or "Covenant" of Saints might make to them *in particular*.

In their manner of celebrating the Lord's Supper or Eucharist, Baptists differ in one notable way from nearly all other forms of the Christian family that either precede the Reformation or flow immediately from it. In Orthodox, Catholic, Anglican, Lutheran, Presbyterian, and most Reformed traditions, the "words of institution" of the meal, associating the bread and cup with the body and blood of Christ (beginning, "In the night when he was betrayed Jesus took bread . . .") are contained in a prayer to the Father. The anamnesis, or remembrance (or "memorial"), that follows thanksgiving is thus addressed to God, with the congregation "overhearing," as it were. Theologically, the idea is no doubt to "plead" the sacrifice of Christ before God, laying the passion of the Son before Father, rather than imagining that God needs to be reminded of these events of our salvation. Among Baptists, by contrast, the words of institution are not addressed to God but are read as a *story* to the congregation. This results from the simple practice of using Paul's account in 1 Corinthians 11 as the framework for the action of the Supper. In accord with the actions of Jesus in the narrative, a prayer of thanksgiving is first offered, and then the story—or the rest of the story following the mention of thanksgiving—is read, so effectively passing on the tradition to the church, as Paul himself claims, "The tradition I received from the Lord I hand on to you" (1 Cor 11:23). The *story* is told that Jesus names the bread as "my body," and the cup as "the new covenant in my blood." The actions of breaking bread and pouring wine are often integrated into the narrative at the point they occur. Thus, thanksgiving is indeed followed by anamnesis, but the anamnesis, or deliberate recollection of the death of Christ, consists in the words of institution themselves, not in a prayer asking God to remember the cross. The memorial is in the story itself.

This is a way of acting out the sequence of thanksgiving and anamnesis that might be a gift to the wider church.[33] In the past it was shared with the Congregationalist tradition within the Reformed life of the English church, and this kind of liturgy still exists in some forms of union between Congregationalists and other Reformed churches.[34] It has also been inherited by other more recent Free Churches such as Brethren and Pentecostals. While not an exclusive Baptist "distinctive," it is nevertheless characteristic of Baptists, and so it is a matter of regret when the gains of "telling the story" are lost. Those presiding at the table often fail in confidence when it comes to assuming the authority of those who pass the story on. Instead of simply declaring with St. Paul "the tradition which *I hand on* to you . . . ," the presiding person will often begin, "The Apostle Paul writes . . ."—thereby distancing the whole story into the third person, and so blunting the effect of telling the story himself or herself.

Here is the point when the doctrine of the Communion of Saints will make a difference. The minister presiding at the table has the confidence of standing in the succession of the saints who, generation after generation following St. Paul, have told the story to the assembled covenant community. The minister will doubtless have in mind those from whom she or he personally heard the story at the table, and can imagine the long chain of those behind them who have said, "I hand this on to you." The congregation too can understand that they are there in the succession of communities that have heard the story over the years. But the doctrine of the Communion of Saints alerts us to the fact that this is not a mere matter of memory and imagination. As the story is told, the voices of those who have told it support the voice of the one who speaks in a spiritual polyphony, and those who have heard it through the years help the hearers to listen. In this act of telling and hearing, the "representation" of the saints by God and the church becomes actual in the here and now.

Baptists, of course, have differed among themselves about the meaning of the Lord's Supper. There are those who maintain that it is an act of remembrance alone, while others follow their seventeenth-century predecessors who readily referred to the Lord's Supper as a means of grace, such as Particular Baptist Benjamin Keach who affirmed that "there is a mystical Conveyance or Communication of all Christ's blessed Merits to our Souls through Faith held forth hereby, and in a glorious manner received, in the right participation of it."[35] However, the experience of the authors of this book, in meeting Baptists from many different parts of the world over the years, is that, despite differences, there is an almost universal agreement that the Supper offers an opportunity for a special depth of "meeting" or "encounter" with Christ.[36] Moreover, Baptists warm to the affirmation that we encounter Christ *in each other* as we gather round the table. This, we suggest, is a second characteristic of the Baptist celebration of the Lord's Supper, a "discerning" of the body of Christ in the body of the people gathered, as much as in the elements of bread and wine. This is in accord with the Apostle Paul's words that "we who are many are one body, for we all partake of the one bread" (1 Cor 10:17), and with the thought of the Reformer Zwingli who wrote: "We eat bread so that we are made into one bread. . . . What we become by this eating . . . is the body of Christ."[37] So also the seventeenth-century Particular Baptist Hercules Collins wrote of the Lord's Supper: "By the Holy Ghost . . . though [Christ] be in Heaven, and we on Earth, yet nevertheless we are Flesh of his Flesh, and Bone of his Bones."[38]

In the seventeenth century, it was common practice for members to hold the church meeting either immediately before or immediately after the Lord's Supper. Indeed, Baptists have held what might be called a highly sacramental understanding of the church meeting, though some would be surprised to hear it described like this. It is because Christ is embodied among the members of the church that they expect to be able to discern his "mind" for them. The church book—which recorded the names of the members, the church covenant, and all the decisions taken in the church meeting—was kept in a drawer in the bench behind the Lord's table, or in the "table pew." Here was a symbol of the sacramental significance of the coming together of human bodies into the body of Christ—table and church book together.

The doctrine of the Communion of Saints makes a difference to this Baptist characteristic. "Body" implies visibility, and the image of the "body" of Christ is about the becoming visible of Christ in the world. Christ becomes manifest through his many human members, each contributing some aspect of the reality of Christ so that in their coming together, like many brushstrokes (or, in computer language, many pixels) making up a picture, the face of Christ stands out and people can touch his hands through the hands of the church. When we discern the body of Christ around the Communion table, we do not find many individual bodies of Christ, but one body to which all the members contribute. To repeat some words from an earlier chapter, the "Christ in me" meets with the "Christ in her."[39] Now, it will be easier to discern the body of Christ if those who make up the image are many and varied, bearing witness to Christ in their bodies in many different cultures, times, and circumstances. To remember the saints when we gather round the table means that they make their contribution to the manifestation of Christ. As we recall their stories—especially the way that the martyrs made a witness that was branded deeply into their own bodies—and as their stories mingle with our stories, colors and shapes come together to make Christ visible. When their stories are known (and told within the life of the church), the mention of their names will be enough to evoke their part in making Christ visible. Nor is it a matter only of memory; the saints share in the celebration of the Eucharist, adding their voices to the prayer of thanksgiving, "represented" as they are by God and the members of the church. By their stories and—more mysteriously—by their presence, the saints add pigments and lines to the picture of Christ that emerges through breaking of bread, pouring of wine, and gathering of disciples. As one modern liturgy puts it:

Heaven is here, and earth,

and the Church above and below is one.

Peter is here, and Paul,

Martha and all the Marys,

Columba and Francis, Theresa and Luther King *[space to add other names]*,

the saints from far back

and those who left us not long ago.[40]

If Baptists differ about the meaning of the Lord's Supper, they differ no less about baptism. There are some who insist that baptism is only a profession of the disciple's faith, bearing witness to an event of salvation that has taken place through the Holy Spirit entirely before baptism. Other Baptists find a convergence in baptism between the personal faith of the candidate and the gracious activity of God, so that baptism is part of an extended process of "being saved" that has begun before baptism but continues during and after it. This they find consistent with the statement from 1 Peter 3:21 (that "baptism now saves you"), with the New Testament attribution to baptism of many gifts of saving grace,[41] and with the convictions of early Baptists such as the General Baptist Thomas Grantham, who writes,

> Baptism in the ordinary way of God's communicating the grace of the Gospel is . . . a means wherein not only the Remission of our sins shall be granted to us, but as a condition whereupon we shall receive the gift of the Holy Ghost. . . . [It] was foreordained to signifie and sacramentally to confer the grace of the pardon of sin, and the inward washing of the Conscience by Faith in the Bloud of Jesus Christ.[42]

As with the Lord's Supper, however, we have found that despite differences among Baptists throughout the world, most Baptists rally around the conviction that in baptism there is a special "encounter" with Christ, and so with the triune God, in a way that has a transforming effect upon the candidate and also upon the congregation that shares in the meeting at the baptismal pool. There is also general agreement that this moment of encounter is the opportunity for a believer to be commissioned for service as a disciple, sharing in God's mission in the world, whether or not this is signified by the laying on of hands.[43] Here, there is a clear distinction between the baptism of a very young infant and someone who can profess faith for him or herself. While aspects of the grace of God and faith (at least the corporate faith of the church) can certainly be discerned in an infant baptism, it is not meaningful to speak of a very young child as receiving gifts of the Spirit to be employed in service in the world.

Thus it is not just the element of faith that differs between different kinds of baptism; there is also a difference in the nature of the grace that is being envisaged as present there. The baptism of an infant can be the opportunity for the prevenient grace of God, beginning a work of regeneration that will come to completion in personally owned faith, but it cannot be the moment for receiving gifts of service. A "spiritual gift" according to the New Testament is not a permanent possession that can be endowed and lie dormant, but the actual *activity* of the Spirit's self-giving through someone, manifested in acts of service such as evangelism, teaching, hospitality, pastoral care, administration, and generosity.[44] These are what begin to show themselves in the life of a disciple, in however elementary a form, following a commissioning at baptism. In other Christian churches, this commissioning and gifting can happen at the moment of confirmation for those baptized as infants, or at baptism as a professing believer if they have newly come to faith and not been baptized as an infant, but it is a characteristic of Baptists (and other baptistic churches) for it to be *always* synchronized with baptism itself.

Now, the doctrine of the Communion of Saints, or Covenant of Saints, makes a difference to this Baptist characteristic, too. The baptismal candidate is being commissioned for service in the glorious company of those who have served faithfully in many times and places. This is not only a communion but a "covenant" of saints, as each member has made a pledge to be a disciple, and this has been marked by high intent and purpose, as well as singularity and communication with others.[45] Recalling the lives of these saints offers a model to the candidate of what the discipleship he or she is undertaking might look like and demand. "This," the candidate is being told, "is what discipleship is like, what it can achieve for God, and what it might require of you." Perhaps particular saints might be remembered who have been personally associated with the candidate if they come from the recent past, or saints of the wider church might be recalled who share a name with the candidate or have some other meaningful connection with the candidate's life and circumstances. It might even be appropriate at this point to offer the candidate a baptismal name to be shared with a saint.

As the Baptist scholars James McClendon and Henk Bakker have emphasized,[46] stories of the saints have rhetorical power to shape character, and the moment of baptism and commissioning is surely a significant focus for this process of formation. Moreover, as the story is being told, the saint of the past is being "represented" by God, in whom the saint is alive and in this sense is truly present. God "stands in" for the saint and allows the church to share in this divine activity, so that the candidate is being challenged to go on representing in his or her life the virtues and the values that made this person such a notable disclosure of the grace of God, and so to "inherit" them today.[47] As in the Lord's Supper, this representation and presence of saints in communion and covenant will make the face of Christ visible in the world today.

As we come to an end of our study, we affirm again the encounter with the triune God that the sacraments of the Lord's Supper and baptism offer to us. God, of course, rejoices to meet with people anywhere at any time, but we know that by the ordinance of Christ himself there is a place and time provided at the table and the pool where we can be assured that God has promised to be present with covenanted people. Such moments offer special opportunity for enrichment of the Christian life. The sacraments are thus doorways into the communion of the triune God, into the interweaving patterns of the dance of life that God enjoys in eternal relations of love. At the same time, they are doorways into the Communion of Saints, since God in overwhelming generosity has made room for created beings in God's uncreated life. With our sight sharpened at the focal point of these sacramental moments, we can recognize invitations in many times and in many places to be drawn into the communion of God and all the saints, so that our vision and our experience is always being enlarged. We discover the depths of communion and the wide horizons of covenant.

NOTES

Introduction

1 In the fall of 2002, the chapel was officially named in honor of Andrew Gerow Hodges, close friend and advisor to the late Ralph Beeson.

2 For this idea, see further below, pp. 146–47.

3 Paul S. Fiddes, *Tracks and Traces: Baptist Identity in Church and Theology* (Milton Keynes, UK: Paternoster, 2003), 15–16.

4 "The Word of God in the Life of the Church: A Report of International Conversations between the Catholic Church and the Baptist World Alliance 2006–2010," *American Baptist Quarterly* 31 (2012): 28–122.

5 See Internet blogs under the names of Baptist scholars Andy Goodliff, Steven Harmon, and Stephen Holmes; also Andy Goodliff, "Towards a Baptist Sanctoral?" *Journal of European Baptist Studies* 13, no. 3 (2013): 24–30.

6 Published by the Baptist Union, London, 1985. The other contributors were Roger Hayden and Keith W. Clements. The book is now out of print, but an electronic version may be obtained free of charge on application to the authors of this book.

Chapter 1

1 Baptist churches have been named after well-known Baptist individuals, such as Fuller Baptist Church, Kettering and Carey Baptist Church, Moulton. More often, however, in the United Kingdom, the building is designated by the name of the road or street on which it is found.

2 Recently, however, there has been an online conversation about creating

a calendar; see the introduction above. The Evangelical Baptist Church of Georgia does have a calendar of saints.

3   Tripp York, *The Purple Crown: The Politics of Martyrdom* (Scottdale, Pa.: Herald, 2007), 30.

4   *The Confession of Faith Of those Churches Which Are Commonly (Though Falsely) Called Anabaptists* (London: Matthew Simmons, 1644), in *Baptist Confessions of Faith*, ed. William L. Lumpkin (Chicago: Judson, 1959), 165.

5   *Confession of Faith Put forth by the Elders and Brethren of Many Congregations of Christians (Baptized upon Profession of Their Faith) in London and the Country* (London, 1677), in Lumpkin, *Baptist Confessions*, 289.

6   *An Orthodox Creed, or A Protestant Confession of Faith, Being an Essay to Unite and Confirm All True Protestants* (London, 1679), XXXV, in Lumpkin, *Baptist Confessions*, 323–24.

7   See, e.g., Peter Brown, *The Cult of the Saints: Its Rise and Function in Latin Christianity* (Chicago: University of Chicago Press, 1981).

8   Translations of the *First Apology* and *Second Apology* of Justin Martyr can be found in Alexander Roberts and James Donaldson, eds., *The Ante-Nicene Fathers* (Grand Rapids: Eerdmans, 1975), 1:163–93.

9   For a full analysis of these stories, see York, *Purple Crown*, 28–60.

10   Origen, *Exhortation to Martyrdom* 16, in *Prayer and Exhortation to Martyrdom*, trans. John J. O'Meara, Ancient Christian Writers, ed. Johannes Quaesten and Joseph C. Plumpe, vol. 19 (Westminster, Md.: Newman Press, 1954); emphasis in original, denoting a quotation.

11   T. S. Eliot, "Murder in the Cathedral," in *The Complete Poems and Plays* (London: Faber & Faber, 1969), 258.

12   *Martyrdom of Polycarp* 4.1, in *A New Eusebius: Documents Illustrative of the Christian Church to AD 337*, ed. James Stevenson (London: SPCK, 1968), 19.

13   *Martyrdom of Polycarp* 18.1–3, in Stevenson, *New Eusebius*, 24.

14   See the argument in Elizabeth Johnson, *Friends of God and Prophets: A Feminist Theological Reading of the Communion of Saints* (London: SCM Press, 1998), 55.

15   Thomas Helwys, *A Short Declaration of the Mystery of Iniquity* (London, 1612), esp. 40–49, 61–62, 69–70.

16   *Confession of Faith Put forth* (1677), in Lumpkin, *Baptist Confessions*, 165.

17   See chapter 6, pp. 130–31.

18   These ideas are considered in more theological detail in chapter 4.

19   Johnson, *Friends of God*, 55.

20   These considerations are expanded in chapter 4, pp. 95–96.

21   Johnson, *Friends of God*, 180.

22 Text in William Brackney and William R. Millar, "Pilgrims in Grace," *American Baptist Quarterly* 2, no. 4 (1983): 290–91.

23 This was held on July 30, 2009, at the Mennonite Church in Amsterdam, with which the part of the earliest Baptist community that remained in Amsterdam had close associations.

24 "Litany of Thanksgiving: Cloud of Witnesses," prepared with the assistance of Paul Sheppy, printed in the program booklet, "Baptist World Alliance Service of Worship in Celebration of the Quadricentennial of Baptist Witness," 3–4.

25 I am grateful to Dr. Anthony Cross for drawing my attention to this manuscript. It can be found in the Angus Library and Archives at Regent's Park College, Oxford, Box 631-660, 1919–1934, among the BMS Archives.

26 "The Church's One Foundation," by Samuel John Stone (1839–1900), in *The Baptist Hymn Book* (London: Psalms and Hymns Trust, 1962), no. 263.

27 Henry Raymond Williamson, *British Baptists in China 1845–1952* (London: Carey Kingsgate, 1957), 65–69.

28 The story is told in J. B. Middlebrook, *In Journeyings Oft: A Memoir of H. R. Williamson* (London: The Baptist Missionary Society, 1969).

Chapter 2

1 Marcel Proust, *In Search of Lost Time*, 6 vols., various translators (London: Penguin Books, 2002).

2 Marcel Proust, *The Way by Swann's*, trans. Lydia Davis, vol. 1 of *In Search of Lost Time* (London: Penguin Books, 2002), 49.

3 Craig Raine, "The Onion, Memory," in *The Onion, Memory* (Oxford: Oxford University Press, 1978), 29. Printed by permission of the publisher.

4 See Jürgen Moltmann, *Theology of Hope*, trans. James Leitch (London: SCM Press, 1965), 26–32.

5 These themes are widely explored in Freud's extensive writings, but find particular theological resonances in Sigmund Freud, *Totem and Taboo*, trans. James Strachey (London: Routledge & Kegan Paul, 1960).

6 See, e.g., Melanie Klein, *Love, Guilt and Reparation: And Other Works 1921–1945* (New York: Macmillan, 1975). These essays explore a wide range of ways in which infant anxieties affect later life.

7 Karl Popper, *Objective Knowledge: An Evolutionary Approach* (Oxford: Oxford University Press, 1972).

8 The classic text was Lovejoy, *The Great Chain of Being: A Study of the History of an Idea* (Cambridge, Mass.: Harvard University Press, 1936).

9 Henri Bergson, *Creative Evolution*, trans. Arthur Mitchell (New York: Random House, 1944).

10   Pierre Teilhard de Chardin, *The Phenomenon of Man*, trans. Bernard Wall (London: Collins, 1961), 257–60.

11   See, e.g., Richard Humphreys, *Futurism* (London: Tate, 1999).

12   The theory of special relativity was first proposed by Albert Einstein in 1905, with general relativity following in a paper of 1916.

13   His formula is $dE \times dT = h$, which is a constant.

14   Alfred North Whitehead, *Process and Reality* (New York: Macmillan, 1929).

15   Whitehead, *Process and Reality*, 27–39, 163–66, 373–75.

16   Stevenson, *New Eusebius*, 21.

17   For a summary of this question and the theological issues it raises, see Paul S. Fiddes, *The Promised End* (Oxford: Blackwell, 2000), 208–15.

18   For an explanation of the rejection of this dualism, see chapter 4, pp. 85–88.

19   A pioneering text was that by Leonardo Boff, *Ecclesiogenesis: The Base Communities Reinvent the Church*, trans. Robert Barr (New York: Orbis, 1986).

20   Gustavo Gutiérrez, *A Theology of Liberation*, trans. Caridad Inda and John Eagleson (New York: Orbis, 1973).

21   José Comblin, *Being Human: A Christian Anthropology*, trans. Robert Barr (New York: Burns & Oates, 1990).

22   This was first highlighted for many British readers in Rosemary Radford Ruether, *Sexism and God-Talk* (London: SCM Press, 1983).

23   The substantive chapter is Marjorie Suchocki, *The End of Evil* (Eugene, Ore.: Wipf & Stock, 1988), chap. 5.

24   See David Griffin, "Marjorie Hewitt Suchocki, 'The End of Evil'" (review), *Process Studies* 18 (1989): 58.

25   Fiddes, *The Promised End*, 208–15.

26   E.g., in Charles Hartshorne, *The Divine Relativity: A Social Conception of God* (1948; repr. New Haven, Conn.: Yale University Press, 1976).

27   Fiddes, *The Promised End*, 211.

28   Thomas Merton's idea of "true" and "false" self is a recurrent theme in his writings. It is concisely expressed in the short chapter "Things in Their Identity" in Thomas Merton, *New Seeds of Contemplation* (Boston: Shambhala, 2003), 31–38. It is explored at length in James Finley, *Merton's Palace of Nowhere* (Notre Dame, Ind.: Ave Maria, 1978).

29   Stephen Hawking, *The Grand Design* (London: Bantam, 2011).

30   Edouard Hoornaert, *The Memory of the Christian People* (New York: Burns & Oates, 1989).

31   This is a major theme in Miroslav Volf, *The End of Memory* (Grand Rapids: Eerdmans, 2006). See, e.g., chap. 4.

32   Whitehead, *Process and Reality*, 521.

33   See another short chapter, entitled "Pray for Your Own Discovery," in Merton, *New Seeds of Contemplation*, 39–48.

34   In Baptist writing, this is nowhere better expressed than in Paul S. Fiddes, *Participating in God: A Pastoral Doctrine of the Trinity* (London: Darton, Longman & Todd, 2000), esp. chap. 3.

Chapter 3

1   Bridget Riley, *The Eye's Mind*, ed. Robert Kudielka (London: Thames & Hudson, 1999).

2   The Gaia theory proposes that the earth is somehow "alive" as a holistic reality. This concept significantly reached the attention of British theologians through the work of Rosemary Radford Ruether. See especially Rosemary Radford Ruether, *Gaia and God: An Ecofeminist Theology of Earth Healing* (New York: Harper Collins, 1992).

3   See the reference in my previous chapter to Teilhard de Chardin's account, *The Phenomenon of Man*.

4   De Chardin, *The Phenomenon of Man*, 77–89, 122–51, 163–83, 254–72.

5   See Paul Tillich, *Systematic Theology*, vol. 3, *Life and the Spirit: History and the Kingdom of God* (Digswell Place, Welwyn, Herts: James Nisbet, 1968), 15–31.

6   This is most famously the case in H. G. Wells' novel *The First Men in the Moon*, published in 1901, more than half a century before the first moon landing became a reality.

7   See my reference to ubuntu in the previous chapter. The core idea is that "my" humanity and the humanity of the whole human community are profoundly interconnected, and that we need to live in ways that respect this fundamental truth.

8   E.g., Eph 3:6 claims that the extraordinary new unity of Jews and Gentiles is grounded in the common membership of one body *in Christ*.

9   The journals and biographical writings of Merton and Nouwen both allude to events that bear the same marks of "strangeness" that I, just occasionally, identify in my own life. See, e.g., Thomas Merton, *The Seven Story Mountain* (New York: Harcourt, 1948); Henri Nouwen, *The Genesee Diary* (New York: Doubleday, 1976).

10   See, e.g., Matt 28:17-20; Luke 24:13-49; John 21:1-14.

11   This is the underlying motif in Thomas Merton's *New Seeds of Contemplation*, to which I referred in the previous chapter.

12   In traditional Christian theology, this has been expressed by the concept of the *logos asarkos*, or the divine Word outside the flesh of the incarnation.

13   For Rahner, this gift is the precondition of the human possibility of forming and working with concepts, constitutive of human being itself. The idea was explored fully in Rahner's early work. See Karl Rahner, *Hearers of the Word* (1941; repr., New York: Seabury, 1969), 146–62. And it was still being developed in his much later work. See Karl Rahner, *Foundations of the Christian Faith*, trans. William Dych (London: Darton, Longman & Todd, 1978), 31–42.

14   See "Anonymous Christians" in Karl Rahner, *Theological Investigations*, vol. 6, *Concerning Vatican Council II*, trans. Karl-H. Kruger and Boniface Kruger (London: Darton, Longman & Todd, 1969), 390–98.

15   See my note 28 on Merton's concepts of the "true" and "false" self in the previous chapter.

16   Paul Tillich, *Systematic Theology*, vol. 1 (Digswell Place, Welwyn, Herts: James Nisbet, 1968), 264.

17   The idea of the preconceptual is ubiquitous in the work of Karl Rahner; but see, for example, his essay "Nature and Grace" in which he develops the idea of "the *a priori* horizon given in consciousness." Karl Rahner, *Theological Investigations*, vol. 4, *More Recent Writings*, trans. Kevin Smith (London: Darton, Longman & Todd, 1966), 165–88. The concept of a horizon also features strongly in David Tracy's work on the analogical imagination. See, e.g., his use of Rahner and the idea of human being as "always-already present to a horizon of radical mystery." David Tracy, *The Analogical Imagination* (London: SCM Press, 1981), 412.

18   See John Hick, *Evil and the God of Love* (London: Collins/Fontana, 1968), 207–24. Later in the century, Jürgen Moltmann has done much to encourage Protestants to look with more openness at the inheritance preserved in contemporary orthodoxy. He was significant in the World Council of Churches' Faith and Order initiative resulting in the Klingenthal Memorandum of 1979, recommending that all churches revert to the original text of the Nicene-Constantinopolitan Creed. See also, his exploration of the *filioque*, in Jürgen Moltmann, *The Trinity and the Kingdom of God*, trans. Margaret Kohl (London: SCM Press, 1981), 188–90.

Chapter 4

1   "Eucharistic Prayer II," in *The Sunday Missal: A New Edition* (London: Collins Liturgical, 1984), 47; texts approved for use in England, Wales, Ireland, and Scotland.

2   "Order One, Eucharistic Prayer B, Order for the Celebration of the Holy Communion," in *Common Worship: Services and Prayers for the Church of England* (London: Church House, 2000), 190.

3 "Thanksgiving and Dismissal," in *The Divine Liturgy of Our Father among the Saints John Chrysostom* (Oxford: Oxford University Press, 1995), 48; Greek text together with a translation into English.

4 Ernest A. Payne and Stephen F. Winward, eds., *Orders and Prayers for Church Worship: A Manual for Ministers* (London: Baptist Union of Great Britain and Ireland, 1967), 13. Prayer taken from the *Book of Common Order* of the Church of Scotland.

5 See, e.g., John Calvin, *Institutes of the Christian Religion*, 2.16.16; 3.20.20; in *Calvin: Institutes of the Christian Religion*, ed. John T. McNeill, trans. F. L. Battles. The Library of Christian Classics 20–21 (London: SCM Press, 1961), 20:524–25; 21:877–78.

6 See the qualms of J. Ivor Wesley, "The Heavenly Intercession of Christ," *Expository Times* 40 (1929): 561–62.

7 See David M. Hay, *Glory at the Right Hand: Psalm 110 in Early Christianity*, SBL Monograph Series 18 (Nashville: Abingdon, 1973), 54–55.

8 See, e.g., (Particular Baptist) *Confession of Faith Put forth* (1677), XXII.2, in Lumpkin, *Baptist Confessions*, 281.

9 Charles Wesley, "And can it be that I should gain / An interest in the Saviour's blood?" [hymn] (1738).

10 The psalmist is evidently referring to the legendary Melchizedek, priest-king of Salem, whose meeting with Abraham is mentioned in Genesis 14:18-20. The allusion enables the psalmist to give the Davidic king, who was not from the line of priests in Israel (Levites), nevertheless the title of "priest." However, it appears to be an early Christian tradition that associates the royal seat "at the right hand" with the sanctuary for worship. Baptist Old Testament scholar Deborah Rooke argues that the sacral kingship theme is more evident in Hebrews than is usually recognized. Deborah Rooke, "Jesus as Royal Priest: Reflections on the Interpretation of the Melkizedek Tradition in Heb 7," *Biblica* 81 (2000): 81–94.

11 W. R. G. Loader, "Christ at the Right Hand—Psalm CX.1 in the New Testament," *New Testament Studies* 24 (1978): 119.

12 Origen, *On Prayer*, trans. William A. Curtis (Grand Rapids: Ethereal Library, 2001), chap. 6; accessible online at www.ccel.org/ccel/origen/prayer.html, p. 18; emphasis added.

13 *Confession of Faith Of those Churches* (1644), XVII, in Lumpkin, *Baptist Confessions*, 160–61.

14 See, e.g., Basil of Caesarea, *Letter* 236.6, in *Creeds, Councils and Controversies*, ed. J. Stevenson (London: SPCK, 1966), 115.

15 Augustine, *De Trinitate* [*The Trinity*] 5.6, trans. Stephen McKenna, The Fathers of the Church 45 (Washington, D.C.: Catholic University of America Press, 1963), 180.

16   Aquinas, *Summa Theologiae* 1a.29.4, ed. Blackfriars (London: Eyre & Spottiswoode, 1965), 6:61.

17   Jürgen Moltmann, *The Crucified God*, trans. R. A. Wilson and John Bowden (London: SCM Press, 1974), 247.

18   See, e.g., Matt 6:6; John 14:16; Heb 7:25; Eph 6:18. The following section employs ideas from my book, Fiddes, *Participating in God*, 36–37.

19   Cf. Rom 8:34.

20   See John 1:14, 13:16, 20:21.

21   See Michael Jacobs, *Living Illusions: A Psychology of Belief* (London: SPCK, 1993), 68–71.

22   "Eucharistic Prayer III," in *Sunday Missal*, 49.

23   William Shakespeare, *Hamlet*, Act 3, scene 1, lines 78–79.

24   N. T. Wright, *Surprised by Hope: Rethinking Heaven, the Resurrection, and the Mission of the Church* (New York: HarperOne, 2008), 151.

25   Jürgen Moltmann, *The Coming of God*, trans. Margaret Kohl (London: SCM Press, 1986), 25–28.

26   For the wide range of meaning of this term, see Aubrey R. Johnson, *The Vitality of the Individual in the Thought of Ancient Israel* (Cardiff: University of Wales Press, 1964), 3–22.

27   See Eberhard Jüngel, "The World as Possibility and Actuality: The Ontology of the Doctrine of Justification" [1969], in *Eberhard Jüngel: Theological Essays*, ed. John Webster (Edinburgh: T&T Clark, 1989), 115–17.

28   Cf. Phil 3:21; 2 Cor 3:18.

29   See John Bowlby, *Attachment and Loss*, vol. 3, *Loss* (Harmondsworth, UK: Penguin, 1981), 86–93.

30   John Hick, "A Possible Conception of Life after Death," in *Death and Afterlife*, ed. Stephen T. Davis (London: Macmillan, 1989), 191–92, 195; cf. John Hick, *Death and Eternal Life*, 279–80, 289–90.

31   John A. T. Robinson, *The Body: A Study in Pauline Theology* (London: SCM Press, 1952), 55–67.

32   Dietrich Bonhoeffer, "Ethics as Formation," in *Ethics*, trans. Reinhard Krauss, Charles West, and Douglas Stott, vol. 6 of *Dietrich Bonhoeffer Works* (Minneapolis: Fortress, 2009), 98–102.

33   See, e.g., Andrew Pollard, *The Sanctuary, the Design of Its Services and the Requisites to Their Acceptableness and Efficiency: A Discourse at the Dedication of the First Baptist Church, Barnstable, Oct. 15, 1845* (Boston: Hallworth, 1845).

34   I have previously worked this out in Fiddes, *The Promised End*, 98–101.

35   Whitehead, *Process and Reality*, ix, 39, 44–47.

36   Charles Hartshorne, "Time, Death and Everlasting Life," in *The Logic of*

Perfection (LaSalle, Ill.: Open Court, 1962), 245–62. Similarly, see Peter Hamilton, *The Living God and the Modern World: A Christian Theology Based on the Thought of A. N. Whitehead* (London: Hodder & Stoughton, 1967), 124–33.

37 Nevertheless, attempts have been made to construct a process Trinitarianism. See, especially Joseph A. Bracken, *The Triune Symbol: Persons, Process and Community* (Lanham, Md.: University Press of America, 1985), 15–34; Lewis Ford, "Contingent Trinitarianism," in *Trinity in Process: A Relational Theology of God*, ed. Joseph A. Bracken and Marjorie Hewitt Suchocki (New York: Continuum, 1997), 41–72; Gregory A. Boyd, "The Self-Sufficient Sociality of God: A Trinitarian Revision of Hartshorne's Metaphysics," in Bracken and Suchocki, *Trinity in Process*, 73–94.

38 See chapter 2 above, pp. 47, 51–52.

39 This also distinguishes my proposal from that of Paul Tillich's understanding of the divine memory. See Tillich, *Systematic Theology*, vol. 3, *Life and the Spirit*, 400–409. A similar view was proposed earlier by the Spanish Catholic writer Miguel de Unamuno. See Miguel de Unamuno, *The Tragic Sense of Life*, trans. J. Crawford Flitch (London: Macmillan, 1931), 149. My proposal is also to be distinguished from "soul sleep" as found in, e.g., Christina Rossetti's poem "Life and Death." The metaphor of sleep, though having some slight New Testament support (1 Thess 4:13-15), is inadequate on its own, projecting too inactive an image of being "in God," as well as transferring too literally the distinction between "conscious" and "unconscious" existence from our present experience. See chapter 1 by Brian Haymes above, pp. 9, 21.

40 See "Eucharistic Prayer I," in *Sunday Missal*, 40; "Prayer of the Trisagion," in *Divine Liturgy*, 13.

41 Anglican-Roman Catholic International Commission, *Mary: Grace and Hope in Christ; An Agreed Statement* (Harrisburg, Pa.: Morehouse, 2005), p. 68 (para. 68).

42 Anglican-Roman Catholic International Commission, *Mary*, pp. 69–70 (para. 69–70).

43 Anglican-Roman Catholic International Commission, *Mary*, pp. 22–23 (para. 23–25), p. 71 (para. 71).

44 See above, p. 21.

45 C. S. Lewis, *Letters to Malcolm* (London: Bles, 1964), 138.

46 With regard to Christ's representing of God, see Dorothee Soelle, *Christ the Representative: An Essay in Theology after the "Death of God,"* trans. David Lewis (London: SCM Press, 1967), 51–56, 137–42.

47 Perhaps only in Psalm 73:24. See Gerhard von Rad, " 'Righteousness'

and 'Life' in the Cultic Language of the Psalms," in *The Problem of the Hexateuch and Other Essays*, trans. E. Trueman Dicken (London: Oliver & Boyd, 1966), 262–66.

48   John Polkinghorne, *Belief in God in an Age of Science* (New Haven, Conn.: Yale University Press, 1998), 90.

49   Jürgen Moltmann, *The Way of Jesus Christ*, trans. Margaret Kohl (London: SCM Press, 1990), 181–95.

50   See Hay, *Glory at the Right Hand*, 88; Loader, "Christ at the Right Hand," 202–8.

51   See above, pp. 23–24.

52   Karl Barth, *Church Dogmatics*, trans. and ed. Geoffrey W. Bromiley and Thomas F. Torrance, 14 vols. (Edinburgh: T&T Clark, 1936-1977), I/2, 140, 191, 195. Barth tries hard, and unconvincingly, to deny that this reception of the Word means a coworking with God. See Paul S. Fiddes, "Mary in the Theology of Karl Barth," in *Mary in Doctrine and Devotion*, ed. Alberic Stacpoole (Dublin: Columba, 1990), 111–26.

53   "The Word of God in the Life of the Church," para. 133, 143; *Marie, comité mixte Baptiste-Catholique en France*, Documents Episcopat 10 (Paris: Le Secrétariat Général de la Conférence des Évêques de France, 2009), para. 15.

54   Barth, *Church Dogmatics*, I/2, 138.

55   Barth, *Church Dogmatics*, I/1, 136.

56   "The Word of God in the Life of the Church," para. 146.

57   "The Word of God in the Life of the Church," para. 148, 150–51.

58   See Eduard Schweizer, *The Good News according to Luke*, trans. D. Green (London: SPCK, 1984), 32–34.

59   See John Nolland, *Luke 1:1–9:20*, Word Commentary 35A (Dallas: Word Books, 1989), 68, 74. Nolland makes a firm attribution to Mary, while recognizing literary development and a Christian liturgical setting for the song in its present form.

60   Anglican-Roman Catholic International Commission, *Mary*, pp. 63–64 (para. 64); cf. p. 48 (para. 51).

61   Quoting from Ps 22:22; Isa 8:17; Isa 8:18. Cf. John 10:29.

62   See above, p. 19.

Chapter 5

1   See the argument in Philip E. Thompson, "Toward Baptist Ecclesiology in Pneumatological Perspective" (unpublished Ph.D. thesis, Emory University, 1995).

2   Two volumes published by the Carey Kingsgate Press in London in 1955

were entitled *Baptists Who Made History: A Book about Great Baptists* and *Great Baptist Women*, both edited by Alberic S. Clement.

3   Samuel Wells, *The Drama of Christian Ethics: Improvisation* (Grand Rapids: Brazos, 2000), esp. 43–70.

4   Michael Pasquarello III, *We Speak Because We Have First Been Spoken: A Grammar of the Preaching Life* (Grand Rapids: Eerdmans, 2009), 20.

5   William Bradford, *History of Plymouth Plantation, 1620–1647*, ed. Worthington Chauncey Ford (Boston: Massachusetts Historical Society, 1912), 1:20-22.

6   See, e.g., the covenants of the Baptist churches at Longworth (1656), Horsley-Down (1697) and Bourton-on-the-Water (1719) in Champlin Burrage, *The Church Covenant Idea* (Philadelphia: American Baptist Publication Society, 1904), 154, 156–59, 161–63.

7   *A Declaration of Faith of English People Remaining at Amsterdam in Holland* (1611), 16, in Lumpkin, *Baptist Confessions*, 121.

8   Martin Buber, *The Eclipse of God* (New York: Harper & Row, 1972).

9   George W. Stroup, *Before God* (Grand Rapids: Eerdmans, 2004), 2.

10 Emmanuel Levinas, *Totality and Infinity: An Essay on Exteriority*, trans. Alphonso Lingis (Pittsburgh: Duquesne, 1969), 194–97.

11 Cf. David Ford, *Self and Salvation: Being Transformed* (Cambridge: Cambridge University Press, 1999), 127.

12 See, e.g., Percy Dearmer and Gerard Moultrie, trans., *Baptist Praise and Worship* (Oxford: Oxford University Press, 1991), no. 441.

13 *Story of a Soul: The Autobiography of St. Thérèse of Lisieux*, trans. John Clarke, OCD, 3rd ed. (Washington, D.C.: ICS, 1996), 17.

14 Thérèse, *Story of a Soul*, 194; emphases in original.

15 Thérèse, *Story of a Soul*, 220; emphasis in original.

16 Thérèse, *Story of a Soul*, 45–46.

17 Hans Urs von Balthasar, *Two Sisters in the Spirits: Thérèse of Lisieux and Elizabeth of the Trinity* (San Francisco: Ignatius, 1992), 221; emphasis in original. Among other important studies, see Ida Friederike Görres, *The Hidden Face: A Study of St. Thérèse of Lisieux* (San Francisco: Ignatius, 1995); Constance Fitzgerald, "The Mission of Thérèse of Lisieux," *Contemporary Carmelite Women, The Way Supplement* 89 (1997): 74–96. Given their very different ways of life and circumstances, Dorothy Day's *Thérèse* makes for a fascinating study. Dorothy Day, *Thérèse* (Springfield, Ill.: Templegate, 1960).

18 The following paragraphs, without extensive direct reference, summarize material from Thérèse, *Story of a Soul*.

19 Ford, *Self and Salvation*, 204.

20   Thérèse, *Story of a Soul* 263.

21   Ford, *Self and Salvation*, 205.

22   Prayer card issued by Office Central de Lisieux, no. 83, n.d. The prayer, designated as "composed by S. Thérèse of the Child Jesus" is printed on the reverse of a drawing of the Holy Face of Jesus, marked "After the Holy Shroud of Turin" and signed "C. de L.".

23   Miroslav Volf, *A Public Faith: How Followers of Christ Should Serve the Common Good* (Grand Rapids: Brazos, 2011), 74; emphasis in original.

Chapter 6

1   Thornton Wilder, *Our Town*, in *Our Town, The Skin of Our Teeth, The Matchmaker* (London: Penguin Books, 2000), 41.

2   Wilder, *Our Town*, 71–72; emphasis in original.

3   Wilder, *Our Town*, 80.

4   This is Fawcett's original version of verse 4, now often slightly rewritten. See John Fawcett, *Hymns: Adapted to the Circumstances of Public Worship and Private Devotion* (Leeds: G. Wright & Son, 1782), no. 104, 188–89.

5   Hymn as printed in *Baptist Praise and Worship*, no. 472. Apart from verse 4, the wording is identical to the publication of 1782 (see n. 4 above).

6   See Hugh Martin, ed., *The Baptist Hymn Book Companion* (London: Psalms and Hymns Trust, 1967), 355. For a less colorful version of events, see John Fawcett [son], *An Account of the Life, Ministry and Writings of the Late Rev John Fawcett* (London: Baldwin, Cradock & Joy, 1818), 173–75. It is reported that the hymn was written to be appended to a sermon preached the following Sunday (August 9, 1772), on the text Luke 12:15, "A man's life consisteth not in the abundance of things he possesseth." However, he did leave Wainsgate in 1777 to be minister of Hebden Bridge, where he remained for the rest of his life.

7   Lincoln Kenkle, *Thornton Wilder and the Puritan Narrative Tradition* (Columbia: University of Missouri Press, 2006), 148–49, 202, 212.

8   Wilder, *Our Town*, 22.

9   See above, p. 107.

10   See the account by Henry Ainsworth, *The Communion of Saincts* (Amsterdam, 1615), 340.

11   *Confession of Faith Of those Churches* (1644), XLVII, in Lumpkin, *Baptist Confessions*, 168-69. This is virtually identical to article 38 of *A True Confession* of the Faith (1596), in Lumpkin, *Baptist Confessions*, 94.

12   See, e.g., Calvin, *Institutes* 2.6.3; 3.14.6; 4.14.6, in McNeill, ed., *Calvin: Institutes*, 20:345–46, 773; 21:1280–81.

13   Calvin, *Institutes* 2.10.23; 2.11.4–10, in McNeill, ed., 20:448–49, 453–60.

Cf. John Gill, *Complete Body of Doctrinal and Practical Divinity: A New Edition in Two Volumes* (London: 1795; repr. Grand Rapids: Baker Book House, 1978), vol. 1, bk. 2, p. 308.

14   *Confession of Faith Put forth* (1677), VII.3, in Lumpkin, *Baptist Confessions*, 260.

15   Benjamin Keach, *The Display of Glorious Grace; or, the Covenant of Peace, Opened: In Fourteen Sermons.* . . . (London, 1698), 285.

16   Keach, *Display of Glorious Grace*, 243.

17   Quoted by John Smyth, *Parallels, Censures, Observations* (1609), in *The Works of John Smyth*, ed. W. T. Whitley (Cambridge: Cambridge University Press, 1915), 2:386-87.

18   John Smyth, *Principles and Inferences Concerning the Visible Church* (1607), in Whitley, *Works*, 1:252.

19   Smyth, *Principles and Inferences*, in *Whitley, Works*, 1:254.

20   See, e.g., Hanserd Knollys, *A Moderate Answer unto Dr. Bastwick's Book Called, "Independency not God's Ordinance"* (London, 1645), 13-14.

21   See, e.g., *Confession of Faith Of those Churches* (1644), XLVII, in Lumpkin, *Baptist Confessions*, 169; *The Faith and Practise of Thirty Congregations, Gathered according to the Primitive Pattern* (London: Will Larnar, 1651), 52, in Lumpkin, *Baptist Confessions*, 183; *Sixteen Articles of Faith and Order [The "Midland Association Confession"]* (1655), 15, in Lumpkin, *Baptist Confessions*, 199; *A Confession of the Faith of Several Churches of Christ [The "Somerset Confession"]* (London: Henry Hills, 1656), XXIV, in Lumpkin, *Baptist Confessions*, 209.

22   *Confession of Faith Put forth* (1677), XXVI.6, in Lumpkin, *Baptist Confessions*, 286.

23   See the unsigned article "Church Covenants," *Baptist Quarterly* 7 (1935): 231.

24   John Fawcett, *The Constitution and Order of a Gospel Church Considered* (Halifax, UK, 1797), 12.

25   Barrington Raymond White, *The English Separatist Tradition: From the Marian Martyrs to the Pilgrim Fathers* (Oxford: Oxford University Press, 1971), 128.

26   *Confession of Faith Put forth* (1677), XXIX–XXXI, in Lumpkin, *Baptist Confessions*, 318-19.

27   Reprinted in Roger Hayden, ed., *Baptist Union Documents 1948–1977* (London: Baptist Historical Society, 1980), 6.

28   See the withering critique by the poet Matthew Arnold, dismissing it as a mechanistic contract or "fairy-tale" of three supernatural persons. Matthew Arnold, *Literature and Dogma*, 2nd ed. (London: Smith, Elder, 1873), 200, 204, 306–10.

29   The following paragraphs follow quite closely the text of my chapter "Walking Together," in Fiddes, *Tracks and Traces*, 35–37.

30   Barth, *Church Dogmatics*, II/2, 79–80, 168–69; IV/1, 6–7, 36–38.

31   Barth, *Church Dogmatics*, II/2, 123–25, 161–65, cf. 6–9, 26; IV/1, 45–46.

32   Barth, *Church Dogmatics*, II/2, 163–64.

33   See Lorelei F. Fuchs, SA, *Koinonia and the Quest for an Ecumenical Ecclesiology* (Grand Rapids: Eerdmans, 2008), 251–368; Walter Kasper, *Harvesting the Fruits: Basic Aspects of Christian Faith in Ecumenical Dialogue* (London: Continuum, 2009), 72–77.

34   The major figure is John Coccejus, *Summa doctrinae de foedere et testamento Dei* (Leiden, 1648). See Barth, *Church Dogmatics*, IV/1, 54–59.

35   Gill, *Complete Body*, vol. 1, bk. 2, p. 305.

36   Bruce McCormack coins the phrase "covenant ontology" for this theme in Barth. See Bruce McCormack, "Grace and Being: The Role of God's Gracious Election in Karl Barth's Theological Ontology," in *The Cambridge Companion to Karl Barth*, ed. John Webster (Cambridge: Cambridge University Press, 2000), 92–109.

37   Barth, *Church Dogmatics*, IV/1, 64–66.

38   Stanley Grenz, *The Social God and the Relational Self: A Trinitarian Theology of the Imago Dei* (Louisville: Westminster John Knox, 2001), 336. Grenz, however, maintains that the covenant is a historical reality rather than an eternal reality in God.

39   Dietrich Bonhoeffer, *Sanctorum Communio*, vol. 1 of *Dietrich Bonhoeffer Works* (Minneapolis: Fortress, 2009), 157–61; Dietrich Bonhoeffer, *Life Together*, vol. 5 of *Dietrich Bonhoeffer Works* (Minneapolis: Fortress, 2005), 31–34, 44–45.

40   In what follows, I draw on chapter 4 of my earlier book, *The Creative Suffering of God*, though placing the concepts there in a new context. See Paul S. Fiddes, *The Creative Suffering of God* (Oxford: Oxford University Press, 1988).

41   Keith Ward, *Religion and Creation* (Oxford: Clarendon, 1996), 185–86; Keith Ward, *Rational Theology and the Creativity of God* (Oxford: Blackwell, 1982), 154.

42   Walther Zimmerli, "Promise and Fulfilment," in *Essays on Old Testament Interpretation*, ed. Claus Westermann and trans. James Luther Mays (London: SCM Press, 1963), 107.

43   See Charles Hartshorne, *Creative Synthesis and Philosophic Method* (London: SCM Press, 1970), 58.

44   William H. Vanstone, *Love's Endeavour, Love's Expense* (London: Darton, Longman and Todd, 1977), 33; see also William H. Vanstone, *The Stature of Waiting* (London: Darton, Longman & Todd, 1982), 89–94.

45   See, e.g., Hos 2:14-20; Isa 43:16-20.

46   So, though not uniformly, see Huw Parri Owen, *Concepts of Deity* (London: Macmillan, 1971), 30–33; Richard Swinburne, *The Coherence of Theism* (Oxford: Oxford University Press, 1977), 175–78. Cf. idem, *The Christian God* (Oxford: Oxford University Press, 1994), 130–34; Ward, *Religion and Creation*, 275–77.

47   Charles Hartshorne, *A Natural Theology for Our Time* (LaSalle, Ill.: Open Court, 1967), 20–21.

48   Fiddes, *The Creative Suffering of God*, 97–98.

49   Wilder, *Our Town*, 68.

50   Wilder, *Our Town*, 76.

51   Wilder, *Our Town*, 83.

52   Wilder, *Our Town*, 81.

53   Wilder, *Our Town*, 89.

54   E. Y. Mullins, *The Axioms of Religion*, ed. C. Douglas Weaver (Macon, Ga.: Mercer University Press, 2010 [1908]).

55   Walter Shurden, "The Baptist Identity and the Baptist Manifesto," *Perspectives in Religious Studies* 25 (1998): 321–40.

56   Malcolm B. Yarnell III, *The Formation of Christian Doctrine* (Nashville: B&H Academic, 2007), 23.

57   Mikael Broadway et al., "Re-envisioning Baptist Identity: A Manifesto for Baptist Communities in North America," *Perspectives in Religious Studies* 24 (1997): 303–10. Signatories are Mikael Broadway, Curtis Freeman, Barry Harvey, James McClendon, Elizabeth Newman, and Philip Thompson. Similar in approach is Steven Harmon, *Towards Baptist Catholicity* (Milton Keynes, UK: Paternoster, 2006).

58   Edith Wyschogrod, *Saints and Postmodernism: Revisioning Moral Philosophy* (Chicago: University of Chicago Press, 1990), 5–14, 33–42, 233–35.

59   Wyschogrod, *Saints and Postmodernism*, 252–54.

60   Wyschogrod, *Saints and Postmodernism*, 192, 222–23, 229, 235, 244. Examples of "ecstatic postmodernism" she offers are Julia Kristeva and Gilles Deleuze; of differential postmodernism, she offers Jacques Derrida and Emmanuel Levinas.

61   Wyschogrod, *Saints and Postmodernism*, 252.

62   Wyschogrod, *Saints and Postmodernism*, 253–56.

63   Wyschogrod, *Saints and Postmodernism*, 253–54.

64   Here Wyschogrod shows the influence of Emmanuel Levinas, whom she helped to introduce to an American audience.

65   Wyschogrod, *Saints and Postmodernism*, 255.

66   Wyschogrod, *Saints and Postmodernism*, 256.

67   To insist that it is unstable does not mean that there is no representa-
     tion at all, but only that truth cannot be established by simple *mimesis*,
     comparing an image (a thought, a sign) with an external thing.

68   Karl Rahner, "A Happy Death: The Witness of Thérèse of Lisieux," in
     idem, *The Great Church Year*, ed. Albert Raffelt and Harvey Egan, 358;
     translation from *Christliche Innerlichkeit* 8 (1977): 34–36, corrected by me.

69   See, e.g., Robert Hall, "On Theories and the Rights of Man," in "The
     Freedom of the Press and for General Liberty," in *The Entire Works of
     the Rev. Robert Hall*, ed. Olinthus Gregory (London: Holdsworth & Ball,
     1831), 3:121–37; General Council of the Baptist World Alliance, "Human
     Rights" (resolution of the General Council of the Baptist World Alliance
     meeting in Vancouver, Canada, July 3–9, 1997 [on the occasion of the fif-
     tieth anniversary of the Universal Declaration of Human Rights of the
     United Nations]), in *1997 Yearbook of the Baptist World Alliance* (McLean,
     Va.: BWA, 1997), 100. Theologians have questioned whether the con-
     cept of "human rights" has any theological foundation (see, e.g., John
     Milbank, "Against Human Rights," *Oxford Journal of Law and Religion* 1,
     no. 1 [2012]: 203–34), but Baptists have grounded talk of "natural rights"
     and "human rights" theologically, in the sovereignty of the rule of God.

70   James Wm. McClendon Jr., *Biography as Theology: How Life Stories Can
     Remake Today's Theology* (Philadelphia: Trinity Press International), 15.

71   McClendon, *Biography as Theology*, 17.

72   McClendon, *Biography as Theology*, 22–23.

73   McClendon, *Biography as Theology*, 86–87.

74   McClendon, *Biography as Theology*, 80, 143.

75   McClendon, *Biography as Theology*, 180.

76   McClendon relates this religious image to Ives' philosophical and politi-
     cal image of "the majority mind," which he suggests derives from the
     "eternal One" of the American transcendentalist school. McClendon,
     Biography as Theology, 126–28.

77   McClendon, *Biography as Theology*, 132–37.

78   Henk Bakker, "A Martyr's Pain Is Not Pain: Mystagogical Directives in
     Tertullian's *Ad martyras*, Origen's *Exhortatio ad martyrium*, and Cyprian's
     Epistula ad Fortunatum de exhortatione martyrii," in *The Mystagogy of the
     Church Fathers*, ed. Paul van Geest et al. (Leuven: Peeters, forthcoming).
     No page numbers yet available.

79   Prudentius, *Peristephanon* 13.11–14 (*deus inditur medullis*).

80   John Milbank, *The Word Made Strange: Theology, Language, Culture*
     (Oxford: Blackwell, 1997), 149.

81   See Morna D. Hooker, *The Son of Man in Mark* (London: SPCK, 1967), 11–32.

82   The NRSV translation is "mortal." See Hooker, *Son of Man*, 182–89.

83   See above, pp. 78–80.

84   Cf. Wolfhart Pannenberg, *Jesus—God and Man*, trans. Lewis Wilkins and Duane Priebe (London: SCM Press, 1968), 334–35. See also above, pp. 99–100.

85   Philip Sheldrake, *Spaces for the Sacred: Place, Memory and Identity* (London: SCM Press, 2001), 50.

86   *Confession of Faith Of those Churches* (1644), XLIV, in Lumpkin, *Baptist Confessions*, 168. This wording is virtually identical to article 26 in the Separatist *A True Confession* (1596), in Lumpkin, *Baptist Confessions*, 90. It is characteristic of Baptist life not to define the relation between personal and corporate oversight by a rule, but to leave the dialectic of *episkope* as a matter of trust.

87   See *Confession of Faith Put forth* (1677), XXVI.13–15, in Lumpkin, *Baptist Confessions*, 288–89; cf. Hanserd Knollys, *The World That Now Is and the World That Is to Come* (London, 1681), bk. 1, pp. 97–98.

88   See John Bunyan's description of hearing "three or four poor women sitting at a door in the sun, and talking about the things of God." Bunyan, *Grace Abounding to the Chief of Sinners* (London: George Larkin, 1666), 10.

89   William Blake, "A Memorable Fancy," in *The Marriage of Heaven and Hell* (etched around 1790 to 1793), plates 12–13. These can be found in Geoffrey Keynes, ed., *Blake: Complete Writings* (London: Oxford University Press, 1966), 153–54.

90   See above, chap. 4, pp. 82–83.

91   Levinas, *Totality and Infinity*, 72, 76.

92   Calvin O. Schrag, *Communicative Praxis and the Space of Subjectivity* (Bloomington: Indiana University Press, 1986), 121.

93   Alistair I. McFadyen, *The Call to Personhood: A Christian Theory of the Individual in Social Relationships* (Cambridge: Cambridge University Press, 1990), 7–8, 72–73.

94   David S. Cunningham, *These Three Are One: The Practice of Trinitarian Theology* (Oxford: Blackwell, 1998), 199.

95   McFadyen, *Call to Personhood*, 162.

96   Alastair Campbell, *Rediscovering Pastoral Care*, new ed. (London: Darton, Longman & Todd, 1986), 99–100.

97   McFadyen, *Call to Personhood*, 185–86.

98   Joe Kapolyo, "An Inheritance Kept in Heaven" (a sermon on 1 Peter 1:1–3 delivered at the Baptist Assembly, Brighton, May 4, 2008). For a strictly

anthropological approach, see Audrey I. Richards, *Chisungu* (London: Routledge, 1982), 38–40.

99   This seems to be in accord with Richard Kidd's westernization of the African idea of ubuntu in chapter 2.

100   McFadyen, *Call to Personhood, 185.*

101   While Pannenberg tends to use this phrase of the Holy Spirit alone, he also applies it to the whole triune life of God as Spirit. See Wolfhart Pannenberg, *Systematic Theology*, trans. Geoffrey Bromiley (Grand Rapids: Eerdmans, 1991-1998), 1:383.

102   Wilder, *Our Town*, 68.

103   Wilder, *Our Town*, 91.

104   Wilder, *Our Town*, 89–90.

105   Wilder, *Our Town*, 89.

Chapter 7

1   John Betjeman, *Collected Poems*, ed. the Earl of Birkenhead, 4th ed. (London: John Murray, 2006), 113.

2   In fact, one of the authors of this book, as a Baptist minister, is an ecumenical prebendary at the Church of St. Endelienta.

3   Ps 95:1; Ps 34:8; Rev 22:17; Jas 4:8-10; Phil 4:6-7; Heb 12:18-22; 1 Pet 2:3-5; Eph 4:3.

4   In George Appleton, ed., *The Oxford Book of Prayer* (Oxford: Oxford University Press), 162–63.

5   Martin Luther King Jr., *"Thou, Dear God": Prayers That Open Hearts and Spirits*, ed. Lewis V. Baldwin (Boston: Beacon, 2011).

6   Personal communication from Andy Goodliff, minister of Belle Vue Baptist Church, Southend-on-Sea.

7   *Georgian Eucharist* (Decatur, Ga.: Cooperative Baptist Fellowship, 2011).

8   Malkhaz Songulashvili, "A Historical Study of the Missiological Convictions of the 'Evangelical Christians and Baptists of Georgia' and Their Role in Relation to National Culture and Life" (unpublished Ph.D. thesis, University of Wales, 2012), 301.

9   Dietrich Bonhoeffer, *Discipleship*, trans. Barbara Green and Reinhard Krauss, in vol. 4 of *Dietrich Bonhoeffer Works* (Minneapolis: Fortress, 2003), 87 n. 11.

10   See the introduction, p. 1.

11   Gregory of Nyssa, *Second Letter* (to Kensitor), sec. 16 in Anna M. Silvas, *Gregory of Nyssa: The Letters. Introduction, Translation and Commentary* (Leiden: Brill, 2007), 121.

12   Augustine, *Ennarationes in Psalmos*, on Psalm 42, sec. 8.

13 See David Brown, *God and the Enchantment of Place* (Oxford: Oxford University Press, 2004), 239–40.

14 Sheldrake, *Spaces for the Sacred*, 65.

15 Rudolf Bultmann, *Jesus Christ and Mythology* (New York: Charles Scribner, 1958), 84. He adds, "Nevertheless, the world is God's world and the sphere of God as acting" (85).

16 Notably, Baptist minister Roy Searle, cofounder of the community, who was president of the Baptist Union of Great Britain, 2005–2006.

17 Quotations are from www.northumbriacommunity.org/who-we-are/introducing-the-community; wwwnorthumbriacommunity/nether-springs/staying-at-nether-springs; and www.northumbriacommunity/who-we-are/introducing-the-community/the-nether-springs (accessed October 27, 2013).

18 Geoffrey Chaucer, "General Prologue," *Canterbury Tales*, lines 12–13.

19 Brown, *God and the Enchantment*, 153–54.

20 See further below, pp. 180–83.

21 See Paul Ricoeur, *Memory, History, Forgetting*, trans. Kathleen Blamey and David Pellauer (Chicago: University of Chicago Press, 2004), 48–49.

22 Sheldrake, *Spaces for the Sacred*, 40–42.

23 The concept of the "hiddenness" was a powerful motif in Karl Rahner's theology of death. See especially Karl Rahner, *Quaestiones disputatae*, vol. 2, *On the Theology of Death* (London: Burnes & Oates, 1961), 46–54.

24 C. S. Lewis [N. W. Clerk, pseud.], *A Grief Observed* (London: Faber & Faber, 1961); reissued as authored by C. S. Lewis in 1964.

25 This first gained momentum with the work of Cecily Saunders and others in the 1970s and is associated with the growth of the hospice movement. A more recent summary of the field is provided in Donna L. Dickenson, Malcolm Johnson, and Jeanne Samson Katz, eds., *Death, Dying and Bereavement*, 2nd ed. (London: Sage, 2000).

26 Lewis, *A Grief Observed*, 7.

27 Lewis, *A Grief Observed*, 49.

28 Lewis, *A Grief Observed*, 49.

29 Lewis, *A Grief Observed*, 56.

30 Paul Fiddes explores the roots of this motif in Lewis' work in his article "On Theology." Paul S. Fiddes, "On Theology," in *The Cambridge Companion to C. S. Lewis*, ed. Robert MacSwain and Michael Ward (Cambridge: Cambridge University Press, 2010), 95–97.

31 Lewis, *A Grief Observed*, 57; emphasis in original.

32 Lewis, *A Grief Observed*, 59.

33 The sequence between thanksgiving and anamnesis is a notable feature

of the account of the Eucharist in World Council of Churches, *Baptism, Eucharist and Ministry*, Faith and Order Paper 111 (Geneva: World Council of Churches, 1982), 10–12.

34   An example is the worship book of the United Reformed Church in England, where the "First Order for Holy Communion" offers as alternatives the "story" form of anamnesis and anamnesis in the prayer of thanksgiving. *Worship: From the United Reformed Church* (London: United Reformed Church, 2003). The "Liturgy for Holy Communion A" in *A Wee Worship Book* also offers the words of institution as a story, noting that this is "following one British historical tradition." Wild Goose Worship Group, *A Wee Worship Book: Fourth Incarnation* (Iona, Scotland: Wild Goose Publications, 1999), 80–92.

35   Benjamin Keach, *Tropologia: A Key to Open Scripture-Metaphors* (London: Enoch Prosser, 1683), bk. 4, p. 45; cf. *Confession of Faith Put forth* (1677), XXX.7, in Lumpkin, *Baptist Confessions*, 293 ("Worthy receivers, outwardly partaking . . . do then also inwardly by faith, really and indeed, yet not carnally and corporally, but spiritual receive, and feed upon Christ crucified and all the benefits of his death").

36   The same approach is found in a work by the Roman Catholic theologian Edward Schillebeeckx. See his *Christ the Sacrament of Encounter with God* (London: Sheed & Ward, 1963), 164.

37   Huldrych Zwingli, Letter to Matthew Alber, November 16, 1524, in *Huldrych Zwingli: Writings*, trans. H. Wayne Pipkin (Allison Park, Pa.: Pickwick, 1984), 2:141. Zwingli is thus often wrongly typecast as having a purely "memorialist" view of the Supper.

38   Hercules Collins, *An Orthodox Catechism: Being the Sum of Christian Religion, Contained in the Law and Gospel* (London, 1680), 39.

39   See pp. 66–67.

40   Wild Goose Worship Group, *Wee Worship Book*, 83.

41   Examples include images of new birth or regeneration (John 3:5; Titus 3:5); forgiveness of sins and cleansing from sin (Acts 2:38; 1 Cor 6:11; Heb 10:22); death and resurrection with Christ (Rom 6:1-6); baptism in the Spirit (1 Cor 12:13; Acts 2:38, 10:47; cf. Mark 1:9-11); deliverance from evil powers (Col 1:13); union with Christ (Gal 3:27); adoption as children of God (Gal 3:26); and membership in the body of Christ (1 Cor 12:13; Gal 3:27-28). See Baptist New Testament scholar George Beasley-Murray, *Baptism in the New Testament* (London: Macmillan, 1963), 263–64.

42   Thomas Grantham, *A Sigh for Peace; or, The Cause of the Division Discovered* (London, 1671), 87–88. There is an echo of 1 Peter 3:21 in the last phrase. Cf. Benjamin Keach, *Gold Refin'd; or, Baptism in its Primitive*

Purity (London, 1689), 173 ("Baptism is a means of conveying this Grace, when the Spirit is pleased to operate with it . . . for 'tis the Sacrament of Regeneration, as the Lord's Supper is of Nourishment").

43 Laying on of hands was practiced by early General Baptists. See, e.g., *The True Gospel Faith Declared according to the Scriptures* (1654), XII, in Lumpkin, *Baptist Confessions of Faith*, 193 ("God gives the Spirit to believers dipped [immersed] through the prayer of faith and the laying on of hands"). The practice has been revived in modern times. See, e.g., Christopher Ellis and Myra Blyth, eds., *Gathering for Worship: Patterns and Prayers for the Community of Disciples* (Norwich, UK: Canterbury, 2005), 74–77.

44 See James D. G. Dunn, *Jesus and the Spirit* (London: SCM Press, 1975), 253–56.

45 See above, pp. 145–50.

46 See above, pp. 146–48.

47 See above, p. 154.

BIBLIOGRAPHY

Ainsworth, Henry. *The Communion of Saincts*. Amsterdam, 1615.

Anglican-Roman Catholic International Commission. *Mary: Grace and Hope in Christ; An Agreed Statement*. Harrisburg, Pa.: Morehouse, 2005.

Appleton, George, ed. *The Oxford Book of Prayer*. Oxford: Oxford University Press.

Aquinas. *Summa Theologiae*. Blackfriars edition. 61 vols. London: Eyre & Spottiswoode, 1965.

Arnold, Matthew. *Literature and Dogma*. 2nd ed. London: Smith, Elder, 1873.

Augustine. *De Trinitate* [*The Trinity*]. Translated by Stephen McKenna. The Fathers of the Church 45. Washington, D.C.: Catholic University of America Press, 1963.

Bakker, Henk. "Martyr's Pain Is Not Pain: Mystagogical Directives in Tertullian's *Ad martyras*, Origen's *Exhortatio ad martyrium*, and Cyprian's *Epistula ad Fortunatum de exhortatione martyrii*." In *The Mystagogy of the Church Fathers*, ed. Paul van Geest et al. Leuven, Belgium: Peeters, forthcoming.

Balthasar, Hans Urs von. *Two Sisters in the Spirits: Thérèse of Lisieux and Elizabeth of the Trinity*. San Francisco: Ignatius, 1992.

Barth, Karl. *Church Dogmatics*. Translated and edited by Geoffrey W. Bromiley and Thomas F. Torrance. 14 vols. Edinburgh: T&T Clark, 1936-1977.

Beasley-Murray, George. *Baptism in the New Testament*. London: Macmillan, 1963.

Bergson, Henri. *Creative Evolution*. Translated by Arthur Mitchell. New York: Random House, 1944.

Betjeman, John. *Collected Poems*. Edited by the Earl of Birkenhead. 4th ed. London: John Murray, 2006.

Blake, William. "A Memorable Fancy." In *The Marriage of Heaven and Hell*. 1789–1790.

Boff, Leonardo. *Ecclesiogenesis: The Base Communities Reinvent the Church*. Translated by Robert Barr. New York: Orbis, 1986.

Bonhoeffer, Dietrich. *Discipleship*. Translated by Barbara Green and Reinhard Krauss. Vol. 4 of *Dietrich Bonhoeffer Works*. Minneapolis: Fortress, 2003.

———. *Ethics*, translated by Reinhard Krauss, Charles West, and Douglas Stott. Vol. 6 of *Dietrich Bonhoeffer Works*. Minneapolis: Fortress, 2009.

———. *Life Together*. Vol. 5 of *Dietrich Bonhoeffer Works*. Minneapolis: Fortress, 2005.

———. *Sanctorum Communio*. Vol. 1 of *Dietrich Bonhoeffer Works*. Minneapolis: Fortress, 2009.

Bowlby, John. *Attachment and Loss*. Vol. 3, *Loss*. Harmondsworth: Penguin, 1981.

Boyd, Gregory A. "The Self-Sufficient Sociality of God: A Trinitarian Revision of Hartshorne's Metaphysics." In Bracken and Suchocki, *Trinity in Process*, 73–94.

Bracken, Joseph A. *The Triune Symbol: Persons, Process and Community*. Lanham, Md.: University Press of America, 1985.

Bracken, Joseph A., and Marjorie Hewitt Suchocki, eds. *A Relational Theology of God*. New York: Continuum, 1997.

Bradford, William. *History of Plymouth Plantation, 1620–1647*. Edited by Worthington Chauncey Ford. 2 vols. Boston: Massachusetts Historical Society, 1912.

Broadway, Mikael, Curtis Freeman, Barry Harvey, James McClendon, Elizabeth Newman, and Philip Thompson. "Re-envisioning Baptist Identity: A Manifesto for Baptist Communities in North America." *Perspectives in Religious Studies* 24 (1997): 303–10.

Brown, David. *God and the Enchantment of Place*. Oxford: Oxford University Press, 2004.

Brown, Peter. *The Cult of the Saints: Its Rise and Function in Latin Christianity*. Chicago: University of Chicago Press, 1981.

Buber, Martin. *The Eclipse of God*. New York: Harper & Row, 1972.

Bultmann, Rudolf. *Jesus Christ and Mythology*. New York: Charles Scribner, 1958.

Bunyan, John. *Grace Abounding to the Chief of Sinners*. London: George Larkin, 1666.

Campbell, Alastair. *Rediscovering Pastoral Care*. New ed. London: Darton, Longman & Todd, 1986.

"Church Covenants." *Baptist Quarterly* 7 (1935): 227–34.

Clement, Alberic S., ed. *Baptists Who Made History: A Book about Great Baptists*. London: Carey Kingsgate, 1955.

———, ed. *Great Baptist Women*. London: Carey Kingsgate, 1955.

Clerk, N. W. *See* Lewis, C. S.

Coccejus, John. *Summa doctrinae de foedere et testamento Dei*. Leiden, 1648.

Collins, Hercules. *An Orthodox Catechism: Being the Sum of Christian Religion, Contained in the Law and Gospel*. London, 1680.

Comblin, José. *Being Human: A Christian Anthropology*. Translated by Robert Barr. New York: Burns & Oates, 1990.

Confession of Faith Put forth by the Elders and Brethren of many Congregations of Christians (baptized upon Profession of their Faith) in London and the Country (London, 1677). In Lumpkin, *Baptist Confessions*, 241–95.

A Confession of the Faith of Several Churches of Christ [The "Somerset Confession"] (London: Henry Hills, 1656). In Lumpkin, *Baptist Confessions*, 203–16.

The Confession of Faith Of Those Churches Which Are Commonly (Though Falsely) Called Anabaptists (London: Matthew Simmons, 1644). In Lumpkin, *Baptist Confessions*, 153–71.

Cunningham, David S. *These Three Are One: The Practice of Trinitarian Theology*. Oxford: Blackwell, 1998.

Day, Dorothy. *Thérèse*. Springfield, Ill.: Templegate, 1960.

Dearmer, Percy, and Gerard Moultrie, trans. *Baptist Praise and Worship*. Oxford: Oxford University Press, 1991.

A Declaration of Faith of English People Remaining at Amsterdam in Holland (1611). In Lumpkin, *Baptist Confessions*, 116–23.

Dickenson, Donna L., Malcolm Johnson, and Jeanne Samson Katz, eds. *Death, Dying and Bereavement.* 2nd ed. London: Sage, 2000.

The Divine Liturgy of Our Father among the Saints John Chrysostom. Oxford: Oxford University Press, 1995. Greek text together with a translation into English. See esp. "Prayer of the Trisagion" and "Thanksgiving and Dismissal."

Dunn, James D. G. *Jesus and the Spirit.* London: SCM Press, 1975.

Eliot, T. S. "Murder in the Cathedral." In *The Complete Poems and Plays.* London: Faber & Faber, 1969, 237–82.

Ellis, Christopher, and Myra Blyth, eds. *Gathering for Worship: Patterns and Prayers for the Community of Disciples.* The Baptist Union of Great Britain. Norwich, UK: Canterbury, 2005.

The Faith and Practice of Thirty Congregations, Gathered according to the Primitive Pattern (London: Will Larnar, 1651). In Lumpkin, *Baptist Confessions*, 174–88.

Fawcett, John [son]. *An Account of the Life, Ministry and Writings of the Late Rev John Fawcett.* London: Baldwin, Cradock & Joy, 1818.

Fawcett, John. *The Constitution and Order of a Gospel Church Considered.* Halifax, UK, 1797.

Fiddes, Paul S. *The Creative Suffering of God.* Oxford: Oxford University Press, 1988.

———. "Mary in the Theology of Karl Barth." In *Mary in Doctrine and Devotion*, edited by Alberic Stacpoole, 111–26. Dublin: Columba, 1990.

———. "On Theology." In *The Cambridge Companion to C. S. Lewis*, edited by Robert MacSwain and Michael Ward, 89–104. Cambridge: Cambridge University Press, 2010.

———. *Participating in God: A Pastoral Doctrine of the Trinity.* London: Darton, Longman & Todd, 2000.

———. *The Promised End.* Oxford: Blackwell, 2000.

———. *Tracks and Traces: Baptist Identity in Church and Theology.* Milton Keynes, UK: Paternoster, 2003.

Fiddes, Paul S., Roger Hayden, Richard L. Kidd, Keith W. Clements and Brian Haymes. *Bound to Love: The Covenant Basis of Baptist Life and Mission.* London: Baptist Union, 1985.

Finley, James. *Merton's Palace of Nowhere.* Notre Dame, Ind.: Ave Maria, 1978.

Fitzgerald, Constance. "The Mission of Thérèse of Lisieux." *Contemporary Carmelite Women, The Way Supplement* 89 (1997): 74–96.

Ford, David. *Self and Salvation: Being Transformed.* Cambridge: Cambridge University Press, 1999.

Ford, Lewis. "Contingent Trinitarianism." In Bracken and Suchocki, *Trinity in Process,* 41–72.

Freud, Sigmund. *Totem and Taboo.* Translated by James Strachey. London: Routledge & Kegan Paul, 1960.

Fuchs, Lorelei F., SA. *Koinonia and the Quest for an Ecumenical Ecclesiology.* Grand Rapids: Eerdmans, 2008.

General Council of the Baptist World Alliance. "Human Rights." Resolution of the General Council of the Baptist World Alliance meeting in Vancouver, Canada, July 3–9, 1997 (on the occasion of the fiftieth anniversary of the Universal Declaration of Human Rights of the United Nations). In *1997 Yearbook of the Baptist World Alliance.,* 100. McLean, Va.: BWA.

Georgian Eucharist. Decatur, Ga.: Cooperative Baptist Fellowship, 2011.

Gill, John. *Complete Body of Doctrinal and Practical Divinity: A New Edition in Two Volumes.* London: 1795; repr. 1839; repr. Grand Rapids: Baker Book House, 1978.

Goodliff, Andy. "Towards a Baptist Sanctoral?" *Journal of European Baptist Studies* 13, no. 3 (2013): 24–30.

Görres, Ida Friederike. *The Hidden Face: A Study of St. Thérèse of Lisieux.* San Francisco: Ignatius, 1995.

Grantham, Thomas. *A Sigh for Peace; or, The Cause of the Division Discovered.* London, 1671.

Grenz, Stanley. *The Social God and the Relational Self: A Trinitarian Theology of the Imago Dei.* Louisville: Westminster John Knox, 2001.

Griffin, David. "Marjorie Hewitt Suchocki, 'The End of Evil'" (Review). *Process Studies* 18 (1989): 57–62.

Gutiérrez, Gustavo. *A Theology of Liberation.* Translated by Caridad Inda and John Eagleson. New York: Orbis, 1973.

Hall, Robert. "On Theories and the Rights of Man." In "The Freedom of the Press and for General Liberty." In *The Entire Works of the Rev.*

Robert Hall, edited by Olinthus Gregory. 6 vols. London: Holdsworth & Ball, 1831.

Hamilton, Peter. *The Living God and the Modern World: A Christian Theology Based on the Thought of A. N. Whitehead*. London: Hodder & Stoughton, 1967.

Harmon, Steven. *Towards Baptist Catholicity*. Milton Keynes, UK: Paternoster, 2006.

Hartshorne, Charles. *Creative Synthesis and Philosophic Method*. London: SCM Press, 1970.

———. *The Divine Relativity: A Social Conception of God*. New Haven, Conn.: Yale University Press, 1976.

———. *A Natural Theology for Our Time*. LaSalle, Ill.: Open Court, 1967.

———. "Time, Death and Everlasting Life." In *The Logic of Perfection*, 245–62. LaSalle, Ill.: Open Court, 1962.

Hawking, Stephen. *The Grand Design*. London: Bantam, 2011.

Hay, David M. *Glory at the Right Hand: Psalm 110 in Early Christianity*. SBL Monograph Series 18. Nashville: Abingdon, 1973.

Hayden, Roger, ed. *Baptist Union Documents 1948–1977*. London: Baptist Historical Society, 1980.

Helwys, Thomas. *A Short Declaration of the Mystery of Iniquity*. London, 1612.

Hick, John. *Evil and the God of Love*. London: Collins, 1968.

———. "A Possible Conception of Life after Death." In *Death and Afterlife*, edited by Stephen T. Davis, 183–96. London: Macmillan, 1989.

Hooker, Morna D. *The Son of Man in Mark*. London: SPCK, 1967.

Hoornaert, Edouard. *The Memory of the Christian People*. New York: Burns & Oates, 1989.

Humphreys, Richard. *Futurism*. London: Tate, 1999.

Jacobs, Michael. *Living Illusions: A Psychology of Belief*. London: SPCK, 1993.

Johnson, Aubrey R. *The Vitality of the Individual in the Thought of Ancient Israel*. Cardiff: University of Wales Press, 1964.

Johnson, Elizabeth. *Friends of God and Prophets: A Feminist Theological Reading of the Communion of Saints*. London: SCM Press, 1998.

Jüngel, Eberhard. "The World as Possibility and Actuality: The Ontology of the Doctrine of Justification" [1969]. In *Eberhard Jüngel:*

Theological Essays, edited by John Webster, 95–123. Edinburgh: T&T Clark, 1989.

Kapolyo, Joe. "An Inheritance Kept in Heaven." A sermon on 1 Peter 1:1-3 delivered at the Baptist Assembly, Brighton, May 2008.

Kasper, Walter. *Harvesting the Fruits: Basic Aspects of Christian Faith in Ecumenical Dialogue*. London: Continuum, 2009.

Keach, Benjamin. *The Display of Glorious Grace; or, the Covenant of Peace, Opened: In Fourteen Sermons. . . .* London, 1698.

———. *Gold Refin'd; or, Baptism in its Primitive Purity*. London, 1689.

———. *Tropologia: A Key to Open Scripture-Metaphors*. London: Enoch Prosser, 1683.

Kenkle, Lincoln. *Thornton Wilder and the Puritan Narrative Tradition*. Columbia: University of Missouri Press, 2006.

Keynes, Geoffrey, ed. *Blake: Complete Writings*. London: Oxford University Press, 1966.

King, Martin Luther, Jr. *"Thou, Dear God": Prayers That Open Hearts and Spirits*. Edited by Lewis V. Baldwin. Boston: Beacon, 2011.

Klein, Melanie. *Love, Guilt and Reparation: And Other Works 1921–1945*. New York: Macmillan, 1975.

Knollys, Hanserd. *A Moderate Answer unto Dr. Bastwick's Book Called, "Independency not God's Ordinance."* London, 1645.

———. *The World That Now Is and the World That Is to Come*. London, 1681.

Levinas, Emmanuel. *Totality and Infinity: An Essay on Exteriority*. Translated by Alphonso Lingis. Pittsburgh: Duquesne, 1969.

Lewis, C. S. [N. W. Clerk, pseud.]. *A Grief Observed*. London: Faber & Faber, 1961. Reissued as authored by C. S. Lewis in 1964.

———. *Letters to Malcolm*. London: Bles, 1964.

Loader, W. R. G. "Christ at the Right Hand—Psalm CX.1 in the New Testament." *New Testament Studies* 24 (1978): 199–217.

Lovejoy, Arthur. *The Great Chain of Being*. Harvard: Harvard College, 1936.

Lumpkin, William L., ed. *Baptist Confessions of Faith*. Chicago: Judson, 1959.

Marie, comité mixte Baptiste-Catholique en France. Documents Episcopat 10. Le Secrétariat Général de la Conférence des Évêques de France, 2009.

Martin, Hugh, ed. *The Baptist Hymn Book Companion*. London: Psalms and Hymns Trust, 1967.

Martyrdom of Polycarp. In Stevenson, *New Eusebius,* 18–26.

McClendon, James Wm., Jr. *Biography as Theology: How Life Stories Can Remake Today's Theology*. Philadelphia: Trinity International, 1990.

McCormack, Bruce. "Grace and Being: The Role of God's Gracious Election in Karl Barth's Theological Ontology." In *The Cambridge Companion to Karl Barth*, edited by John Webster, 92–110. Cambridge: Cambridge University Press, 2000.

McFadyen, Alistair I. *The Call to Personhood: A Christian Theory of the Individual in Social Relationships*. Cambridge: Cambridge University Press, 1990.

McNeill, John T., ed. *Calvin: Institutes of the Christian Religion*, trans. F. L. Battles. The Library of Christian Classics 20–21. London: SCM Press, 1961.

Merton, Thomas. *New Seeds of Contemplation*. Boston: Shambhala, 2003.

———. *The Seven Story Mountain*. Fla.: Harcourt, 1948.

Middlebrook, J. B. *In Journeyings Oft: A Memoir of H. R. Williamson*. London: The Baptist Missionary Society, 1969.

Milbank, John. "Against Human Rights." *Oxford Journal of Law and Religion* 1, no. 1 (2012): 203–34.

———. *The Word Made Strange: Theology, Language, Culture*. Oxford: Blackwell, 1997.

Moltmann, Jürgen. *The Coming of God*. Translated by Margaret Kohl. London: SCM Press, 1986.

———. *The Crucified God*. Translated by R. A. Wilson and John Bowden. London: SCM Press, 1974.

———. *Theology of Hope*. Translated by James Leitch. London: SCM Press, 1965.

———. *The Trinity and the Kingdom of God*. Translated by Margaret Kohl. London: SCM Press, 1981.

———. *The Way of Jesus Christ*. Translated by Margaret Kohl. London: SCM Press, 1990.

Mullins, E. Y. *The Axioms of Religion*. Edited by C. Douglas Weaver. 1908; repr. Macon, Ga.: Mercer University Press, 2010.

Nolland, John. *Luke 1:1–9:20*. Word Commentary 35A. Dallas: Word Books, 1989.

Nouwen, Henri. *The Genesee Diary*. New York: Doubleday, 1976.

"Order One, Eucharistic Prayer B, Order for the Celebration of the Holy Communion." In *Common Worship: Services and Prayers for the Church of England*, 188–90. London: Church House, 2000.

Origen. *Exhortation to Martyrdom*. In *Prayer and Exhortation to Martyrdom*, translated by John J. O'Meara. Ancient Christian Writers, edited by Johannes Quaesten and Joseph C. Plumpe, vol. 19. Westminster, Md.: Newman, 1954.

———. *On Prayer*. Translated by William A. Curtis. Grand Rapids: Ethereal Library, 2001. Accessible online at www.ccel.org/ccel/origen/prayer.html.

———. *An Orthodox Creed, or a Protestant Confession of Faith, Being an Essay to Unite and Confirm All True Protestants* (London, 1679). In Lumpkin, *Baptist Confessions*, 297–334.

Owen, Huw Parri. *Concepts of Deity*. London: Macmillan, 1971.

Pannenberg, Wolfhart. *Jesus—God and Man*. Translated by Lewis Wilkins and Duane Priebe. London: SCM Press, 1968.

———. *Systematic Theology*. Translated by Geoffrey Bromiley. 3 vols. Grand Rapids: Eerdmans, 1991–1998.

Pasquarello, Michael, III. *We Speak Because We Have First Been Spoken: A Grammar of the Preaching Life*. Grand Rapids: Eerdmans, 2009.

Payne, Ernest A., and Stephen F. Winward, eds. *Orders and Prayers for Church Worship: A Manual for Ministers*. London: The Baptist Union of Great Britain and Ireland, 1967.

Polkinghorne, John. *Belief in God in an Age of Science*. New Haven, Conn.: Yale University Press, 1998.

Pollard, Andrew. *The Sanctuary, the Design of Its Services and the Requisites to Their Acceptableness and Efficiency: A Discourse at the Dedication of the First Baptist Church, Barnstable, Oct. 15, 1845*. Boston: Hallworth, 1845.

Popper, Karl. *Objective Knowledge: An Evolutionary Approach*. Oxford: Oxford University Press, 1972.

Proust, Marcel. *In Search of Lost Time*. 6 vols. Various translators. London: Penguin Books, 2002.

———. *The Way by Swann's*. Translated by Lydia Davis. Vol. 1 of *In Search of Lost Time*. London: Penguin Books, 2002.

Rahner, Karl. *Foundations of the Christian Faith*. Translated by William Dych. London: Darton, Longman & Todd, 1978.

————. *Hearers of the Word.* 1941; repr. New York: Seabury, 1969.

————. *Quaestiones disputatae.* Vol. 2, *On the Theology of Death.*, London: Burnes & Oates, 1961.

————. *Theological Investigations.* Vol. 4, *More Recent Writings.* Translated by Kevin Smith. London: Darton, Longman & Todd, 1966.

————. *Theological Investigations.* Vol. 6, *Concerning Vatican Council II.* Translated by Karl-H. Kruger and Boniface Kruger. London: Darton, Longman & Todd, 1969.

Raine, Craig. "The Onion, Memory." In *The Onion, Memory,* 28–29. Oxford: Oxford University Press, 1978.

Richards, Audrey I. *Chisungu.* London: Routledge, 1982.

Ricoeur, Paul. *Memory, History, Forgetting.* Translated by Kathleen Blamey and David Pellauer. Chicago: University of Chicago Press, 2004.

Riley, Bridget. *The Eye's Mind.* Edited by Robert Kudielka. London: Thames & Hudson, 1999.

Roberts, Alexander, and James Donaldson, eds. *The Ante-Nicene Fathers.* 10 vols. Grand Rapids: Eerdmans, 1975.

Robinson, John A. T. *The Body: A Study in Pauline Theology.* London: SCM Press, 1952.

Rooke, Deborah. "Jesus as Royal Priest: Reflections on the Interpretation of the Melkizedek Tradition in Heb 7." *Biblica* 81 (2000): 81–94.

Ruether, Rosemary Radford. *Gaia and God: An Ecofeminist Theology of Earth Healing.* New York: Harper Collins, 1992.

————. *Sexism and God-Talk.* London: SCM Press, 1983.

Schillebeeckx, Edward. *Christ the Sacrament of Encounter with God.* London: Sheed & Ward, 1963.

Schrag, Calvin O. *Communicative Praxis and the Space of Subjectivity.* Bloomington: Indiana University Press, 1986.

Sheldrake, Philip. *Spaces for the Sacred: Place, Memory and Identity.* London: SCM Press, 2001.

Shurden, Walter. "The Baptist Identity and the Baptist Manifesto." *Perspectives in Religious Studies* 25 (1998): 321–40.

Sixteen Articles of Faith and Order [The "Midland Association Confession"] (1655). In Lumpkin, *Baptist Confessions,* 198–200.

Smyth, John. *Paralleles, Censures, Observations* (1609). In Whitley, *Works,* 2:327–546.

―――. *Principles and Inferences Concerning the Visible Church* (1607). In Whitley, *Works*, 1:249–68.

Soelle, Dorothee. *Christ the Representative: An Essay in Theology after the "Death of God."* Translated by David Lewis. London: SCM Press, 1967.

Songulashvili, Malkhaz. "A Historical Study of the Missiological Convictions of the 'Evangelical Christians and Baptists of Georgia' and Their Role in Relation to National Culture and Life." Unpublished Ph.D. thesis, University of Wales, 2012.

Stevenson, James, ed. *Creed, Councils and Controversies: Documents Illustrative of the History of the Church A.D. 337–461.* London. SPCK, 1972.

―――. *A New Eusebius: Documents Illustrative of the Christian Church to AD 337.* London: SPCK, 1968.

Stroup, George W. *Before God.* Grand Rapids: Eerdmans, 2004.

Suchocki, Marjorie. *The End of Evil.* Eugene, Ore.: Wipf & Stock, 1988.

The Sunday Missal: A New Edition. London: Collins Liturgical, 1984. Texts approved for use in England, Wales, Ireland, and Scotland. See esp. "Eucharistic Prayer I," "Eucharistic Prayer II," and "Eucharistic Prayer III."

Swinburne, Richard. *The Christian God.* Oxford: Oxford University Press, 1994.

―――. *The Coherence of Theism.* Oxford: Oxford University Press, 1977.

Teilhard de Chardin, Pierre. *The Phenomenon of Man.* Translated by Bernard Wall. London: Collins, 1961.

Thérèse. *Story of a Soul: The Autobiography of St. Thérèse of Lisieux.* Translated by John Clarke, OCD. 3rd ed. Washington, D.C.: ICS, 1996.

Thompson, Philip E. "Toward Baptist Ecclesiology in Pneumatological Perspective." Unpublished Ph.D. thesis, Emory University, 1995.

Tillich, Paul. *Systematic Theology.* Vol. 1. Digswell Place, Welwyn, Herts: James Nisbet, 1968.

―――. *Systematic Theology.* Vol. 3, *Life and the Spirit: History and the Kingdom of God.* Digswell Place, Welwyn,Herts: James Nisbet, 1968.

Tracy, David. *The Analogical Imagination.* London: SCM Press, 1981.

A True Confession of the Faith (1596). In Lumpkin, *Baptist Confessions*, 82–97.

The True Gospel-Faith Declared according to the Scriptures (1654). In Lumpkin, *Baptist Confessions of Faith*, 192–95.

Unamuno, Miguel de. *The Tragic Sense of Life*. Translated by J. Crawford Flitch. London: Macmillan, 1931.

Vanstone, William H. *Love's Endeavour, Love's Expense*. London: Darton, Longman & Todd, 1977.

———. *The Stature of Waiting*. London: Darton, Longman & Todd, 1982.

Volf, Miroslav. *The End of Memory*. Grand Rapids: Eerdmans, 2006.

———. *A Public Faith: How Followers of Christ Should Serve the Common Good*. Grand Rapids: Brazos, 2011.

von Rad, Gerhard. "'Righteousness' and 'Life' in the Cultic Language of the Psalms." In *The Problem of the Hexateuch and Other Essays*, translated by E. Trueman Dicken, 243–66. London: Oliver & Boyd, 1966.

Ward, Keith. *Rational Theology and the Creativity of God*. Oxford: Blackwell, 1982.

———. *Religion and Creation*. Oxford: Clarendon, 1996.

Wells, Samuel. *The Drama of Christian Ethics: Improvisation*. Grand Rapids: Brazos, 2000.

Wesley, J. Ivor. "The Heavenly Intercession of Christ." *Expository Times* 40 (1929): 559–63.

White, Barrington Raymond. *The English Separatist Tradition: From the Marian Martyrs to the Pilgrim Fathers*. Oxford: Oxford University Press, 1971.

Whitehead, Alfred North. *Process and Reality*. New York: Macmillan, 1929.

Whitley, W. T. *The Works of John Smyth*. 2 vols. Cambridge: Cambridge University Press, 1915.

Wilder, Thornton. *Our Town*. In *Our Town, The Skin of Our Teeth, The Matchmaker*. London: Penguin, 2000.

Wild Goose Worship Group. *A Wee Worship Book: Fourth Incarnation*. Iona: Wild Goose Publications, 1999.

Williamson, Henry Raymond. *British Baptists in China 1845–1952*. London: Carey Kingsgate, 1957.

"The Word of God in the Life of the Church: A Report of International Conversations between the Catholic Church and the Baptist World Alliance 2006–2010." *American Baptist Quarterly* 31 (2012): 28–122.

World Council of Churches. *Baptism, Eucharist and Ministry*. Faith and Order Paper III. Geneva: World Council of Churches, 1982.

Worship: From the United Reformed Church. London: United Reformed Church, 2003.

Wright, N. T. *Surprised by Hope: Rethinking Heaven, the Resurrection, and the Mission of the Church*. New York: HarperOne, 2008.

Wyschogrod, Edith. *Saints and Postmodernism: Revisioning Moral Philosophy*. Chicago: University of Chicago Press, 1990.

Yarnell, Malcolm B., III. *The Formation of Christian Doctrine*. Nashville: B&H Academic, 2007.

York, Tripp. *The Purple Crown: The Politics of Martyrdom*. Scottdale, Pa.: Herald, 2007.

Zimmerli, Walther. "Promise and Fulfilment." In *Essays on Old Testament Interpretation*, edited by Claus Westermann and translated by James Luther Mays, 89–122. London: SCM Press, 1963.

Zwingli, Huldrych. Letter to Matthew Alber, 16 November 1524. In *Huldrych Zwingli: Writings*, translated by H. Wayne Pipkin, 2:127–46. Allison Park, Pa.: Pickwick, 1984.

Author Biographies

PAUL S. FIDDES was principal of Regent's Park College, Oxford (a Baptist foundation) (1989–2007) and has been chair of the Doctrine and Unity Commission of the Baptist World Alliance (2005–2010). At present he holds the title of Professor of Systematic Theology in the University of Oxford.

BRIAN HAYMES was principal of Northern Baptist College, Manchester (1985–1994), principal of Bristol Baptist College (1994–2000), and president of the Baptist Union of Great Britain (1993–1994). He is active in retirement in writing and preaching.

RICHARD KIDD was principal of Northern Baptist College, Manchester (1994–2009) and co-principal of Northern Baptist Learning Community (2009–2012). His life at present includes voluntary work with the Baptist Missionary Society in India.

All three authors are ordained ministers of the Baptist Union of Great Britain and have been friends for more than thirty years.

CREDITS

INDEX